GREAT SCIENTISTS

Chemists

Cavendish Square

New York

Published in 2014 by Cavendish Square Publishing, LLC
303 Park Avenue South, Suite 1247, New York, NY 10010

Library of Congress Cataloging-in-Publication Data
Van Koevering, Thomas E.
Chemists / by Thomas E. Van Koevering, et. al.
p. cm. — (Great scientists)
Includes index.
ISBN 978-1-62712-554-3 (hardcover) ISBN 978-1-62712-555-0 (paperback) ISBN 978-1-62712-556-7 (ebook)
1. Chemists — Biography — Juvenile literature. 2. Chemistry —Juvenile literature. I. Van Koevering, Thomas E., 1941-. II. Title.
QD21.V35 2014
540—d23

Editorial Director: Dean Miller; Editorial Assistant: Amy Hayes; Art Director: Jeffrey Talbot; Designer: Joseph Macri; Production Manager: Jennifer Ryder-Talbot; Production Editor: Andrew Coddington; Photo Researchers: Laurie Platt Winfrey, Carousel Research, Inc.; Joseph Marci; Amy Greenan; and Julie Alissi, J8 Media

The photographs in this book are used by permission and through the courtesy of: Front cover photos by David Freund/Photodisc/Getty Images, Massachusetts Institute of Technology, Ralph Morse/Contributor/Time & Life Pictures/Getty Images, © The Print Collector/Alamy; Back cover photos by David Freund/Photodisc/Getty Images, UniversalImagesGroup/Contributor/Universal Images Group/Getty Images, Stock Montage/Contributor/Archive Photos/Getty Images, © IMAGE ASSET MANAGEMEN; David Freund/Photodisc/Getty Images, 1; Massachusetts Institute of Technology, 6; Ralph Morse/Contributor/Time & Life Pictures/Getty Images, 6; © The Print Collector/Alamy, 6; UniversalImagesGroup/Contributor/Universal Images Group/Getty Images, 7; Stock Montage/Contributor/Archive Photos/Getty Images, 7; © IMAGE ASSET MANAGEMEN, 7; Time Life Pictures/Contributor/Time & Life Pictures/Getty Images, 8; Fox Photos/Stringer/Hulton Archive/Getty Images, 12; Accurate Art, Inc., 13, 15, 28, 31, 33, 39, 73, 83, 87, 96, 110, 149, 151; Paul Nadar/ Portrait of Antoine-Henri Becquerel/ Portrait of Antoine-Henri Becquerel (1852-1908), Physicist (www.flickr.com/photos/25053835@N03/2536015971/), 14; BSIP/Contributor/Universal Images Group/Getty Images, 18; DEA PICTURE LIBRARY/Contributor/De Agostini/Getty Images, 21; Leemage/Universal Images Group/Getty Images, 24; UniversalImagesGroup/Contributor/Universal Images Group/Getty Images, 26; Photo Researchers/Photo Researchers/Getty Images, 30; Keystone/Stringer/Hulton Archive/Getty Images, 32; Nancy R. Schiff/Contributor/Archive Photos/Getty Images, 35; Unknown/ Pierre and Marie Curie/ hp.ujf.cas.cz, 38; Time Life Pictures/Contributor/Time & Life Pictures/Getty Images, 42; British Library/Robana/Contributor/Hulton Fine Art Collection/Getty Images, 45; Imagno/Contributor/Hulton Archive/Getty Images, 48; UniversalImagesGroup/Contributor/Universal Images Group/Getty Images, 51; Keystone/Stringer/Hulton Archive/Getty Images, 53; © AP Images, 56; AP Photo/ Tobbe Gustavsson, 59; François Séraphin Delpech/ Gaylussac 2/ United States Library of Congress's Prints and Photographs division, 61; AP Photo/Clarence Hamm, 64; STF/Staff/AFP/Getty Images, 67; Smithsonian Institution from United States/ Irène Joliot-Curie (1897-1956), c. 1935 (4406405158)/www.flickr.com/photos/smithsonian/4406405158/ uploaded by Magnus Manske, 71; SCIENCE SOURCE/Photo Researchers/Getty Images, 74; Alfred Eisenstaedt/Contributor/Time & Life Pictures/Getty Images, 77; FPG/Staff/Archive Photos/Getty Images, 79; Jean-Marie Lehn/GNU Free Documentation License/Creative Commons Attribution-Share alike 3.0 Unported, 2.5 Generic, 2.0 Generic, and 1.0 Generic license, 82; NYPL/Science Source/Photo Researchers/Getty Images, 85; Rex Features via AP Images, 89; Nobel Foundation/ McMillan, signature/Les Prix Nobel en 1951, 92; Sovfoto/Contributor/Universal Images Group/Getty Images, 94; NPLY/Science Source/Photo Researchers/Getty Images, 98; © AP Images, 101; Jan COLISIOO/Stringer/AFP/Getty Images, 103; Smithsonian Institution from United States/ Linus Pauling with rope/www.flickr.com/photos/smithsonian/4729473975/ uploaded by PDTillman, 106; Ron Case/Stringer/Hulton Archive/Getty Images, 109; DEA PICTURE LIBRARY/De Agostini Picture Library/Getty Images, 112; Bain News Service, publisher/ Ellen Richards/Library of Congress Prints and Photographs Division, 115; Keystone/Staff/Hulton Archive/Getty Images, 118; Interim Archives/Contributor/Archive Photos/Getty Images, 121; Atomic Energy Commission/ Glenn Seaborg – 1964/NAIL Control Number: NWDNS-326-COM-12 NARA, 124; Fine Art Images/SuperStock/Getty Images, 127; AP Photo/Bob Child, 129; NYPL/Science Source/Photo Researchers/Getty Images, 132; © AP Images, 135; © iStockphoto.com/JacobH, 137; George Karger/Contributor/TIME & LIFE Images/Getty Images, 139; Unknown/ PSM V66 D198 J H vant Hoft/Popular Science Monthly Volume 66, 143; © AP Images, 145; © AP Images, 148; Rudolph Hoffmann/ Friedrich Wöhler Litho/ Eigenes Foto einer Originallithographie der ÖNB (Wien), 151.

Front cover (left to right): Ellen Richards Swallow, Linus Pauling, Marie Curie; back cover (left to right): Ernest Rutherford, Robert Boyle, Dmitry Mendeleev

Printed in the United States of America

Contents

An Introduction to Great Scientists: *Chemists*

Science offers an ever-expanding and seemingly ever-changing array of facts and theories to explain the workings of life and the universe. Behind its doors, we can explore fascinating worlds ranging from the tiny—the spiral ladder of DNA in every human cell and the particle zoo of quarks and mesons in every atom—to the unimaginably vast—the gradual, often catastrophic shifting of tectonic plates and the immense gravitational fields surrounding black holes in space. Unfortunately, the doors of science often remain shut to students and the general public, who worry they are unable to understand the work done in these technical fields.

Great Scientists seeks to serve as a key. Its goal is to introduce many notable researchers and concepts, sparking interest and providing jumping-off points for gaining further knowledge. To this end, these books offer a select survey of scientists and their accomplishments across disciplines, throughout history, and around the world. The life stories of these individuals and the descriptions of their research and achievements will prove both informational and inspirational to budding scientists and to all those with inquisitive minds. For some, learning the paths of these scientists' lives will enable ambitious young students to follow in their footsteps.

Science disciplines are foundational by nature. The work done by the earliest pioneers in a specific field often leads to inspire and inform the next generation of minds, who take the findings and discoveries of their heroes and mentors, and further the body of knowledge in a given area. This progression of knowledge increases the world's understanding of existing theories and tenants, blazing trails into new directions of study. Perhaps by reading this work, the next great chemists will discover their spark of creativity. Whether interested in the theoretical sciences, mathematics, or the applied fields of engineering and invention, students will find these life stories proof that individuals from any background can be responsible for key discoveries and paradigm-shifting thoughts and experiments.

The Organization of *Chemists*

This volume profiles more than four dozen representative figures in the history of chemistry. Entries are generally 800 to 1,700 words in length, with some longer essays covering individuals who made numerous significant contributions to the development of their fields, such as Marie Curie, Linus Pauling, Svante Arrhenius, Dmitri Mendeleev, John Dalton, and Georg Wittig. In addition to celebrating famous names that made great strides in scientific inquiry and paved the way for others to follow, this book gives credit to individuals and groups who have gone largely unrecognized, such as women and minorities, as well as introducing many contemporary scientists who are making advancements in their field.

The profile of each scientist begins with a list of their areas of achievement, as a good number of these individuals' work influenced more than one discipline. For example, the seventeenth-century scientist Robert Boyle made significant contributions in the fields of medicine, invention, and physics, as well as chemistry. Many of the names in this volume had such impact in multiple fields of study that inclusion in several different books would be logical, but decisions were made to place each scientist in the field most emblematic of his or her work. After a brief statement of each individual's contribution to science, a time line covers the major life events, including birth and death dates, major awards and honors, and milestones in the scientist's education, research, employment, and private life. The entry then details the struggles and triumphs that characterize the lives of so many who pursue knowledge as a career.

The Science Behind the Scientist

An important goal of the Great Scientist series is to expand a reader's understanding of science, not just cover the biographical data of specific scientists. To that end, each profile contains one or more sidebars within the article that provide a simple snapshot introduction to a key topic within the featured scientist's achievements, including theories, research, inventions, or discoveries.

While the subjects are not covered in painstaking detail, there is enough information for readers to gain a working knowledge of topics important to the field of chemistry and its applications.

Illustrating the Science

Several of the sidebars in this book are accompanied by diagrams that help to reinforce the information covered through graphical representation of complex theories and discoveries. In addition, wherever possible, a photograph, painting, or sculpture of the profiled scientist is provided, although there are no likenesses for some of history's earliest contributors.

Additional Resources

Each profile ends with a two-part bibliography, pointing readers to some of the most significant books and papers written by the particular scientist, as well as other content written about the subject. It's worth noting that these bibliographies are selected works and by no means a complete listing—many of these scientists have contributed dozens of works. The book concludes with a glossary that offers clear definitions of selected terms and concepts, and a comprehensive index that allows readers to locate information about the people, concepts, organizations, and topics covered throughout the book.

Skill Development for Students

Great Scientists: Chemists can serve as a basic biographical text on a specific individual or as a source of enrichment for students looking to know more about an entire scientific field. It's an excellent reference for reading and writing assignments, and can be a foundational work for major research and term papers. The bibliographies at the end of the profiles and sidebars are invaluable for students looking to learn more about a specific individual or topic.

Svante A. Arrhenius

Disciplines: Chemistry and physics
Contribution: Arrhenius developed an explanation for electrolysis from which he was able to define acids, bases, and salts. He also developed the Arrhenius equation, which describes the effect on temperature on the speed of a chemical reaction.

Feb. 19, 1859	Born in Castle of Vik, near Uppsala, Sweden
1884	Defends his doctoral thesis on the theory on ionic dissociation
1886	Receives a traveling fellowship from the Swedish Academy of Sciences
1895	Professor of physics at the Royal Institute of Technology in Stockholm
1901	Elected to the Swedish Academy of Sciences
1902	Awarded the Davy Medal of the Royal Society of London
1903	Receives the Nobel Prize in Chemistry
1905	Director of the Nobel Institute for Physical Chemistry in Stockholm
1911	Visits the United States, where he gives the Sillman Lectures at Yale University and receives the Willard Gibbs Medal
1912	Publishes *Theories of Solutions*
1915	Publishes *Quantitative Laws in Biological Chemistry*
Oct. 2, 1927	Dies in Stockholm, Sweden

Early Life

Svante August Arrhenius (pronounced "ahr-RAY-nee-uhs") was born near Uppsala, Sweden, in 1859. He was a very bright child, and it is said that he taught himself to read at the age of three. He developed his interest in mathematics by watching his father add up columns of numbers. He pursued his interests in chemistry, mathematics, and physics at Uppsala University.

Arrhenius moved to Stockholm to work with Erik Edlund, a well-known chemist at that time. Arrhenius developed an explanation for why certain substances conduct electric currents in solutions. This area was a difficult to research because little was known about the structure of atoms at that time.

The significance of Arrhenius' work was not appreciated, however, and he received a low passing grade when he submitted his theory as the thesis for his doctoral degree.

Arrhenius' Ionic Hypothesis

Arrhenius proposed that electrolytes in solution conduct electricity as a result of molecules splitting into positive and negative ions.

Chemists used electrochemical cells to isolate and identify many elements more than fifty years before Arrhenius began his work in the 1880s. It was known that electrical currents were conducted by certain substances and had no impact on other substances. Arrhenius proposed that some substances, when dissolved in an appropriate solvent such as water, separate (disassociate) into positively and negatively charged particles called ions. This process occurs because of an interaction between the molecules of the dissolved material and the molecules of the solvent.

Arrhenius believed that the kinds of ions present in a solution determine whether the dissolved substance (the solute) should be classified as an acid, a base, or a salt. He defined acids as substances that produce hydrogen ions and bases as substances that produce hydroxide ions. The ions produced by salts are neither hydrogen ions nor hydroxide ions. Prior to this time, acids and bases were characterized as molecules with certain properties in common, such as whether they produce reactions with indicators, taste sour or bitter, feel slippery, or neutralize the expressed properties of another substance. Acids and bases were also defined as substances derived from reactions when metals or nonmetals react with oxygen. Such later scientists as Johannes Brønsted and Gilbert N. Lewis developed more comprehensive definitions of acids, bases, and salts.

Many chemists were skeptical about the ionic hypothesis. Problems resulted from attempts to extend the concept of the ionization of dissolved materials to nearly every chemical reaction and assumptions that molecules do not react at all. J. W. Mellor, a famous inorganic chemist, noted that "in spite of the ionic hypothesis, chemical reactions do take place in nonconducting solutions, and these reactions are similar in result and speed to those which occur in conducting aqueous solutions." Chemists at the beginning of the twentieth century had little knowledge about the interactions that occur between solutes and solvents. These interactions cannot be fully appreciated unless the "polar" character of many molecules is understood. This information was not widely available for another thirty years.

The ionic hypothesis did help explain why some substances when dissolved in solution produce changes in the physical properties of the solution that are inconsistent with the number of molecules that are present. When a substance dissolves in water or some other solvent, the normal freezing point, boiling point, osmotic pressure, and some other properties of the liquid change. The magnitude of the change depends on the number of particles present. When molecules form ions, the number of particles increases, thus increasing the boiling point or lowering the freezing point of the solution more than would be anticipated from a substance that remains in molecular form.

Bibliography

Foundations of the Theory of Dilute Solutions. Svante Arrhenius. 1887. Reprint. Edinburgh, Scotland: Alembic Club, 1929.

Modern Inorganic Chemistry. J. W. Mellor. London: Longmans, Green, 1916.

Theories of Solutions. Svante Arrhenius. Cambridge, Mass.: Harvard University Press, 1912.

The Arrhenius Equation

Arrhenius developed the mathematical relationship between the temperature of a chemical reaction and the rate at which reactants are converted into products.

Each chemical reaction has a reaction rate constant that is determined by the chemical nature of the molecules and the numbers of molecules involved in the reaction. The rate constant, which is sensitive to temperature, is determined by the individual reaction step that requires the most time. The activation energy, which determines the stability of the reactants, is the energy needed for reacting molecules to undergo "molecular damage" in collisions with other molecules. The higher the temperature of a chemical reaction, the easier it is to supply reacting molecules with the required amount of activation energy.

The equation proposed by Arrhenius has the form $k = se^{-Ea/RT}$, where k is the reaction rate constant, s is a numerical constant for the reaction, Ea is the activation energy of the reaction, R is the thermo-dynamic constant, and T is the absolute temperature of the reaction.

The significance of the Arrhenius equation is that it allows scientists to predict how the rate of a reaction will change with temperature if the activation energy is known. Reaction rates can be measured easily at various temperatures, and this information can be used to calculate the activation energy.

Bibliography

Daniels, Farrington and Robert Alberty. *Physical Chemistry: Svante Arrhenius.* 2d ed. New York: John Wiley & Sons, 1961.

Chemists at that time were more interested in accurate experimental work than they were in theoretical explanations for why certain chemical reactions occurred. Arrhenius was also working in an area that was not clearly defined as either chemistry or physics.

Professional Development

From 1886 to 1890, Arrhenius used his traveling fellowship from the Swedish Academy of Sciences to work with many of the prominent scientists in Germany and the Netherlands. During this time, he refined his theory of ionization and gradually gained a following. When he was offered a post at one of the prominent universities in Germany, he soon received a position at the Royal Institute of Technology in Sweden.

The international fame for Arrhenius reached its high point in 1903 when he was awarded the Nobel Prize in Chemistry. He was the first person from Sweden to win a Nobel Prize. The offer of a position as chair at the University of Berlin in 1905, the most prominent post available to an academic chemist in Europe, promoted the creation of a position for him in Sweden as the director of the Nobel Institute for Physical Chemistry in Stockholm. This job gave him an opportunity to continue his research and writing.

Arrhenius, the Scientist

Arrhenius was unusual in that he was able to look beyond data and identify mathematical relation-ships. This talent was appreciated by only the more imaginative scientists of his time. His theory of ionization and its application in defining acids, bases, and salts have been cornerstones of chemistry. Other chemists have used the Arrhenius definitions as starting points for developing more comprehensive descriptions of the chemical activi-ties of acids, bases, and salts. Arrhenius was able to use the work of J. J. Hood to develop an explana-tion of the impact of temperature on the velocity of a wide range of chemical reactions. This work has practical applications in nearly every aspect of chemical research today.

Arrhenius was awarded the Nobel Prize at the midpoint of his career, and, as the director of the Nobel Institute, he was able to spend time pursuing scientific interests in immunology, geology, and cosmology. He even proposed an explanation for the propagation of the universe; although it is not supported by the theories of modern cosmology.

Bibliography

By Arrhenius

Theorien der Chemie, 1906 (Theories of Chemistry, 1907).

Immunochemistry, 1907.

Theories of Solutions, 1912.

Quantitative Laws in Biological Chemistry, 1915.

Kemien och der moderna livet, 1919 (Chemistry in Modern Life, 1925)

About Arrhenius

Crawford, Elisabeth. *Arrhenius: From Ionic Theory to the Greenhouse Effect*. Sagamore Beach, Mass: Science History Publications, 1996.

"Styles in Scientific Explanations: Paul Ehrlich and Svante Arrhenius on Immunochemistry." *Journal of the History of Medicine and Allied Sciences* 35, 1980.

Magill, Frank N., ed. "Svante August Arrhenius." *The Nobel Prize Winners: Chemistry*. Pasadena, Calif.: Salem Press, 1990.

(Thomas E. Van Koevering)

Sir Derek H. R. Barton

Discipline: Chemistry

Contribution: Barton is best known for the studies of steroids and other complex molecules in nature. The chemical role played by the various geometric patterns that these molecules formed won him the Nobel Prize in Chemistry in 1969.

Sept. 8, 1918	Born in Kent, England
1940	Granted a B.S. degree from Imperial College, University of London
1942	Earns a Ph.D. at Imperial College
1949	Acts as a visiting professor at Harvard University
1950-1954	Serves on the faculty of Imperial College
1955-1957	Serves as a professor at Glasgow University, Scotland
1956	Wins the Fitzche Medal from the American Chemical Society
1957-1977	Serves as a professor at Imperial College
1961	Wins the Davy Medal from the Royal Society of London
1969	Awarded the Nobel Prize in Chemistry
1977-1985	Serves as director of research at the Centre Nationale de la Recherche Scientifique in Gif-sur-Yvette, France
1985	Becomes a Distinguished Professor at Texas A & M University
Mar. 19, 1998	Dies in College Station, Texas

Early Life

Derek Harold Richard Barton was born in Kent, England, in 1918. He actually worked in his father's wood business for a few years. After this manual labor, Barton wrote in his autobiography, "I felt there must be something more interesting in life. I decided to go to the university." In spite of his good elementary education, there was little indication of Barton's future scientific career, much less a Nobel Prize.

Early Education

After a year at Gillingham Technical College, he decided to go to Imperial College at the University of London. Barton's reasoning in this selection might suggest his general approach to problem solving: "Since the fees at Imperial College were 50 percent higher . . . I concluded that Imperial College was 50 percent better . . . This was, in fact, an underestimate."

A Wandering, Productive Scholar

The course of Barton's career was unusual. Most scientists spend a career in one setting, but from the beginning, Barton held positions at a variety of academic, industrial, and research laboratories. He took part in a large number of scientific meetings, colloquia, and conferences and also held posts as visiting professor at an impressive number of universities. Barton showed an unusual desire to communicate with his colleagues. He was amazingly productive despite the special demands imposed by adjustments to new surroundings and the time required to prepare talks. During his ten years in France, Barton published more than two hundred scientific articles. This accomplishment, he once noted, equaled his previous best decade.

The reasons for Barton's achievements extend beyond brilliance and hard work. His style of studying many different chemical problems—for example, steroids, alkaloids, terpenes, kinetics, energetics, and chemical physics—accounts for his seminal contributions to a wide range of chemical areas. In addition, his efforts to communicate the results and application of his studies to a broad spectrum of other chemists led him to forums where exciting new ideas were constantly being discussed.

A Roaming Chemist

One of Barton's remarkable traits is the ease with which he moved from one culture to another. Moving from England to France, and then finally to the United States, where he moved in 1985 to become a Distinguished Professor at Texas A & M University.

Throughout his career, Barton displayed both a talent for finding the most important idea in a new science problem and an amazing ability to discover the most promising aspects of stimulating colleagues in every new locale.

The Shape and Movement of Carbon Molecules

A successful physical model of molecules demands a specific geometry and consists of spherical beads that represent atoms; the pegs or springs holding them together are chemical bonds. These simple models are widely used for teaching and research.

The small molecule methane, natural heating gas, is represented as:

The Three-Dimensional Structure of Methane

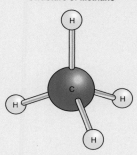

The shaded bonds imply that the molecule has the three-dimensional structure of Plato's simplest regular solid, the tetrahedron.

Yet, however useful this model is for simple molecules and even for much larger molecules found in nature, it is deficient. The model appears to be static (that is, without motion), but appearances are sometimes deceiving. Scientific theory and experimentation show that all matter is in constant motion.

Bond movement creates an infinite number of possible structures, each one having its own potential energy. Each of these specific structures is called a conformer; the study of such structures, pioneered by Barton, is termed conformational analysis.

Understanding chemical reactions depends on this vibrant, three-dimensional model and its energy. The breaking and forming of chemical bonds is usually represented in terms of bond vibrations. Chemical changes that facilitate or retard the rate of a reaction are frequently understandable only on the basis of bonds in motion.

Bibliography

Carey, Francis A. and Richard J. Sundberg. *Advanced Organic Chemistry.* 3d ed. New York: Plenum Press, 1990.

Allinger, Norman L. "Conformational Analysis in the Elementary Organic Course." *Journal of Chemical Education* (1964).

McMurry, John and Mary E. Castellion. *Fundamentals of General, Organic, and Biological Chemistry.* 2d ed. Upper Saddle River, N.J.: Prentice Hall, 1992.

Bibliography

By Barton

"The Principles of Conformational Analysis" *Les Prix Nobel en 1969,* 1970.

"Some Approaches to the Synthesis of Tetracycline," *Proceedings of the Royal Society of London, A,* 1970.

"Chemical Relationships Between Cephalosporins and Penicillins," *Proceedings of the Royal Society of London, B,* 1971.

Reason and Imagination: Reflections on Research in Organic Chemistry, 1996.

About Barton

Finley, K. T. and P. J. Siegel. "Barton and Hassel Share the Nobel Prize for Determining the Three-Dimensional Shapes of Organic Compounds." *Great Events from History II: Science and Technology.* Pasadena, Calif.: Salem Press, 1991.

Bezoari, Massimo D. . "Derek H. R. Barton." *The Nobel Prize Winners: Chemistry,* edited by Frank N. Magill. Pasadena, Calif.: Salem Press, 1990.

"Sir Derek H. R. Barton; Nobel-Winning Chemist" *Los Angeles Times,* March 19, 1998.

(K. Thomas Finley)

Antoine-Henri Becquerel

Disciplines: Chemistry, earth science, and physics

Contribution: Becquerel discovered radioactivity, for which he jointly received the Nobel Prize in Physics in 1903 with Marie and Pierre Curie.

Dec. 15, 1852	Born in Paris, France
1872-1874	Studies at the École Polytechnique
1874-1877	Studies at the École des Ponts et Chaussées
1879	Succeeds his father as *aidenaturaliste* at the Musée d'Histoire Naturelle
1888	Receives a doctorate from the Faculté des Sciences of Paris
1889	Elected to the Académie des Sciences
1894	Becomes engineer in chief at the École des Ponts et Chaussées
1896	Learns of the discovery of X-rays
1899-1900	Identifies electrons in the radiation of radium
1901	Publishes the first evidence of a radioactive transformation
1903	Receives the Nobel Prize in Physics jointly with Marie and Pierre Curie
1906	Elected vice president of the Académie des Sciences
1908	Becomes president of the Académie des Sciences
Aug. 25, 1908	Dies in Le Croisic, Brittany, France

Early Life

Antoine-Henri Becquerel (pronounced "beh-KRE-HL") was born in Paris on December 15, 1852. Both his father, Alexandre-Edmond Becquerel, and his grandfather, Antoine-César Becquerel, were physicists, members of the Académie des Sciences and, in turn, professors of physics at the Musée d'Histoire Naturelle (museum of natural history) in Paris. Antoine-Henri Becquerel would represent the third generation in his family to become a physicist and to hold these positions.

Becquerel attended school at the Lycée Louis-le-Grand. From there, he went to the École Polytechnique from 1872 to 1874 and to the École des Ponts et Chaussées, the French department of bridges and highways, from 1874 to 1877, where he was trained in engineering. He then entered the École des Ponts et Chaussées as an engineer.

In 1874, Becquerel married Lucie-Zoé-Marie Jamin, the daughter of J.-C. Jamin, a professor of physics in the Faculté des Sciences in Paris.

Lucie-Zoé-Marie died only a few years later, in March, 1879, following the birth of their son, Jean.

Early Research and Professional Life

Becquerel began his research career at the École Polytechnique in 1875 and began teaching there in 1876. In 1879, he succeeded his father as *aide-naturaliste* at the Musée d'Histoire Naturelle. Afterward, his professional life was shared between the museum, the École Polytechnique, and the École des Ponts et Chaussées.

Becquerel's early research was optical and dealt in part with the rotation of plane-polarized light by magnetic fields. He also studied infrared spectra by examining light emitted from phosphorescent crystals in infrared light and the absorption of light in crystals.

Becquerel earned his doctorate from the Faculté des Sciences in Paris in 1888 and in 1889 he was elected to the Académie des Sciences. After receiving his doctorate, Becquerel became largely inactive in research. In 1890, he married his second wife.

Becquerel's father died in 1891. The following year, he took over his father's two positions as chair of physics at the Conservatoire National des Arts et Métiers and at the Musée d'Histoire Naturelle. About the same time, he also took over the physics teaching duties of Alfred Potier at the École Polytechnique. In 1894, he became *ingénieur en chef* (engineer in chief) at the École des Ponts et Chaussées.

The Discovery of Radioactivity

X-rays were discovered accidentally by the German physicist Wilhelm Röntgen in 1895 while he was studying cathode rays in a high-voltage gaseous-discharge tube. Becquerel learned of this discovery on January 20, 1896, when two physicians, Paul Oudin and Toussaint Barthélemy, submitted an X-ray image of a hand to the Académie des Sciences. Noting that visible light and invisible X-rays were produced by the same mechanism, Becquerel wondered whether X-rays might be associated with all types of light.

Penetration of Matter by Various Types of Radiation

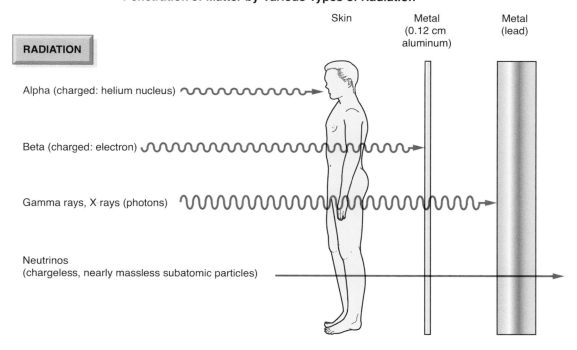

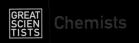

Radioactivity

Radioactivity is the spontaneous breakdown of the nucleus of an atom, which releases subatomic particles and radiation.

Radioactivity was discovered by Becquerel in 1896, shortly after the discovery of X-rays by Wilhelm Röntgen in 1895. Becquerel learned that invisible radiation from a cathode-ray tube could penetrate through a black cardboard box and cause a nearby barium platinocyanide screen to fluoresce; these invisible rays were termed X-rays. Becquerel began searching for a fluorescent crystal that could emit penetrating radiation, and he soon found that crystals of potassium uranyl sulfate would darken a photographic plate wrapped in black paper. Uranium was the source of the penetrating radiation. This radiation was initially called uranium rays or Becquerel rays, but it came to be known as radioactive radiation or radioactivity.

Elements that are unstable and spontaneously break down, or decay, to form other elements are referred to as radioactive elements. When the nucleus of a radioactive element decays, it releases subatomic particles, called alpha particles and beta particles, and radiation. An alpha particle (α) consists of two protons bound to two neutrons (a helium nucleus). A beta particle (β) is an electron that forms when a neutron splits into a proton and an electron. Gamma rays (γ) are high-energy photons, invisible electromagnetic radiation with a shorter wavelength than X-rays.

A loss of subatomic particles from the nucleus changes the atomic number and produces a different element, called a daughter element. For example, carbon 14 decays to the daughter element nitrogen 14 through the release of a beta particle. Uranium 238 decays to lead 206 through a multistep process in which eight α particles and six β particles are released, forming more than a dozen intermediate radioactive daughter elements, such as thorium and radon, in the process. The stable daughter product of the radioactive decay of uranium is lead.

An isotope is a form of an element with a different number of neutrons. There are several isotopes of uranium, such as uranium 238 and uranium 235. The number following the name of an element is called the mass number; it is the sum of the number of protons and the number of neutrons. All uranium atoms have 92 protons, so uranium 238 has 146 neutrons and uranium 235 has 143 neutrons. Both of these isotopes of uranium are radioactive, and each has its own unique half-life (the time that it takes for half of a given quantity of radioactive element to decay). After one half-life, half of the original number of radioactive atoms remain; the others have decayed to daughter atoms.

Radioactivity has many useful applications in science, medicine, engineering, and industry. Radioactive tracers can be used to monitor the movement of biochemical components in the bloodstream, to measure flow rates through systems of pipes, and to clarify complex chemical reactions such as photosynthesis. A drawback is that radioactive materials are hazardous and must be handled using protective measures.

Bibliography

Spinks, J. W. T. and R. I. Woods. *An Introduction to Radiation Chemistry*. 3d ed. New York: John Wiley & Sons, 1990.

Mas, A. W. H. *An Introduction to Radiobiology*. New York: John Wiley & Sons, 1990.

Faure, G. *Principles of Isotope Geology*. 2d ed. New York: John Wiley & Sons, 1986.

Choppin, G., J. Rydberg, and J. O. Liljenzin. *Radiochemistry and Nuclear Chemistry*. Oxford, England: Butterworth-Heinemann, 1995.

Because he had studied phosphorescent crystals, he began to seek a crystal that could emit penetrating radiation. He soon found that fluorescent crystals of uranium salt would expose a photographic plate wrapped in black paper, and he reported his findings to the academy on February 24 and March 2, 1896.

Becquerel experimented with other luminescent crystals and found that only those containing uranium emitted the penetrating radiation. Ultimately, he found that pure uranium metal produced penetrating radiation several times more intense than that produced by uranium salts. The significance of this finding, which was announced on May 18, 1896, was that penetrating radiation, or radioactivity, was a property of uranium.

This discovery opened the field of nuclear physics and set the stage for the research that Marie and Pierre Curie would perform, resulting in the discovery of radium. Becquerel later identified electrons in the radiation of radium and published the first evidence of a radioactive transformation in 1901.

It was soon found that radioactivity causes biological damage. When Becquerel went to London to make a presentation to the Royal Society, he carried a small amount of radium in a tube in his vest pocket and received a nasty burn on the skin of his stomach.

The Nobel Prize

In 1903, the Nobel Prize in Physics was shared by Becquerel and the Curies for their work with radioactive materials. In 1906, Becquerel was elected vice president of the Académie des Sciences, and he became its president in 1908. He was elected as one of two permanent secretaries of the academy later that year.

He died soon afterward at the age of fifty-five on August 25, 1908, at the home of his wife's family in Le Croisic, Brittany, France.

Bibliography
By Becquerel
"Sur les radiations émises par phosphorescence," *Comptes rendus de l' Académie des Sciences, Paris,* 1896.

"Sur les radiations invisibles émises par les sels d'uranium," *Comptes rendus de l' Académie des Sciences, Paris,* 1896.

"Sur diverses propriétés des rayons uraniques," *Comptes rendus de l' Académie des Sciences, Paris,* 1896.

"Sur la loi de décharge dans l'air de l'uranium électrisé," *Comptes rendus de l'Académie des Sciences, Paris,* 1897.

"Contribution à l'étude du rayonnement du radium," *Comptes rendus de l' Académie des Sciences, Paris,* 1900.

About Becquerel
Magill, Frank N., ed. "Antoine-Henri Becquerel." *The Nobel Prize Winners: Physics.* Pasadena, Calif.: Salem Press, 1989.

Jaffe, Bernard Jaffe. *Crucibles: The Story of Chemistry.* New York: Dover, 1976.

(Pamela J. W. Gore)

Claude Louis Berthollet

Discipline: Chemistry

Contribution: Berthollet showed that the simple laws of affinity between acidic and basic radicals were not enough to explain all compound formation, and factors like quantity of material and temperature must be considered.

Dec. 9, 1748	Born in Talloire, Savoy, Italy
1768	Graduates as a physician from the University of Turin, Italy
1772	Studies chemistry with P. J. Macquer and J. B. M. Bucquet in Paris
1778	Earns a DMed at the University of Paris
1780	Elected a member of the Académie des Sciences
1792-1796	Serves in many positions, scientific and otherwise, under several governments and sovereigns
1798	Travels to Egypt with Gaspard Monge, at Napoleon's request, to look into natural resources
1801	Publishes *Recherches sur les lois de l'affinité* (Researches into the Laws of Chemical Affinity, 1804)
1803	Publishes *Essai de statique chimique* (An Essay on Chemical Statics, 1804), his definitive statement on the laws of affinity
1805	Partially retires to Arceuil, a suburb of Paris
1807	With Pierre Laplace, founds Société d'Arceuil to discuss scientific matters
Nov. 6, 1822	Dies in Arceuil, France

Early Life

Claude Louis Berthollet (pronounced "behr-toh-LAY") was born to a family from the minor aristocracy that had fallen on hard times. His connections opened doors, however, and he became the physician to Mme de Montesson in Paris, which gave him access to a private laboratory. His work brought him to the attention of the new chemists surrounding Antoine-Laurent Lavoisier and to the Académie des Sciences, where he presented seventeen memoirs between 1778 and 1780. In the latter year, he became a member of the academy.

Investigations in Chemical Theory

Berthollet began his career as an adherent to the "phlogiston" theory of chemistry, which held that combustible materials contained an element of fire, called phlogiston, that was released when burning took place. The "calx" that remains (for example, a metal oxide) was seen as having lost its phlogiston

Chemical Affinity

Compound formation by simple affinity of one chemical fragment for another is affected by physical and chemical circumstances.

The theory of compound formation at the beginning of Berthollet's career rested on the doctrine of "chemical affinity." This theory stated that in any mixture of chemical fragments (now called ions or small molecules), those with the greatest affinity for each other would form a compound, leaving all others behind. Thus—to use the example that changed Berthollet's thinking in this matter—in a mixture of sodium chloride and calcium carbonate, the calcium and carbonate ions would seek out each other to form calcium carbonate, regardless of any interfering circumstances

During his Egyptian expedition, Berthollet observed the formation of sodium carbonate from such a combination of reactants (salt, or sodium chloride, from surface evaporation, and limestone, or calcium carbonate, in rock formations) at the shores of Lake Natron. He reasoned that the tremendous amount of carbonate leached out of the limestone, together with the large quantity of sodium from the salt, must tip the scales to favor the formation of sodium carbonate rather than the calcium carbonate predicted by simple affinity theory.

Back in Paris, he tested his ideas on this and other chemical systems and found that quantity of reactants did indeed alter product formation, as did temperature. Berthollet stopped short of the actual cause, the solution concentration of reactants, but he opened the way for a broader and subtler theory of compound formation that lasted for half a century.

Bibliography

Kapoor, Satish C. "Berthollet, Claude-Louis." in *Dictionary of Scientific Biography.* Vol. 2. New York: Charles Scribner's Sons, 1970.

LeGrand, H. E. "Claude-Louis Berthollet's *Essai de statique chimique and Acidity." Isis* 67 (1976).

but the metal could be reclaimed by transferring phlogiston from soot, oils, resins, sulfur, and the like, through heating.

This doctrine was radically opposed by Lavoisier, who showed that the calx was actually heavier than the metal, contrary to what the phlogiston theory would predict. Lavoisier correctly attributed this result to reaction with atmospheric oxygen and the recovery of the metal to the removal of oxygen. Berthollet became associated with Lavoisier's school because he thought that both sides of the argument could be modified to produce a unified chemistry. Later, he abandoned the phlogiston theory altogether.

Later Positions

By the turn of the nineteenth century, Berthollet had begun to study the laws of chemical affinity, an investigation that occupied his later years and produced his most important publication, *Essai de statique chimique* (1803; An Essay on Chemical Statics, 1804). In it, he introduced a broader view of chemical combination that served for nearly half a century before it was replaced with a theory that led to the current understanding of the subject.

Berthollet held influential positions under four separate regimes before and after the French Revolution. He was at various times a member of commissions on monetary reform, munitions, agriculture, and the arts. With Gaspard Monge and Louis B. Guyton de Morveau, he founded and taught at the École Polytechnique. He was commissioned to bring back Italian paintings to Paris and restore them. He was also sent to Egypt in 1798 by Napoleon. He was to investigate Egypt's natural resources.

Napolean made Berthollet a count, a senator from Montpellier, administrator of the mint, and a grand officer of the Legion of Honor.

Berthollet died in 1822.

Bibliography

By Berthollet

Éléments de l' art de la teinture, 1791 (2 vols.; Elements of the Art of Dyeing, 1791).

Recherches sur le lois de l'affinité, 1801 (Researches into the Laws of Chemical Affinity, 1804).

Essai de statique chimique, 1803 (2 vols.; An Essay on Chemical Statics, 1804).

Mémoires de physique et de chimie de la Société d'Arceuil, 1807-1817 (3 vols.).

About Berthollet

Partington. J. R. "Berthollet and the Antiphlogistic Theory." *Chymia* 5 (1959).

Kapoor, S. C. "Berthollet, Proust, and Proportions." *Chymia* 10 (1965).

Le Grand H. E. "The 'Conversion' of C. L. Berthollet to Lavoisier's Chemistry." *Ambix* 22 (1975).

Holmes, Frederic L. "From Elective Affinities to Chemical Equilibria: Berthollet's Law of Mass Action." *Chymia* 8 (1962).

(Robert M. Hawthorne, Jr.)

Jöns Jacob Berzelius

Discipline: Chemistry

Contribution: Berzelius contributed to analysis of chemistry, atomic and equivalent weights and combining proportions, nomenclature, and the discovery of new minerals and elements.

Aug. 20, 1779	Born in Östergötland, Sweden
1796-1798	Begins medical studies at Uppsala University
1798-1800	Analyzes the mineral content at Medevi mineral springs
1800	Builds a voltaic pile, using its electric current to treat patients
1802	Receives an M.D. from Uppsala
1803	Discovers the element cerium
1805	Practices as a physician to the poor in Stockholm
1807	Becomes a professor of medicine and pharmacy at the Medical College, Stockholm
1808	Made a member of Swedish Academy of Science
1810	Becomes the president of the Swedish Academy of Science
1817	Isolates the element selenium
1819	Elected secretary of the Swedish Academy of Science, a paid position
1829	Discovers the element thorium
1835	Is made a baron
Aug. 7, 1848	Dies in Stockholm, Sweden

Early Life

The forebears of Jöns Jacob Berzelius (pronounced "bur-ZEE-lee-us") on both sides of his family were clergymen. His father died when he was four years old, and Jöns lived with various relatives thereafter. Although he was expected to study to join the ministry, Berzelius was an indifferent student, preferring to collect and classify birds, flowers, and insects.

His choice of medicine was almost the only one available to a science-minded student of the day; the sciences as they are now known were not offered as degree studies in the universities. Berzelius was introduced to chemistry by a cousin, and he worked for a time in a pharmacy where he learned glassblowing, a necessary art for chemists of the time.

Early Research and Academia

Berzelius' work in mineral water analysis and voltaic current caused the physician Sven Hedin to recommend him in 1802 as an unpaid assistant to the professor of medicine and pharmacy at the Medical College in Stockholm. At this time, he met Wilhelm Hisinger, a mine owner who had the money and supported investigations in electrochemistry and mineralogy.

The appointments in the Medical College finally gave Berzelius a secure position in the world of chemistry, although he spent many years repaying debts contracted through no fault of his own. The secretary position at the Swedish Academy of Science, which provided a salary and excellent laboratory facilities, consolidated his position both academically and financially. By about 1820, he began to take his place as an authority among the chemists of England and the Continent.

Later Research

Although Swedish chemistry excelled in the discovery of elements and minerals at the time that Berzelius began his career, it was unequally developed and lacked broad grounding in both theory and laboratory practice. Berzelius, virtually uneducated in the science, changed all that during his lifetime, becoming, for a time, the European authority in chemistry.

After he summed up his voltaic chemistry in an 1802 volume and finished his research in the area a decade later, Berzelius turned to a determination of combining weights in compounds, to atomic and equivalent weights, and to elemental analysis of chemical substances. He began by reviewing and tightening up existing analytical procedures, and even inventing new ones.

From sample selection and analytical reagents (which he had to produce for himself) and balance techniques to the handling of solutions and precipitates—all were subjected to his relentless self-criticism. The results that Berzelius obtained on atomic weights and percent elemental composition of compounds were usually within a few hundredths of a percent of values accepted today.

Notation and Compound Formation

As Berzelius published the compositions of many chemical compounds, he realized that the symbols representing the elements and their proportions in the compounds could no longer be the geometrical and alchemical icons of the past; instead, an easy-to-remember, rational set of symbols was required.

By 1818, Berzelius and his students analyzed and produced the chemical formulae of nearly 2,000 chemical compounds. They also published accurate atomic weights of forty-five of the forty-nine known elements. Concurrently, Berzelius developed his system of element and compound notation.

Although Antoine-Laurent Lavoisier and others had developed a logical nomenclature based on the elements actually contained in the compound, notation was still at the stage of alchemical symbols—circles with dots, lines, and letters. Numbers of elements or radicals were shown by drawing the symbol more than once, in cluster fashion.

Berzelius' notation was the kind of innovation that seems almost foolishly obvious after it is adopted.

He suggested that they simply represent each element by the first letter of its Latin name, or the first two letters if necessary, and the numbers of atoms by superscript numbers following the symbol: Ag^2O or SnO^2, for example. Today's subscript numbers quickly came into use in all countries but France. Thereafter, all the carefully determined compounds, expressed in dualistic, acid-base nomenclature (Berzelius' other major contribution), had rational names and formulae and could be readily listed in alphabetical order along with their molecular weights and appropriate physical data.

Bibliography

Leicester, Henry M. "Berzelius, Jöns Jacob." In *Dictionary of Scientific Biography*. Vol. 2. New York: Charles Scribner's Sons, 1970.

Melhado, Evan N. and Tore Frangsmyr. *Enlightenment Science in the Romantic Era: The Chemistry of Berzelius and Its Cultural Setting*. Cambridge, England: Cambridge University Press, 1992.

Effect on Chemistry

The new information thus obtained about compounds required an improved notation and theory of compound formation. The notation that Berzelius devised is substantially that used today: elements represented by one-letter or two-letter symbols and proportions by numbers in the compound formula. The only difference being that Berzelius' numbers were superscripts rather than subscripts (for example, SO^3 rather than SO_3).

His new theory of compound formation was dualistic, with all compounds formed by the addition of a base to an acid (for example, the base K^2O and the acid SO^3 to make the compound K^2SO^4). This is a clear forerunner of the modern notation of inorganic salts, although it fell short when applied to organic compounds.

Nevertheless, he recognized and named isomerism in organic compounds, allotropy in elements, and the effect of catalysts in reaction.

Influence

Many chemists made the pilgrimage to Stockholm during Berzelius' heyday, roughly 1820 to 1840. His findings were published in textbooks that were translated into several languages.

In his later years Berzelius became less able to absorb new ideas, particularly in organic chemistry where molecular fragments that he knew clearly to be bases seemed to substitute freely for acids—chlorine for hydrogen, for example. He became engaged in polemics with other chemists and produced ever-smaller investigations with often unsatisfying results.

Berzelius' marriage at the age of fifty-six to twenty-four-year-old Elizabeth Poppius provided comfort and intellectual companionship in his declining years. Honors came his way, such as twelve royal orders and membership in ninety-four learned societies. He was made a baron in 1835. He died in 1848, just short of his sixty-ninth birthday.

Bibliography

By Berzelius

Holmberg, Arne, ed. *Bibliografi över Berzelius*, 1933-1953.

Partington, J. R., ed. *History of Chemistry*, vol. 4, 1964.

About Berzelius

Jorpes, J. Erik. *Jacob Berzelius, His Life and Work*, trans Barbara Steele. Berkeley, Calif.: University of California Press, 1970.

Melhado, Evan N. *Jacob Berzelius: The Emergence of His Chemical System*. Madison, Wis.: University of Wisconsin Press, 1981.

Berzelius, Jöns Jacob. *Jöns Jacob Berzelius: Autobiographical Notes*, trans Olof Larsell. Baltimore: Williams & Wilkins, 1934.

(Robert M. Hawthorne, Jr.)

Joseph Black

Disciplines: Chemistry and physics

Contribution: Black has been called the founder of modern quantitative chemistry. He applied precise measurements to the study of chemical reactions and to the study of heat exchange between substances at different temperatures.

Apr. 16, 1728	Born in Bordeaux, France
1740	Sent to Ireland for schooling
1746	Enters the University of Glasgow, Scotland
1754	Earns an M.D. from the University of Edinburgh, Scotland
1756	Publishes his classic dissertation *Experiments upon Magnesia Alba, Quicklime, and Some Other Alcaline Substances*
1756	Assumes the chair of anatomy and chemistry at the University of Glasgow
1757	Teaches a course in chemistry
1759	Begins his research on heat
1766	Assumes the chair of chemistry at the University of Edinburgh
Nov. 10, 1799	Dies in Edinburgh, Scotland
1803	Black's chemistry lectures are published posthumously

Early Life

Joseph Black was born in 1728 in Bordeaux, France to John and Margaret Black . He was one of fifteen children. His father, John Black, was a wine merchant. His father was a native of Belfast, so Joseph was sent to Ireland for schooling at the age of twelve. Six years later, he entered the University of Glasgow in Scotland, where he developed an interest in chemistry. Black earned an M.D. in 1754 from the University of Edinburgh, in Scotland.

Chemical Research at Edinburgh

Black did the chemical work for which he is most famous as part of his dissertation at Edinburgh, entitled *Experiments upon Magnesia Alba, Quicklime, and Some Other Alcaline Substances* (1756). In the course of his medical studies, he became interested in the chemistry of lime because of its properties as an antacid. A lot of work had already been done with lime, so Black decided to work with magnesia alba ($MgCO_3$), which had similar properties.

He heated the $MgCO_3$, decomposing it to magnesium oxide, and then regenerated the $MgCO_3$ by reacting the oxide with potassium carbonate. By careful weighing, Black showed that the loss in weight in the first reaction was almost equal to the gain in the second.

Black had demonstrated that the decomposition and regeneration of the magnesia alba had involved driving off and then replacing a gas that he called "fixed air." Black collected some of the gas and determined that it would put out a flame, and that it would not support life. At that time, air was considered to be a single substance and the only gas. Black's demonstration that ordinary air and fixed air had very different properties showed that this was not true. Fixed air is now called carbon dioxide.

Black as a Teacher

In 1756, Black became professor of chemistry at the University of Glasgow. He was said to be a brilliant teacher and students from the United States and a number of European countries traveled to Scotland to attend his lectures.

Black had little interest in publishing his research, so his lectures, which were published posthumously in 1803, contain the only record of some of his work.

Research on Heat

Black's major work in physics involved heat. For example, he was struck by an observation by Gabriel Daniel Fahrenheit that water can be cooled below its freezing point of 32 degrees Fahrenheit while remaining a liquid but then will quickly solidify when shaken. This solidification of the water is accompanied by a sharp rise in temperature to 32 degrees Fahrenheit. The thermometer gives no indication of the presence of this heat in the supercooled water, and only the temperature rise on solidification reveals that it is there. Black called it latent heat.

The Nature of Heat

Black's greatest contributions as a scientist were the result of his studies on heat. Since he never published any of his results, the only record of his work can be found in his lecture notes, which were published posthumously.

When Black began his work on heat, the distinction between quantity of heat and intensity of heat as measured by a thermometer was not appreciated. Black clarified the difference by showing that different heating times were required to produce the same increase in temperature for different substances. This fact led to the development of the concept of specific heat. Specific heat is now defined as the quantity of heat required to change the temperature of a substance by 1 degree Celsius. It is an essential concept in calorimetry, the science of the measurement of heat changes in physical and chemical processes.

The other important contribution from Black's work on heat was the development of the concept of latent heat. His measurements indicated that when water froze, it gave up a certain quantity of heat. He then showed that the same quantity of heat had to be added to ice in order to melt it. Black surmised that the same had to be true for the vaporization and condensation of water. These observations were essential to an understanding of the processes involved in phase changes.

Black's development of techniques for the careful measurement of heat changes gained him the title of the founder of calorimetry.

Bibliography

Roller, Duane E. ed. *The Early Development of the Concepts of Temperature and Heat: The Rise and Decline of the Caloric Theory.* Cambridge, Mass.: Harvard University Press, 1950.

Neidig, H. A., H. Schneider, and T. G. Teates. "Thermochemical Investigations for a First-Year College Chemistry Course." *Journal of Chemical Education* 42, no. 1 (1965).

Black also postulated that the same amount of heat should be given off in freezing as was required to melt a given weight of water. To verify this theory, Black had to wait until winter when ice was readily available.

Black had never been especially healthy and had suffered from lung problems as a child and rheumatism as an adult. He died on November 10, 1799, in Edinburgh, at the age of seventy-one.

Bibliography

By Black

Dissertatio medica inauguralis ..., 1754 (trans. in *Journal of Chemical Education*, 1935).

Experiments upon Magnesia Alba, Quicklime, and Some Other Alcaline Substances, 1756.

Lectures on the Elements of Chemistry Delivered in the University of Edinburgh, 1803.

About Black

Gillispie, Charles Coulston. ed. Vol. 2. *Dictionary of Scientific Biography.* New York: Charles Scribner's Sons, 1970.

Ramsay, Sir William. *Life and Letters of Joseph Black, M.D.* London: Constable, 1918.

(Francis P. Mac Kay)

Robert Boyle

Disciplines: Chemistry, invention, medicine, and physics

Contribution: Boyle is known for his development of the experimental method and for his careful recording and reporting of results. His work with air pressure and gases provided the basis for the kinetic theory of gases. His work in differentiating chemistry from alchemy earned him the title of founder of chemistry.

Jan. 25, 1627	Born in Lismore, Waterford, Ireland
1635-1639	Studies at Eton College, England
1639-1644	Travels throughout continental Europe with tutors
1655	Moves to Oxford, England to work with other leading scientists
1660	Becomes a founding member of the Royal Society of London
1660	Publishes *New Experiments Physio-Mechanicall, Touching the Spring of the Air and Its Effects*
1661	Publishes *The Sceptical Chymist*
1662	Publishes Boyle's Law
1668	Moves to London, England
1679	French physicist Edme Mariotte publishes his version of what is commonly called Boyle's law
Dec. 31, 1691	Dies in London, England

Early Life

Robert Boyle was an Anglo-Irish chemist and natural philosopher born in Lismore, Ireland, in 1627. His father was Richard Boyle, one of the richest men in Great Britain and the Lord High Treasurer (chief financial officer) of Ireland.

Boyle was educated at Eton College, England from 1635 to 1639. He spent the next five years with private tutors touring the European continent, where he studied French, Latin, Italian, history, mathematics, theology, and philosophy.

In 1644, he returned to England, where he began his experimental scientific work and also wrote moral essays. From 1656 to 1668, Boyle lived in Oxford, England. His father's fortune enabled Boyle to finance several scientific laboratories with trained associates to assist him in his experiments.

Experimental Methods

The seventeenth century was a time of rapid scientific advances. The century began with the studies of Galileo and ended with the monumental work of Sir Isaac Newton, who, along with many later scientists, was greatly influenced by Boyle.

Boyle is considered one of the founders of modern science and the chief founder of modern thinking in chemistry. He is noted for the development of the experimental method to test scientific theory. Boyle believed that experimental demonstration, as opposed to simple observation and speculation, was the only path to knowledge. This methodology necessitated collecting facts as a foundation for theories. It was in contrast to the school of René Descartes, which attempted to deduce a comprehensive description of nature from principles, with the aid of mathematics. Boyle believed that such a description was an ultimate aim of science but that it could be derived only from a preliminary experimental examination of nature.

Boyle was also noted for recording and reporting his experiments in great detail so that others could repeat his work. In doing so, he established the scientific tradition of carefully documented research and the repeatability of experiments. Boyle's theoretical explanations followed the mechanical (clockwork) philosophy, which can be verified through laboratory demonstration.

The Classification of Chemical Properties

Considered by many philosophers of science as the founder of chemistry, Boyle succeeded in changing chemists' outlook in the whole field. It appears that he was the first to suggest that matter can be classified in terms of similar chemical properties and to distinguish between atoms and elements. Thinking about matter in this way separated chemistry from alchemy. Such classification replaced the obscure medieval theories based on Aristotle's view of the four elements (earth, air, fire, and water) and served as a forerunner of the modern theory of chemical elements and atomic theory.

The Study of Gases and the Vacuum Pump

One of Boyle's greatest accomplishments was in the field of pneumatics, or the study of gases. Indeed, he is probably best known for summarizing the properties of gases by the law that is given his name, Boyle's Law. Boyle's Law states that at a constant temperature, the pressure and volume of a gas are inversely related. He also showed that air had weight and that gases have elastic properties.

This view led Boyle to spend much time, money, and effort on the development of a vacuum pump for his investigations of the properties of gases. He developed an improved vacuum pump and developed air pressure gauges and compression pumps. Boyle conducted pioneering experiments in which he demonstrated the physical characteristics of air and the necessity of air for combustion and for the transmission of sound.

Other Experiments

Boyle's research threw light on such physiological processes as the digestion of food and the role of air in the respiratory mechanism. In his experiments, Boyle also studied the calcination of metals and proposed a means of distinguishing between acid and alkaline substances, which was the origination of the use of chemical indicators.

In 1660, Boyle became a founding Fellow of the Royal Society of London, in which he challenged the widely held view that the writings of the great classical philosophers were the only fountain of wisdom. In 1668, he moved to London, England and lived with his sister until his death on December 31, 1691.

Throughout his life, Boyle regarded himself as dedicated to God by the practice of charity and science in lay life. His inherited wealth provided money for religious and charitable endeavors, and in his will he endowed a yearly series of Boyle's Lectures, sermons to defend Christianity against atheism. The lectures continue to this day.

Boyle's Law

Boyle's Law states that at a given temperature, the volume occupied by a gas is inversely proportional to the pressure.

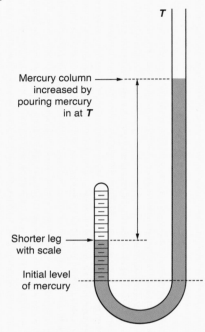

Mercury column increased by pouring mercury in at **T**

Shorter leg with scale

Initial level of mercury

At a constant temperature, the pressure (*P*) of a fixed amount of gas is inversely proportional to its volume (*V*). Mathematically, $P \times V = K$, where *K* is a constant. The Law applies only to ideal gases, that is, gases in which molecules are considered to be mathematical points with totally elastic collisions. On the European continent, the relationship of pressure and volume is referred to as Mariotte's law, after the French scientist Edme Mariotte, who published his results in 1679.

Boyle's law was first published in 1662. In his experiment, Boyle fashioned a J-shaped tube, with the short end of the J-tube sealed. He poured some mercury into the open end of the tube, waited until the mercury came to rest, and measured the volume of the gas trapped above the mercury in the enclosed end of the J-tube. Finally, Boyle measured the pressure in

inches of mercury from the top of the mercury in the open end of J-tube to the top of the mercury in the shorter leg of the J-tube.

Boyle then added more mercury to the tube and measured the new pressure and volume. He added the atmospheric pressure in inches of mercury to the pressure readings that he had obtained. Boyle compared the products of pressure and volume in these two instances and found that they were the same within experimental error (plus or minus a few points). He added more mercury, took further measurements, and found the same value for the pressure-volume product.

As an example, if the volume of the gas in the J-tube is 50 cubic centimeters and the mercury in the open end of the tube is 10 inches with the barometer reading 30 inches of mercury, the total pressure on the gas is 40 inches of mercury. The product of the pressure and the volume is 200. If enough mercury is added to the tube to increase the volume to 40 cubic centimeters, the mercury in the open end will be 20 inches above the mercury in the closed end. The total pressure will be 30 inches plus 20 inches, or 50 inches of mercury. The pressure-volume product again will be 200.

Boyle's law holds for real gases only over a small range of temperatures and pressures. The law makes poorer predictions at higher pressures and lower temperatures, where the gas molecules are closer together.

Bibliography

Conant, James B., ed. *Robert Boyle's Experiments in Pneumatics*. Cambridge, Mass.: Harvard University Press, 1950.

Brush, Stephen G., *Statistical Physics and the Atomic Theory of Matter from Boyle and Newton to Landau and Onsager*. Princeton, N.J.: Princeton University Press, 1983.

Bibliography

By Boyle

New Experiments Physio-Mechanicall, Touching the Spring of the Air and Its Effects, 1660.

The Sceptical Chymist, 1661.

The Works of the Honourable Robert Boyle, 1744.

Stewart, M.A. ed. *Selected Philosophical Papers of Robert Boyle,* 1979.

About Boyle

Shapin, Stephen and Simon Schaffer. *Leviathan and the Air-Pump: Hobbes, Boyle, and the Experimental Life.* Princeton, N.J.: Princeton University Press, 1985.

Conant, James B., ed. *Robert Boyle's Experiments in Pneumatics.* Cambridge, Mass.: Harvard University Press, 1950.

Brush, Stephen G. *Statistical Physics and the Atomic Theory of Matter from Boyle and Newton to Landau and Onsager.* Princeton, N.J.: Princeton University Press, 1983.

(Michael J. Wavering)

Henry Cavendish

Disciplines: Chemistry and physics

Contribution: In addition to making the first accurate measurement of the gravitational constant, Cavendish also discovered the element hydrogen and carried out experiments on electricity and on gases.

Oct. 10, 1731	Born in Nice, France
1742	Enrolls at Dr. Newcome's Academy
1749-1753	Attends St. Peter's College, University of Cambridge
1760	Elected a member of the Royal Society of London
1765	Writes an unpublished work on specific heat
1766	Reports the discovery and properties of hydrogen to the Royal Society of London
1767	Begins to study the composition of water
1771	Publishes a theory on the nature of electricity
1783	Publishes a study on the composition of air
1783-1788	Studies the freezing points of liquids
1784	Shows that the reaction of hydrogen with oxygen produces water
1785	Determines the composition of nitric acid
1798	Provides the first experimental determination of the gravitational constant and of Earth's mass
Feb. 24, 1810	Dies in London, England

Early Life

Henry Cavendish was born in Nice, France, in 1731. His father, Lord Charles Cavendish, was a member of the Royal Society of London and a noted experimental scientist. Lord Cavendish encouraged his son's interest in science, making his own scientific equipment available for his son's use.

At the age of eleven, Henry Cavendish enrolled at Dr. Newcome's Academy, a school for upper-class children. From 1749 to 1753, he attended St. Peter's College at the University of Cambridge. After leaving Cambridge, Cavendish moved to London, where he lived for the remainder of his life.

Early Scientific Work

Because Cavendish pursued his investigations for his own pleasure, he was often careless in publishing his results. As a result, it has proven difficult to develop a chronology for his research. It appears, however, that his early research was in the areas of heat and the dynamics of moving bodies.

Cavendish developed conservation laws for mechanical motion and in the early 1760s rediscovered the concept of specific heat.

Cavendish's first published work, appearing in 1766, concerned the properties of gases. He found differences in density between ambient air and gases produced by various chemical processes such as fermentation and the reaction of metals with strong acids or bases. In the course of his studies, Cavendish isolated a light gas that he identified as "phlogiston," the substance that was then believed to flow between objects during the transfer of heat. In fact, he had discovered hydrogen.

In the early 1770s Cavendish developed a fluid model for electricity. He devised an experimental test to confirm the inverse square law for the interaction of charged objects. Cavendish carried out a number of additional experiments that anticipated later work by other researchers, including studies on the attractive and repulsive forces acting on charged bodies, and on the relationship between charge and electrical potential for objects of various shapes and sizes.

The Chemistry of Gases and Solutions

In the 1780s, Cavendish returned to experimental work on the properties of gases. A paper in 1783 reported the results of his studies on the composition of air. The following year, he showed that the chemical reaction of hydrogen with oxygen produced water, thereby proving that water was a chemical compound and not an element, as had previously been thought.

In 1785, Cavendish carried out a series of experiments in which he passed an electrical discharge through air. When the product gases were bubbled through water, nitric acid was produced. During the course of these experiments, Cavendish found a component of air that would not combine with oxygen in the discharge. A century later, it was shown that this unreactive component of air was argon, a chemically inert element.

The Determination of the Value for the Gravitational Constant

Cavendish used a modified torsion balance to determine the value for G, the gravitational constant.

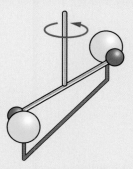

Cavendish used a torsion balance to determine the gravitational constant.

Sir Isaac Newton discovered that the gravitational attraction between bodies follows an inverse square law of the form "$F = GM_1M_2/r^2$," where F is the force of attraction, M_1 and M_2 are the masses of the bodies that are interacting, and r is the distance between the centers of mass of M_1 and M_2. G, the constant of proportionality in the equation, is called the gravitational constant. Because of the weakness of the gravitational attractive force compared to that for electrostatic attraction, it proved difficult to obtain a value for the gravitational constant.

In 1798, Cavendish used a modified torsion balance to make the first accurate experimental determination of G. The apparatus consisted of two small spherical masses connected to opposite sides of a rod that was suspended from a thin wire. The movement of the rod as two large spheres were brought close to the masses and the change in the frequency in the oscillation of the rod allowed Cavendish to determine the force of attraction, from which G could be obtained.

The Cavendish experiment remains the most accurate method by which the gravitational constant can be found. It has also been used to search for small differences in G based on time or on the composition of the interacting bodies.

Bibliography

Dicke, Robert H. *Gravitation and the Universe*. Philadelphia, PA: American Philosophical Society, 1970.

Nardo, Don. *Gravity, the Universal Force*. San Diego, Calif: Lucent Books, 1990.

At the same time that he was investigating the properties of air, Cavendish also began a series of measurements on the freezing of liquids. He was able to show that mercury thermometers become unreliable at low temperatures because of the freezing of liquid mercury and the corresponding decrease in volume.

Bibliography

In his later years, Cavendish gradually became interested in astronomy. From the gravitational constant, he was able to determine the mass and density of Earth. During the last years of his life, he gradually gained recognition for his scientific achievements. Cavendish died in London in 1810.

Bibliography

By Cavendish

Maxwell, James Clerk ed. *The Electrical Researches of the Honourable Henry Cavendish*, 1879.

About Cavendish

Berry, A. J. *Henry Cavendish: His Life and Scientific Work*. London, England: Hutchinson, 1960.

Wilson, George. *The Life of the Honourable Henry Cavendish*. London, England: Cavendish Society, 1851.

Crowther, James G. *Scientists of the Industrial Revolution*. London, England: Cresset Press, 1962.

(Jeffrey A. Joens)

Sir John Cornforth

Discipline: Chemistry
Contribution: Cornforth showed the power of associating a molecule's exact structure, or stereochemistry, with its synthesis in nature.

Sept. 7, 1917	Born in Sydney, Australia
1937	Graduated with first-class honors from Sydney University
1937-1941	Studies the synthesis of steroids at Oxford University, England, with Sir Robert Robinson
1941-1945	Works on the synthesis of penicillin
1946	Joins the National Institute for Medical Research
1946	Begins his collaboration with George Popják
1953	Elected a Fellow of the Royal Society of London
1962	Becomes co-director of the Milstead Laboratory of Chemical Enzymology for Shell Research Ltd.
1966	Wins the CIBA Medal of the British Biochemical Society
1968	Wins the Davy Medal of the Royal Society of London
1972-1982	Serves as professor at University of Sussex
1975	Wins the Nobel Prize in Chemistry
1977	Receives a knighthood
1978	Elected to the U.S. National Academy of Sciences
1991	Made Companion of the Order of Australia

Early Life

John Warcup Cornforth was born in Sydney, Australia, in 1917. His father was a teacher and is mother a nurse. Cornforth spent his youth in Sydney and in rural New South Wales. His progressive loss of hearing and ultimate deafness before entering college did not prevent him from attaining an excellent education.

At fourteen, Cornforth began chemical experiments in his home laboratory. He chose to study at Sydney University because of its excellent facilities. Receiving his degree with honors in 1937, Cornforth won a scholarship to continue at Oxford University, England. His choice was dictated by the presence of Sir Robert Robinson, the chemist who would win the 1947 Nobel Prize.

Research and World War II

Another scholarship winner, Rita H. Harradence, was also involved in studying the synthesis of steroids. Harradence and Cornforth fell in love

Stereochemical Road Maps

In its most fundamental form, stereochemistry involves the comparison of two molecules, as one compares right and left hands. Many molecules possess symmetry making them achiral, meaning that the left-hand and right-hand forms are identical or can be superimposed.

In the world of living plants and animals, most molecules exist in nonidentical right and left forms that are related as an object and its image in a mirror. The modern term describing this comparison is "chirality," derived from the Greek word "cheri," meaning hand. Furthermore, these two molecules are rarely interchangeable in natural chemistry. Efforts to study the benefits of using only a right-handed or left-handed form of a drug, in order to reduce the dosage and/or side effects, has attracted considerable research.

In many cases, the chiral molecule results from a carbon atom attached to four different atoms or groups of atoms. The differences among the atoms need not be very great, although the smaller the difference, the more difficult it becomes to detect the change. In John and Rita Cornforth's study of cholesterol, the differences were made as small as possible, involving atoms of a single element that differed only in their mass.

Acetic acid, found in vinegar, is an achiral molecule that is important in biosynthesis. The Cornforths used deuterium and tritium, the heavy and radioactive isotopes of hydrogen, to construct the right-handed and left-handed forms of acetic acid.

Left-Handed and Right-Handed Forms of Acetic Acid

In this diagram of acetic acid, O is oxygen, H is hydrogen, C is carbon, OH is hydroxide, D is deuterism, and T is tritium.

Bibliography

Lehninger. Albert L. *Biochemistry*. 2d ed. New York: Worth, 1993.

Ramsay, O. Bertrand. *Stereochemistry*. London: Heyden, 1981.

Devlin, Thomas M. *Textbook of Biochemistry*. 3d ed. New York: Wiley-Liss, 1992.

and married in 1941. Not only was Harradence's early research in the same area that would eventually win her husband a Nobel Prize, but she would also play a vital role in the success of his work. The two scientists continued to work together on the synthesis of penicillin during World War II.

Following the war, John Cornforth continued to work with Robert Robinson until 1946, when he joined the National Institute for Medical Research.

These early studies illustrate Cornforth's self-description as an organic chemist. While he constantly employed the latest and most powerful theoretical and practical tools available, he never lost sight of his goal. He was always dedicated to discovering the ways in which complex molecules are created from simpler structures—that is, their synthesis.

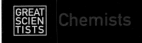
How Complex Can a Molecule Be?

As a result of public concern with proper diet, cholesterol is one of the most widely known of the molecules found in nature, and it was not by chance that the Cornforths and their collaborator, George Popják, decided to study it. Popják's training as a biochemist complemented that of John Cornforth's by placing a greater emphasis on cellular behavior.

Both noticed the molecule's unique geometry, obtained from relatively simple starting material. Squalene, for example, is an open-chain molecule that represents the immediate source of cholesterol. Cholesterol, by contrast, contains a complex system of four rings attached to one another in a specific fashion. Furthermore, squalene appeared to form from two identical molecules of a substance called farnesyl pyrophosphate.

These facts would intrigue any chemist, and the detailed story is even more astonishing. The conversion of farnesyl to squalene involves only the exchange of a single hydrogen atom from each of the carbon atoms that unite. Cornforth saw in this delicate choice of nature an opportunity to examine the exact functioning of the powerful natural catalysts called enzymes. The results revolutionized the understanding of stereochemistry.

Honors and Awards

Cornforth was named a Fellow of the Royal Society of London in 1953 and was elected to the U.S. National Academy of Sciences in 1978. In 1966, he won the CIBA Medal of the British Biochemical Society, and in 1968 he was awarded the Davy Medal of the Royal Society of London. He was named a Commander of the British Empire in 1972. In 1975 came Cornforth's greatest honor: the Nobel Prize in Chemistry and in 1977, he received a knighthood.

In 1982 Cornforth retired from teaching. He continues to work at the University of Sussex, England.

Bibliography

By Cornforth

Clarke, (Hans T. ed., "Oxazoles and Oxazolones" in *The Chemistry of Penicillin*, 1949.

"Absolute Configuration of Cholesterol," *Nature*, 1954.

"A Stereoselective Synthesis of Squalene," *Journal of the Chemical Society*, 1959.

"Exploration of Enzyme Mechanisms by Asymmetric Labeling," *The Chemical Society Quarterly Reviews*, 1969.

"Asymmetry and Enzyme Action" in *Les Prix Nobel*, 1975.

About Cornforth

Magill, Frank N. ed. "John Warcup Cornforth." In *The Nobel Prize Winners: Chemistry*, Pasadena, Calif.: Salem Press, 1990.

Eliel, Ernest L. and Harry S. Mosher. "The 1975 Nobel Prize for Chemistry" *Science* (1975).

Greene, Jay E. ed. "Sir John (Warcup) Cornforth." In *McGraw-Hill Modern Scientists and Engineers*. New York: McGraw-Hill, 1980.

"Sir John Warcup Cornforth," Faculty of Science, The University of Sydney, http://sydney.edu.au/science/about_us/fame_cornforth.shtml

(K. Thomas Finley)

Donald J. Cram

Discipline: Chemistry

Contribution: Cram mapped out the retention of three-dimensional molecular form in a wide variety of substitution and elimination reactions. He then concentrated on host-guest chemistry.

Apr. 22, 1919	Born in Chester, Vermont
1941	Receives a B.S. in chemistry from Rollins College in Winter Park, Florida
1942	Receives an M.S. in chemistry from the University of Nebraska
1942-1945	Helps develop penicillin and streptomycin at Merck & Co.
1947	Receives a Ph.D. at Harvard University
1947	Carries out postdoctoral studies with John D. Roberts at the Massachusetts Institute of Technology (MIT)
1947	Becomes assistant professor of chemistry at the University of California, Los Angeles (UCLA)
1956	Becomes a full professor at UCLA
1960	Publishes *Organic Chemistry*, a textbook arranged by reaction mechanism
1966	Named Saul Winstein Professor of Chemistry at UCLA
1987	Awarded the Nobel Prize in Chemistry
1990	Publishes the autobiography *From Design to Discovery*
June 27, 2001	Dies in Palm Desert, California

Early Life

Donald James Cram was born in Vermont in 1919. His father was of Scottish descent, while his mother was of German descent. Cram's family moved to Brattleboro, Vermont, in 1921. Two years later, his father died of pneumonia. There were five children to be fed and housed, giving Cram an early appreciation for a strong work ethic. It also led him to a conviction that he wanted no part of futureless, repetitive employment.

At Winwood, a small private school on Long Island, Cram read all the classics, but he also played varsity sports. His undergraduate studies in chemistry at Rollins College in Winter Park, Florida, gave him the first hint that here might be the nonrepetitive, ever-fresh work for which he was looking. His M.S. and Ph.D. research confirmed this, and thereafter he never looked back. Teaching and research, with their continuous surprises, would be his life.

First Years at UCLA

Cram began research work at the University of California, Los Angeles (UCLA), while he was still getting his feet under him in the classroom. His investigation of natural products from Merck & Co.'s penicillin studies during World War II quickly led to the observation of the retention or exact inversion of configuration (the three-dimensional structure around carbon atoms with four different groups attached to them). Cram attributed this to the bridging of two adjacent carbons by a phenonium ion (essentially a benzene ring) during the course of the reaction, so that the atoms could not rotate about their bond and thereby change their configuration.

The phenonium and other bridging ions occupied the attention of Cram and his graduate students for two decades, allowed the synthesis of many biological and pharmaceutical compounds in which configuration is all-important for medicinal effectiveness, and gave birth to a broad generalization about product structure called Cram's rule. Parenthetically, it should be noted that the earliest part of this work was a hands-on effort by Cram himself; he later expressed pride that he "earned tenure with my personal research."

Later Research

At the age of fifty, fearing that the bridging-ion work was becoming repetitive, Cram shifted his interests to the research in host-guest chemistry that would earn him the Nobel Prize in Chemistry.

Host-guest chemistry is akin to the pattern of catalysis carried out by enzymes in the cell, in which enzymes hold other molecules in particular patterns or positions so that they can react only one way, giving a specific, physiologically necessary product. Early efforts in this field were much simpler than cell chemistry, but the success achieved and the clear-cut importance of the concept led the Nobel Committee to recognize Cram and his fellow awardees, Jean-Marie Lehn and Charles J. Pedersen.

Host-Guest Chemistry

Organic molecules can be synthesized with three-dimensional shapes that allow them to pick up atoms, ions, or other molecules to hold in position for very specific reactions.

Cram's first success in host-guest chemistry was obtained with a crown ether, a cyclic molecule of carbon and oxygen atoms, the latter regularly spaced about the ring. He found that in the 18-crown-6 molecule—with eighteen atoms in the ring, every third one an oxygen, with the oxygens sticking up like points on a crown—that Charles J. Pedersen had synthesized at DuPont, the spacing of the oxygen points was exactly right for holding a potassium ion. That ion could be selectively removed from a solution containing other ions. The resulting crown ether can be a useful tool in analytical chemistry.

Within a few years, Cram and his graduate students synthesized a series of crown ethers and similar molecules to select a wide range of ions from solutions. He then turned his attention to what he called "cavitands," molecules large enough to contain a cavity that could fix another molecule in place for reaction with yet another molecule. The analogy between cavitands and the enzymes that catalyze cell reactions was so compelling that it led to the 1987 Nobel Prize in Chemistry for Cram, Pedersen, and Jean-Marie Lehn.

Bibliography

"The Design of Molecular Hosts, Guests, and Their Complexes." Donald J. Cram. *Angewandte Chemie: International Edition in English* 27 (1988).

"Molecular Cells: Their Guests, Portals, and Behavior." Donald Cram. *CHEMTECH* (1987).

Marriage and Awards

Cram married Jean Turner, in 1940, and then Jane Maxwell, in 1969. Both marriages were childless.

Throughout his career Cram received numerous awards, including honorary doctorates and various medals from the American Chemical Society. He became an avid surfer and downhill skier, as well as a folksinger and guitarist. Cram died of cancer in 2001.

Bibliography

By Cram

Fundamentals of Carbon Chemistry, 1965.

Elements of Organic Chemistry, 1970 (with Jane Cram).

"Host-Guest Chemistry," *Science*, 1974 (with Jane Cram).

"Molecular Cells: Their Guests, Portals, and Behavior," *CHEMTECH*, 1987.

"The Design of Molecular Hosts, Guests, and Their Complexes," *Angewandte Chemie: International Edition in English*, 1988

About Cram

Peterson, Ivars. "Cages, Cavities, and Clefts." *Science News* 132 (August 8, 1987).

Hawthorne, Robert M. Jr., "Donald J. Cram, 1919-." In *Notable Twentieth-Century Scientists*, edited by Emily J. McMurray. Detroit: Gale Research, 1995.

James, Laylin K., ed. *Nobel Laureates in Chemistry, 1901-1992*. Washington, D.C.: American Chemical Society, 1993.

(Robert M. Hawthorne, Jr.)

Marie Curie

Disciplines: Chemistry and physics
Contribution: Curie helped lay the foundations of modern nuclear physics; with her husband, Pierre, she discovered the highly radioactive elements radium and polonium. She was an early advocate of the medical use of X-rays and radioactivity.

Nov. 7, 1867	Born in Warsaw, Poland
1891	Moves to Paris to study at the Sorbonne
1898	With her husband, isolates polonium
1902	Separates out a decigram of pure radium
1903	Presents her work in radioactivity as a Ph.D. thesis
1903	Receives the Nobel Prize in Physics jointly with Pierre Curie and Antoine-Henri Becquerel
1906	Assumes her husband's position on the faculty of the Sorbonne after he is killed in an accident
1911	Receives the Nobel Prize in Chemistry for her work with radium and polonium
1914	Equips ambulances with portable X-ray equipment during World War I
1918	Becomes the first director of the Radium Institute in Paris
1920	Creates the Curie Foundation
July 4, 1934	Dies in Sancellemoz, near Sallanches, France

Early Life

Marie Curie was born Marya Sklodowska on November 7, 1867, in Warsaw, Poland. Her father taught mathematics and physics at a government secondary school in Warsaw. Her mother was the principal of a private boarding school for girls until shortly after Marie's birth, when she contracted tuberculosis and had to give up her position.

At that time, Poland was under Russian rule; it was difficult for the family to make ends meet. Marie attended public schools and was always a star pupil. When her sister Bronia left to study medicine in Paris, Marie took a position as a governess with the Zorawski family in order to help with the finances. After a day's work, she would give lessons to the peasant children.

Student Days in Paris

In 1891, Marie collected her meager savings and went to Paris to study at the Sorbonne.

Although she could have lived comfortably with Bronia and her husband, who were both doctors, Marie insisted on living alone in a modest room in order to concentrate more on her studies. Her hard work paid off when, in 1893, she passed her examination for the licentiate in physics with high honors, ranking first. In 1894, she passed her examination for the licentiate in mathematics with honors, ranking second.

In that year, she met Pierre Curie, with whom she found a kindred spirit in their love of and devotion to the sciences. They were married in July 1895, in a simple civil service. For their honeymoon, they toured the French countryside on bicycles, sharing their fondness for nature. They would have two daughters, Irène and Eve.

Research in Radioactivity

Upon returning to Paris, Marie Curie began looking for a topic for her doctoral research. She was excited by Antoine-Henri Becquerel's discovery that uranium emits X-rays. Curie, suggesting the term radioactivity, decided to further investigate this phenomenon. Finding no other elements besides uranium and thorium that emit radiation, she began looking more closely at pitchblende, the ore from which uranium is obtained. Curie found a curious inconsistency: The pitchblende contained more radioactivity than could be accounted for by the uranium and thorium that it contained.

This led Curie to the conclusion that the ore must contain some new, previously unknown element that although present in only minute quantities, was much more radioactive than uranium. She plunged into the search for this element, and Pierre abandoned his own research to help her. In the yard of the School of Physics and Chemistry, in a tumbledown shed with no heat and a leaky roof they set out to process tons of pitchblende.

After many years of arduous work, they finally succeeded in identifying two new elements: polonium and radium.

The Radioactive Decay of Uranium

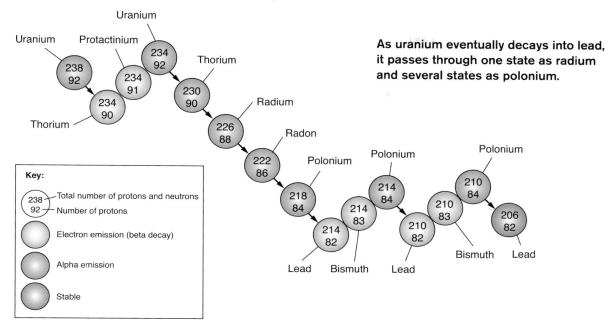

As uranium eventually decays into lead, it passes through one state as radium and several states as polonium.

Radioactivity

Radioactivity is a property of the nucleus. Some nuclei are unstable and will disintegrate spontaneously to form different nuclei, with the subsequent emission of particles and energy. This transmutation can occur even when the nucleus is isolated from any external influences.

The most common types of radioactivity are alpha (α) decay, beta (β) decay, and gamma (γ) decay. An alpha particle consists of two protons and two neutrons and is essentially a helium nucleus. There are three different types of beta decay: β^- decay, β^+ decay, and electron capture. A β^- is really an electron; it was given a different name since it originates in the nucleus. In β^- decay, a neutron decays into a proton, an electron, and an antineutrino. A β^+ is a positron, or an antielectron. In β^+ decay, a proton decays into a neutron, a β^+, and a neutrino. In electron capture, the nucleus captures an atomic electron and then transforms into a different nucleus with the emission of a neutrino. A gamma particle is a high-energy photon.

When a nucleon (a proton or a neutron) decays from an excited energy level within the nucleus to a lower level, excess energy is given off in the form of a gamma particle.

The number of nuclei present at any time is dependent on the number of nuclei originally present and the probability that a decay will occur, called the decay constant, λ. The decay constant is a characteristic of the nucleus. The number of nuclei decreases exponentially with time. The time for half of the nuclei to decay is called the half-life.

Bibliography

Beiser, Arthur. *Concepts of Modern Physics*. New York: McGraw-Hill, 1987.

Lerner, Rita G. and George L. Trigg, eds. *Encyclopedia of Physics*. New York: VCH, 1991.

Thornton, Stephen T. and Andrew Rex. *Modern Physics for Scientists and Engineers*. Fort Worth, Tex.: W. B. Saunders, 1993.

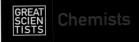
Finally, in 1902, they were able to separate out a decigram of pure radium. In 1903, Marie presented this research for her Ph.D. That year, the Curies were awarded the Nobel Prize in Physics for the discovery of radioactivity.

The Curies at last were gaining the international recognition that they deserved. Honors were heaped upon them, much to their dismay. They continued their research, refusing to take out patents or to claim royalties for their processes, giving away a fortune.

Going on Alone

In 1906, Pierre was killed in an accident on the streets of Paris. Marie was devastated but continued with her research in his memory. She was appointed to the chair of physics originally created for Pierre and became the first woman to teach at the Sorbonne. In 1911, Curie was awarded the Nobel Prize in Chemistry for her discovery of polonium and radium.

During World War I, Curie used private donations to equip ambulances that she accompanied to the front lines with portable X-ray machines. Assisted by her daughter Irène, she created accelerated courses for doctors to learn the new methods of locating foreign objects in the human body.

In 1918, the Radium Institute was opened, and Curie served as its director until she became too ill to continue.

Polonium and Radium

Wherever uranium and thorium are found, small amounts of polonium and radium are also found. These elements were first discovered by Pierre and Marie Curie.

The Curies found that pitchblende, a uranium ore, contained more radioactivity than could be accounted for from the amount of uranium that it contained. The implication of this extra radioactivity was that some previously unknown element must exist in the pitchblende that, although present in minute quantities, emitted large amounts of radioactivity.

The Curies began processing tons of pitchblende, and, after years of work, they were able to isolate a small amount of black powder that was 400 times more radioactive than uranium. They named this new element "polonium" in honor of Marie's homeland of Poland. Its chemical properties are similar to those of tellurium, and it was later found to have an atomic number of 84, placing it in the same group.

The polonium that they had isolated, however, still did not account for all the extra radioactivity. After five years of work, they were able to produce a decigram (hardly enough to see) of another new element, which they named "radium." Radium's properties are very similar to those of barium, and it was later determined to have an atomic number of 88.

Polonium and radium are much more radioactive than uranium because of their very short half-lives; they decay much faster than uranium. Their lifetimes are so short that no polonium or radium should be left in the world by now. The reason that one still finds these elements is that they are continually being formed in the decay of uranium and thorium. Both of these elements are intermediate products on the way to lead. This fact led to the discovery of three other new elements: actinium, radon (a radioactive gas), and protactinium, which are also intermediate steps in the uranium decay series.

Bibliography

Asimov, Isaac. *Asimov's New Guide to Science*. New York: Basic Books, 1984.

Lerner, Rita G. and George L. Trigg, eds. *Encyclopedia of Physics*. New York: VCH, 1991.

Suffering from cataracts and lesions on her hands from handling radium, Marie Curie died of leukemia in 1934.

Bibliography

By Curie

"Sur une substance nouvelle radioactive dans la pechblende," *Comptes Rendus*, 1898 (with Pierre Curie).

"Nouvelle substance fortement radioactive, contenu dans la pechblende," *Comptes Rendus*, 1898 (with Pierre Curie and G. Bémont).

Traité de radioactivité, 1910 (2 vols.).

Radioactivité, 1935 (2 vols.; Irène and Frédéric Joliot-Curie, eds.).

Joliot-Curie, Irène ed. *Oeuvres de Marie Sklodoioska-Curie*, 1954.

About Curie

Christie, J. "The Discovery of Radium." *Journal of Franklin Institute* 167, no. 5 (May, 1909).

Curie, Eve. *Madame Curie*. New York: Garden City, 1943.

Reid, Robert. *Marie Curie*. New York: E. P. Dutton, 1974.

(Linda L. McDonald)

John Dalton

Disciplines: Biology, chemistry, earth science, mathematics, and physics

Contribution: Dalton developed the first modern atomic theory to explain chemical behavior, and researched the behavior of gas mixtures, meteorology, and color blindness.

Sept. 6, 1766	Born in Cumberland, England
1792	Appointed Professor of Mathematics at The New College, Manchester
1793	Publishes *Meteorological Observations and Essays*
1794	Elected a member of the Manchester Literary and Philosophical Society
1794	Publishes the first description of color blindness
1801	Publishes a formal statement of the partial pressure law
1803	Issues the first statement of the law of multiple proportion
1808-1810	Publishes the first two parts of *A New System of Chemical Philosophy*
1822	Elected a member of the Royal Society of London
1827	Publishes the third volume of *A New System of Chemical Philosophy*
1831	Helps found the British Association for the Advancement of Science
1832	Awarded an honorary degree from Oxford University
July 27, 1844	Dies in Manchester, England

Early Life

John Dalton was born on or about September 6, 1766, in Eaglesfield, Cumberland, England. His father, Joseph, was a weaver and a devout Quaker. As a boy, Dalton was educated at a local Quaker school, but in his early teens he was forced to work as a common laborer to support himself.

In 1781, Dalton was hired to replace his older brother as an assistant in a boarding school in Kendal, 40 miles from his home. His new position gave him access to the school's facilities and was also able to attend lectures by notable visitors to the region.

During the next few years, Dalton was given increasing responsibilities at the boarding school. As was common at the time, he began offering public lectures in astronomy, mechanics, and other areas of science. In 1792 he moved to Manchester, where he obtained an appointment as a professor of mathematics and natural philosophy at the New College.

Initial Scientific Work

In 1793 Dalton published a series of observations and essays on meteorology. The next year, following his election as a member of the Manchester Literary and Philosophical Society, he presented a paper containing the first detailed discussion of color blindness, an affliction from which Dalton himself suffered. While his explanation for the cause of color blindness turned out to be incorrect, the condition is sometimes called daltonism in honor of his work on the subject.

Dalton's interest in chemistry and meteorology led him to consider the behavior of mixtures of gases. In 1801 he proposed that in a mixture of gases, each component acts independently of the other gases present. This behavior, true for mixtures of ideal gases, is now known as Dalton's Law of Partial Pressures.

In his work with gas mixtures, Dalton had assumed that gases were composed of individual particles of matter. In 1803, he applied this concept to chemistry, arguing that when elements combine to form chemical substances, compounds appear for only certain fixed ratios of each element. This law of multiple proportions allowed him to find relative values for the atomic weights of elements.

Atomic Theory

Dalton's work on gas mixtures, the law of multiple proportions, and relative atomic weights led him to consider the nature of matter itself. During the next few years, he used his previous work to develop a systematic atomic theory.

Dalton presented his theory in 1808 in his book, *A New System of Chemical Philosophy*. The basic idea behind Dalton's atomic theory was that all matter is composed of atoms, which represent the smallest particles of an element. All atoms of a particular element are identical in mass and chemical properties and differ in these characteristics from atoms of different elements.

Dalton's Atomic Theory

Dalton developed the first atomic theory based on quantitative chemical principles and experimental observations.

The idea that matter is composed of small particles dates back to ancient times. The first known atomic theory was proposed by the Greek philosopher Democritus in the fifth century BC. Early atomic theories, however, were based on philosophical considerations instead of empirical evidence.

The first modern comprehensive atomic theory was proposed by Dalton in 1808. His theory was an attempt to explain a body of observations from his own experiments and those of other scientists.

In modern language, his atomic theory consisted of the following five ideas. First, elements are composed of small particles called atoms. Second, all atoms of a particular element are identical in mass and other physical and chemical properties. Third, atoms of different elements have different masses and properties. Fourth, in a chemical compound, the relative number of each type of atom making up a compound is constant. Fifth, in chemical reactions, the atoms making up chemical compounds can be rearranged, but atoms themselves cannot be created or destroyed.

Dalton's atomic theory provided a simple and consistent explanation for a number of experimental observations, including the conservation of mass, the law of definite proportions, and the law of multiple proportions. Atomic theory also made it possible for Dalton and others to determine relative values for mass for each of the known elements.

Dalton's theory was quickly accepted as a useful means of summarizing and explaining a large body of experimental data on the chemical behavior of substances. Many scientists, however, while agreeing as to the usefulness of the theory, remained skeptical concerning the reality of atoms themselves. In large part, this reaction was attributable to the inability to observe atoms directly. It was only in the early twentieth century, when Albert Einstein used the concepts of atoms and molecules to explain Brownian motion, that the existence of real atoms became generally accepted as fact.

Subsequent advances in the understanding of the nature of matter have required modification of Dalton's ideas. It was discovered that atoms themselves possess an underlying structure and that it is possible by nuclear reactions to convert atoms of one element into those of another element. Further, it was found that atoms of the same element can differ slightly in mass. These different forms of elements, called isotopes, differ slightly in their physical and chemical properties, primarily because of mass differences. Separation methods based on the small mass differences of isotopes, such as thermal diffusion, can be used to obtain nearly pure samples of particular isotopes of an element.

While there are shortcomings to the atomic theory advanced by Dalton, it remains a starting point in the discussion of the nature of matter. The theory remains a useful means of summarizing and predicting the behavior of chemical substances.

Bibliography

Atom. Isaac Asimov. New York: E. P. Dutton, 1991.

Atoms and Powers. A. W. Thackray Cambridge, Mass.: Harvard University Press, 1970.

Mystery of Matter. Louise B. Young, ed. New York: Oxford University Press, 1965.

Nature of Matter. Ginestra Amaldi. Chicago: University of Chicago Press, 1966.

Atoms can be rearranged to form various chemical substances, but it is impossible to create, destroy, or transform the atoms themselves.

Dalton's theory gave a simple explanation for a variety of observations that had been made concerning the properties of matter and it quickly gained acceptance among scientists as a useful model for explaining the chemical behavior of substances.

Later Life

While Dalton continued to conduct research in chemistry after the development of his atomic theory, his later work was of little importance when compared to his earlier discoveries.

He maintained an active role in the Manchester Literary and Philosophical Society and served as its president from 1817 until his death. Dalton was elected a member of the Royal Society of London in 1822, and in 1826, he received the Royal Medal from the Society. He was also a founding member of the British Association for the Advancement of Science, which was organized in 1831.

In 1837 Dalton suffered a stroke. Seven years later he died in Manchester.

Bibliography

By Dalton

Meteorological Observations and Essays, 1793.

A New System of Chemical Philosophy, part 1, 1808; part 2, 1810.

A New System of Chemical Philosophy, 1827 (vol. 2).

About Dalton

Greenaway, Frank. *John Dalton and the Atom.* Ithaca, N.Y.: Cornell University Press, 1966.

Patterson, Elizabeth C. *John Dalton and the Atomic Theory.* Garden City, N.Y.: Doubleday, 1970.

Cardwell, Donald S. L. ed. *John Dalton and the Progress of Science.* Manchester, England.: Barnes & Noble Books, 1968.

(Jeffrey A. Jones)

Sir Humphry Davy

Disciplines: Chemistry and invention

Contribution: Davy's work on electrochemistry was fundamental in revealing the electrical nature of matter. He discovered and isolated many new elements from compounds.

Dec. 17, 1778	Born in Cornwall, England
1795	Apprenticed to an apothecary and surgeon
1798	Appointed chemical superintendent of the Pneumatic Institution
1800	Publishes *Researches, Chemical and Philosophical*
1801	Begins lecturing and research at the Royal Institution of Great Britain
1803	Becomes a Fellow of the Royal Society of London
1807	Isolates sodium and potassium from compounds
1810	Uses the process of electrolysis to establish that what had been called oxymuratic acid (chlorine)
1812	Knighted
1815	Appoints Michael Faraday as an assistant
1815	Invents a miners' safety lamp
1820	Elected president of the Royal Society of London
May 29, 1829	Dies in Geneva, Switzerland

A chance meeting with Davies Gilbert, a member of Parliament who had an interest in science, provided him with an invitation to use his library in Tradea and to visit well-equipped chemistry laboratories.

In 1798, Davy was appointed chemical superintendent of the Pneumatic Institution in Bristol, England. There, he studied the properties and possible therapeutic uses of gases, including the anesthetic properties of nitrous oxide (laughing gas). He frequently inhaled samples of gases to determine their physiological effect, and he nearly died on several occasions as a result.

In 1801, Davy began lecturing on chemistry at the Royal Institution (RI) in London. There, he developed his electrochemical theories and isolated many new elements. His invention of the miners' safety lamp brought him popular acclaim. Despite having no formal college training, Davy became a prominent scientist of his day.

Early Life

Humphry Davy was born in Penzance, Cornwall, England, in 1778. He attended grammar school until the age of sixteen and was considered clever but was by no means an outstanding student. He was good at composing verse, translating the classics into English, and was an enthusiastic storyteller. He developed a keen interest in nature and enjoyed fishing, shooting, and collecting mineral specimens.

In 1795, Davy was apprenticed to Bingham Borlase, an apothecary and surgeon in Penzance, and hoped eventually to study medicine. While working, he planned a program of intensive self-study that included theology, science, medicine, languages, and mathematics.

At the age of nineteen, he became interested in chemistry after reading Antoine-Laurent Lavoisier's *Traité élémentaire de chimie* (1789; Elements of Chemistry, 1790). Davy soon began devising his own experiments at home.

The Electrical Nature of Matter

In 1800, Count Alèssandro Volta produced a battery composed of alternating silver and zinc discs. The battery soon became a powerful tool enabling chemists to analyze matter. Davy postulated that chemical reactions were responsible for the battery's source of electricity. He experimented with different combinations of metals and determined that one of the metals always underwent the process of oxidation.

During his tenure at the RI, Davy's electrochemical work brought him public recognition. He suggested that when electricity is passed through a solution—a process later termed "electrolysis" by Michael Faraday—compounds are broken down into elements. Since electricity is capable of breaking down the natural forces that hold elements together in compounds, Davy concluded that these forces themselves are electrical in nature. Using electrolysis, Davy decomposed molten potassium hydroxide. In 1807 he isolated the element potassium.

Electrochemical Work and Electrolysis

Davy used electricity to decompose compounds into their constituent elements, successfully isolating many group 1 and group 2 elements.

Davy experimented with ionic compounds, such as potassium hydroxide, which are composed of positive and negative ions. When an ionic compound is melted and subjected to an electric current, the positive ions migrate toward the negative electrode (cathode), while the negative ions are attracted to the positive electrode (anode). At the cathode, electrons react with positive ions, causing them to be reduced. When a battery is used to push electrons through the system, electrochemical reactions at the electrodes are initiated.

When Davy subjected molten potassium hydroxide to electrolysis, he observed the formation of small metallic globules similar in appearance to mercury at the cathode. This metallic substance was molten potassium, which formed as a result of reduction of the potassium ions through reaction with electrons generated at the cathode. Davy also observed the ease with which the potassium underwent combustion as soon as it was formed. Potassium, like all the alkali (group 1) metals, is extremely reactive. It readily decomposes on contact with water and ignites spontaneously, burning with a violet flame. Davy noticed that the surface of some of the newly formed potassium quickly tarnished and became coated with a white film. The alkali metals react rapidly with oxygen, especially when heated, to form white metal-oxygen compounds such as oxides.

Davy also isolated sodium by the electrolysis of molten sodium hydroxide. Its chemical properties (very reactive with water and oxygen) are similar to potassium. In fact, all the group 1 metals share similar chemical and physical properties—soft, low melting point metals with low densities—because all elements in the group have the same number of outer (valence) electrons. Davy also isolated a number of metals from group 2, including calcium, barium, and strontium. Likewise, the group 2 elements are similar but they differ slightly in their properties compared with the group 1 metals.

The alkali metals, potassium in particular, are strong reducing agents. Consequently, when they react with other compounds and elements, they readily add electrons to them. Davy used this property of potassium to isolate the element boron from a heated mixture of potassium and boric acid in a copper tube. Other elements such as silicon, thorium, and zirconium were similarly isolated. In each case, the strong reducing power of the potassium provided the driving force to break compounds into their elements.

Bibliography

Weeks, Mary E. and Henry L. Leicester. *Discovery of the Elements*. 7th ed. Easton, Pa.: Journal of Chemical Education, 1968.

Heiserman, David L. *Exploring the Chemical Elements*. Blue Ridge Summit, Pa.: Tab Books, 1991.

Oldham, Keith B. and Jan C. Myland. *Fundamentals of Electrochemical Science*. San Diego, Calif: Academic Press, 1994.

He soon used electrolysis to isolate the elements sodium, calcium, strontium, barium, and magnesium.

Davy's work helped form the framework of the dualistic theory of Jöns Jakob Berzelius in 1812. The theory was an early attempt to explain the fundamental forces that hold matter together.

The Safety Lamp

Mine explosions were common in the eighteenth century. Davy's safety lamp used a wire gauze to dissipate the heat from the flame of a miner's lamp and so greatly reduced the risk of igniting underground pockets of explosive gases, such as methane. The safety lamp not only saved the lives of many miners but it also illustrated to the public how the complex theoretical concepts of science could have practical value in everyday life.

An Early Acid Theory

Toward the end of the eighteenth century, the French chemist Lavoisier had proposed that oxygen was the essential constituent of all acids. In 1810, Davy used electrolysis to show that oxymuriatic acid contains no oxygen and is, in fact, the element chlorine. It soon became evident to Davy and others that hydrogen, rather than oxygen, is the element common to all acids.

Davy was knighted in 1912 and elected president of the Royal Society of London in 1820. He died on May 29, 1829, in Geneva, Switzerland.

Bibliography

By Davy

Beddoes, Thomas ed. "An Essay on Heat, Light, and the Combinations of Light," *Contributions to Physical and Medical Knowledge, Principally from the West of England*, 1799.

"An Account of Some Galvanic Combinations, Formed by the Arrangement of Single Metallic Plates and Fluids, Analogous to the New Galvanic Apparatus of Mr. Volta," *Philosophical Transactions of the Royal Society of London*, 1801.

"Electrochemical Researches," *Philosophical Transactions of the Royal Society of London*, 1808.

Elements of Chemical Philosophy, 1812.

"On the Wire-Gauze Safe-Lamp," *Quarterly Journal of Science and the Arts*, 1816 *Collected Works*, 1839–1840 (9 vols.).

About Davy

Knight, David M. *Humphry Davy*. Oxford, England: Blackwell Scientific Publications, 1992.

Hartley, Harold. *Humphry Davy*. London, England: Thomas Nelson, 1966.

(Nicholas C. Thomas)

Peter J. W. Debye

Disciplines: Chemistry and physics
Contribution: Debye studied the bonding and structure of compounds. He investigated the polarity of molecules through a study of their dipole moments and their X-ray diffraction patterns.

Mar. 24, 1884	Born in Maastricht, the Netherlands
1905	Earns a degree in electrical engineering at Technische Hochschule in Aachen, Germany
1908	Receives a Ph.D. from the University of Munich, Germany
1911–1912	Teaches physics at the University of Zurich, Switzerland
1912	Advances the concept of a permanent molecular dipole moment
1914–1919	Teaches physics at the University of Göttingen, Germany
1914	Studies the effect of temperature on the X-ray patterns of substances
1916	With Paul Scherrer, develops powder X-ray diffraction
1919–1927	Serves as director of the Physical Institute in Zurich
1927–1935	Acts as director of the Physical Institute in Leipzig, Germany
1935–1940	Teaches physics at the University of Berlin while acting as director of the Kaiser Wilhelm Institute
1936	Awarded the Nobel Prize in Chemistry
1940–1952	Teaches at Cornell University
Nov. 2, 1966	Dies in Ithaca, New York

Early Life

Peter Joseph William Debye (pronounced "dee-BI"), whose name was originally Petrus Josephus Wilhelmus Dibije, was born in Maastricht, the Netherlands. He attended college in Germany just across the boarder from his birthplace, receiving his degree in electrical engineering in 1905. Debye accompanied one of his favorite teachers from college to Munich, Germany, where he completed his Ph.D. in physics in 1908.

In 1911, he accepted a professorship of physics in Zurich, Switzerland, a position recently vacated by Albert Einstein. What followed were a series of professorships at various universities. Debye moved each time to a location with better facilities for his studies.

The Study of Molecular Structure

Debye conducted research on the structure of molecules. His studies took various forms, but each procedure had as its goal a better understanding of how atoms are joined together to form molecules and how these molecules interact with one another.

One of his earliest studies dealt with the measurement of specific heat capacity, which is the amount of heat that 1 gram (0.03 ounces) of a substance can absorb to raise its temperature 1 degree centigrade. Metals, for example, require less heat to become hotter than does wood. Debye derived a formula for predicting the specific heat capacity of materials at very low temperatures.

Another of his studies dealt with the effect that a substance exhibits when placed between two electrically charged metal plates. Different substances respond differently, as the charged particles within each atom of a molecule are attracted to the positively and negatively charged plates. This situation allows one to theorize on how the atoms within the molecule are joined together and how tightly they are bonded.

Debye used X-rays to study molecular structure. The patterns photographed from X-rays passed through a material, a process called X-ray diffraction, are used to calculate the distances between atoms in a substance. Debye and coworker Paul Scherrer were the first scientists to use powdered samples for this study.

Debye extended his study of bonding within molecules to investigate how substances interact in dilute solutions. He and a coworker derived a formula to account for these interactions.

Moving to America

Debye was not a German citizen so he was forced to leave Germany during World War II. After briefly returning to the Netherlands, he visited the United States in 1940 and settled there to accept a professorship with the chemistry department of Cornell University, New York. Although he wished to help the Allies, his affiliation with Germany prohibited him from working in classified areas. Instead he found a way to contribute by studying methods for improving rubber and plastic.

Dipole Moments

Debye was the first to observe that some materials have a permanent dipole moment; scientists had thought that only induced dipole moments were possible.

A covalent chemical bond exists when the electrons of one atom intermingle with those of another, forming a molecule of a chemical compound. Within the molecule, a pull from the positive center of each atom occurs for these electrons. If the joining atoms are identical, as in a hydrogen molecule (H_2), the attraction for the electrons is equal from each hydrogen atom center, resulting in an equal distribution of charge throughout the molecule. To an observer outside the molecule—if it were possible to observe a single molecule in this manner—the molecule appears neutral. Such a molecule is termed nonpolar.

If, however, the molecule consists of different atoms, such as hydrogen bromide (HBr), there is an unequal attraction for the electrons within the molecule. Bromine, with its thirty-five protons, attracts electrons more strongly than hydrogen, with only one proton. As a result, the electrons within the molecule spend most of their time at the bromine end. To an observer outside the molecule, the electron-rich end appears more negative and the hydrogen end appears less negative or more positive. The molecule is polar.

The degree to which the molecules of a substance are polar, or have a separation of electrical charge, depends on which atoms compose the molecule and on the arrangement of atoms within the molecule. Molecules that are symmetrical about a central atom are nonpolar. Molecules that are nonsymmetrical show unequal attractions for the electrons within them, have a separation of charge, and are polar.

It was known before the work of Debye that nonpolar molecules could be made polar, an induced polarity, by placing a sample between electrically charged metal plates. The positive plate pulls the electrons within the molecules toward itself, and the negative charged plate pushes electrons away.

It is possible to measure the extent of polarization for a substance experimentally. This measurement is called the dipole moment of the material. The larger the dipole moment, the more polar the molecule, that is, the greater the separation of positive and negative centers within the molecule.

Knowing the dipole moment of a substance allows one to speculate regarding not only the structure within a molecule but also the interactions between molecules. If the intermolecular interactions are strong or weak, many of the properties of the substance can be explained.

Dipole moments are on the order of 1×10^{-18} electrostatic unit (esu). In honor of the contributions made by Debye, the quantity 1×10^{-18} esu is called 1 debye, the unit in which dipole moments are generally expressed.

Bibliography

Gray, Harry B. *Chemical Bonds*. Menlo Park, Calif.: W. A. Benjamin, 1973.

Ebbing, Darrell D. *General Chemistry*. Boston, Mass.: Houghton Mifflin, 1987.

Parker, Sybil P. ed. *McGraw-Hill Encyclopedia of Science and Technology*. New York: McGraw-Hill, 1992.

After the war, he continued his study of polymers, devising a method for measuring the molecular mass of large polymer material by observing light scattered from their surfaces.

Debye was highly regarded for his contributions to science and became known as "the master of the molecule" for the many ways in which he studied molecular bonding and structure.

He died in New York in 1966.

Bibliography

By Debye

Quantentheorie und Chemie, 1928.
Polare Molekeln, 1929 (Polar Molecules, 1929).
Dipolmoment und Chemische Struktur, 1929 (The Dipole Moment and Chemical Structure, 1931).
Magnetismus, 1933.
Kernphysik, 1935.

About Debye

Miles, W. D. ed. *American Chemists and Chemical Engineers.* Washington, D.C.: American Chemical Society, 1976.
James, Laylin K. ed. *Nobel Laureates in Chemistry, 1901-1992.* Philadelphia: Chemical Heritage Foundation, 1993.
Magill, Frank N. ed. "Peter Debye." In *The Nobel Prize Winners: Chemistry*, Pasadena, Calif.: Salem Press, 1990.
Davies, Mansel. "Peter J. W. Debye (1884-1966)." *Journal of Chemical Education* 45 (July, 1968).

(Gordon A. Parker)

Jean-Baptiste-André Dumas

Discipline: Chemistry
Contribution: Dumas is best known for his study of organic substitution reactions and his measurement of atomic masses, molecular masses, and nitrogen levels in organic compounds.

Jul. 14, 1800	Born in Alais (now Aiès), France
1816	Moves to Geneva, Switzerland to study physiological chemistry
1823	Moves to Paris, France and begins teaching at the École Polytechnique
1826	Develops a vapor density method for measuring molecular masses
1831	Proposes structural isomerism for organic compounds
1832	Joins the chemistry faculty at the Sorbonne in Paris
1833	Develops a method for the quantitative determination of nitrogen in organic compounds
1834	Proposes substitution reactions for organic compounds
1840	Accurately measures the atomic mass of carbon
1848	Launches his political career during the time of Napoleon III
1858	Begins publishing his list of new atomic mass values
1868	Appointed permanent secretary of the Académie des Sciences
1870	His political career ends with the fall of the Second Empire
Apr. 10, 1884	Dies in Cannes, France

Early Life

Jean-Baptiste-André Dumas (pronounced "dyoo-MAH") was born in Alais (now Alès), France, in 1800. His father was the town clerk. At the age of sixteen, he left home and went to live in Geneva, Switzerland. There, he studied physiological chemistry including muscle action and the use of iodine for the treatment of goiter.

In 1823, Dumas moved to Paris and began studies in chemistry. Also at this time, he started a teaching career that was to last for many years. He was considered an excellent teacher and was among the first to introduce laboratory work as part of his courses.

Molecular Mass Measurement

Dumas developed a method for determining the molecular mass values of volatile compounds through the measurement of vapor density. As a result of misunderstandings at the time between the relationship between atoms and molecules,

his measured values, although correct, did not always agree with the incorrect thinking of his colleagues. Dumas himself could not always explain properly the interpretation of his findings. Later, he accurately measured the atomic mass values of carbon and other elements. These values were readily accepted by other chemists.

Studies in Organic Chemistry

Over the years, Dumas made many contributions to the field of organic chemistry. He was the first to study several important compounds derived from natural sources, including anthracene from coal and some essential oils used in perfumes, camphor, and menthol. He also recognized the concept of a homologous series, in which related organic compounds are identified by a given, constant increase in chemical composition.

Dumas initially accepted but later proved erroneous the dualistic theory as applied to organic compounds. This theory held that organic compounds are formed from the electrical attraction of positive and negative components, analogous to the manner in which inorganic ionic compounds are formed. By preparing certain compounds from components that were uncharged, he recognized and proposed the concept of substitution reactions, in which one component replaces another in a compound without the joining of any charge particles. In time, other chemists accepted his work and discarded the dualistic approach for the formation of organic compounds.

International Fame and a Political Career

Dumas became one of the best-known chemists in the world. He cofounded a scientific journal, published numerous articles, and held important offices in various scientific societies.

Dumas decided set aside his chemical studies for a time in order to assume political office. In 1848, he was elected to the French National Assembly.

The Formation of Organic Molecules

Dumas developed the theory of organic substitution reactions, which replaced the dualistic theory of bond formation for organic compounds.

During the earlier years of Dumas' rise to prominence, the dualistic theory was applied to both inorganic and organic substances. This theory based on the electrical attraction between positive and negative particles accounted correctly for the formation of inorganic substances. Dumas carried out a series of reactions with a class of organic compounds called esters that could not be explained by this theory. Other evidence unresolved by the dualistic theory concerned Dumas' study of the substitution of chlorine for hydrogen in acetic acid, an organic compound.

When Dumas first questioned the dualistic theory based on his experiments, he met with considerable opposition. Not wishing to offend the scientific community, he did not press his discovery. One of his coworkers, however, was more adamant in seeking its acceptance of what Dumas had termed the unitary theory. Dumas himself later took up the cause, and the idea of organic substitution reactions, in which one molecule can replace another in an organic compound without any charged particles being joined, is now firmly accepted by chemists.

Bibliography

Cobb, Cathy and Harold Gold White. *Creations of Fire: Chemistry's Lively History from Alchemy to the Atomic Age.* New York: Plenum Press, 1995.

Salzberg, Hugh W. *From Caveman to Chemist: Circumstances and Achievements.* Washington, D.C.: American Chemical Society, 1991.

Asimov, Isaac. *A Short History of Chemistry.* Westport, Conn.: Greenwood Press, 1979.

This era is known as the Second French Republic. At various periods, he was minister of agriculture and commerce, minister of education, master of the mint, and a member (and later, the president) of the Municipal Council of Paris. With the downfall of Napoleon III, however, he ended his political activities and again concentrated on his scientific studies, which continued until his death in 1884.

Bibliography

By Dumas

Phénomènes qui accompagnent la contraction de la fibre musculaire, 1823.

Traité de chimie appliquée aux arts, 1828–1848 (8 vols.).

Leçons sur la philosophie himique, 1837.

Thèse sur la question de l'action du calorique sur les corps organiques, 1838.

Essai sur la statique chimique des êtres organisés, 1841.

About Dumas

Ihde, Aaron J. *The Development of Modem Chemistry.* New York: Harper & Row, 1964.

Gillispie, Charles Coulston. ed. "Jean Baptiste André Dumas." In *Dictionary of Scientific Biography,* New York: Charles Scribner's Sons, 1973.

Also-brook, Jane W. "Jean Baptiste André Dumas." *Journal of Chemical Education* 28 (December, 1950).

Brock, William H. *The Norton History of Chemistry.* New York: W. W. Norton, 1992.

(Gordon A. Parker)

Ernst Otto Fischer

Discipline: Chemistry

Contribution: An authority on metallocenes, Fischer shared the Nobel Prize in Chemistry with Sir Geoffrey Wilkinson for pioneering research into the chemistry of organometallic compounds.

Nov. 10, 1918	Born in Solln, near Munich, Germany
1939-1945	Serves in Poland, France, and Russia during World War II
1941-1942	Studies chemistry at the Technische Hochschule München
1946	Resumes his studies at the re-opened Technische Hochschule
1949	Earns a chemistry diploma
1949-1952	Works as an assistant to Walter Hieber and earns a Ph.D.
1954	Admitted into the faculty at the Technische Hochschule
1957-1959	Named an associate professor at the University of Munich
1959-1964	Becomes a professor at Munich
1964	Becomes a professor at the Technische Universität München and director of its Institute for Inorganic Chemistry
1969	Named Firestone Lecturer at the University of Wisconsin, Madison
1973	Named Arthur D. Little Visiting Professor at the Massachusetts Institute of Technology (MIT) and Visiting Distinguished Lecturer at the University of Rochester
1973	Awarded the Nobel Prize in Chemistry
July 23, 2007	Dies in Munich

Early Life

Ernst Otto Fischer, whose father was a professor of physics at the Technische Hochschule München, Germany, was educated and spent his entire life in his hometown of Munich, except for two years of compulsory military service and foreign travels and lectureships. He began to study chemistry at the Technische Hochschule München during a study leave from the military in the winter of 1941-1942, but he received most of his formal education there after World War II ended.

In 1949, Fischer became the assistant to Walter Hieber, the founder of modern carbonyl chemistry. Hieber supervised Fischer's research on organometallic chemistry that led to his Ph.D. in 1952 with a dissertation entitled "The Mechanisms of Carbon Monoxide Reactions of Nickel (II) Salts in the Presence of Dithionites and Sulfoxylates."

Fischer completed his university teaching thesis, "The Metal Complexes of Cyclopentadienes and Indenes" in 1954. The thesis lead not only to his

appointment as privatdozent (lecturer) in 1955 but also to a Nobel Prize in Chemistry in 1973, almost twenty years later.

Organometallic Chemistry

In 1957, Fischer moved to the University of Munich, where, as associate professor and then professor, he and his students continued his research on the chemistry and structure of metallocenes (sandwich compounds of metal atoms and cyclopentadienyls).

He then succeeded Hieber as professor and director of the Institute for Inorganic Chemistry at the Technische Universität München (formerly the Technische Hochschule München), which, under his direction, became one of the world's leading centers for research in organometallic chemistry.

Metallocenes

Fischer confirmed Sir Geoffrey Wilkinson and Robert B. Woodward's determination of the structure of ferrocene as a sandwich compound, a complex consisting of a metal atom and an aromatic organic compound, with the metal ion "sandwiched" between the rings.

He also synthesized other metallocenes and extended the concept of organic aromatic molecules π-bonded to transition metals by correctly predicting and proving by an X-ray diffraction study with E. Weiss that bis (benzene) chromium (0) is a sandwich compound. Together-er with Walter Hafner, he developed a high-yield synthesis for this compound, using a reductive-ligation process known as the Fischer-Hafner method.

Ferrocene and the Metallocenes

An analysis of the structure of ferrocene, an unusually stable organic iron complex, led to the discovery of a new type of chemical bonding and many other organometallic compounds.

In 1951, ferrocene, a stable complex of one iron atom and two cyclopentadienide anions, was discovered. Its structure was determined to consist of a central iron atom with a single (σ) bond on either side attached to one of the five carbon atoms of the flat, planar cyclopentadienide ring. Sir Geoffrey Wilkinson recognized, however, that this structure could not account for the compound's unusually high stability.

He proposed that all five carbon atoms of each ring contribute equally to the π-bonding to the iron atom, with the iron atom "sandwiched" between two cyclopentadienyls. With Robert B. Woodward, Wilkinson measured the compound's infrared and ultraviolet spectra, magnetic susceptibility, and dipole moment and proved this structure to be correct.

In 1952, Fischer and W. Pfab confirmed the structure by X-ray diffraction. They also showed that the two cyclopentadienide rings are reversed, giving an overall pentagonal, antiprismatic structure. Fischer and his coworkers also prepared and determined the crystal structures of the cobalt and nickel analogues.

The entire class of transition metal and cyclopentadienyl compounds became known as metallocenes. The discovery and recognition of this new type of bonding between metals and unsaturated organic molecules or ions led to a renaissance in organometallic chemistry.

Bibliography

Miller, S. A. Miller, J. A. Tebboth, and J. F Tremaine. "Dicyclopentadienyliron." *Journal of the Chemical Society* (1952).

"The Discovery of Ferrocene, the First Sandwich Compound." George B. Kauffman. *Journal of Chemical Education* 60 (March, 1983).

Carbene and Carbyne Complexes

Fischer extended his work on transition metal complexes of aromatic hydrocarbons to include the synthesis and characterization of entirely new compounds—those of transition metal complexes of carbenes, in 1964, and carbynes, in 1973. These short-lived, highly reactive organic compounds contain a metal-carbon double bond and a metal-carbon triple bond, respectively.

Transition metal alkoxycarbenes were found to react with primary and secondary amines to yield compounds that led Fischer and his coworkers into peptide chemistry. The use of transition metal carbene residues as protective groups for the amino groups of amino acids and peptides has found wide use in organic chemistry and biochemistry.

Bibliography

By Fischer

"Cyclopentadien-Metallkomplexe: Ein neuer Typ metallorganischer Verbindungen," *Zeitschrift für Naturforschung*, 1952 (with W. Pfab).

"Zur Kristallstruktur und Molekelgestalt des Dibenzol-chrom(0)," *Zeitschrift für anorganische und allgemeine Chemie*, 1956 (with E. Weiss).

"Trans-Halogeno[alkyl(aryl)carbyne]tetracarbonyl Complexes of Chromium, Molybdenum, and Tungsten—A New Class of Compounds Having a Transition Metal-Carbon Triple Bond," *Angewandte Chemie, International Edition in English*, 1973 (with Cornelius G. Kreiter et al).

About Fischer

Encyclopedia Britannica Online, s.v. "Fischer, Ernst Otto," http://www.britannica.com/

Magill, Frank N. "Ernst Otto Fischer." In *The Nobel Prize Winners: Chemistry*, edited by Pasadena, Calif.: Salem Press, 1990.

Seyferth, Dietmar and Alan Davison. "The 1973 Nobel Prize in Chemistry." *Science* (1973).

(George B. Kauffman)

Paul J. Flory

Discipline: Chemistry
Contribution: Flory studied plastics and rubbers, and was a contributor to the theory of the physical conformation of the long molecular chains that make up polymers. He was awarded the Nobel Prize in Chemistry for achievements in macromolecular science.

June 19, 1910	Born in Sterling, Illinois
1934	Earns a Ph.D. in chemistry from Ohio State University
1934	Becomes a research scientist at DuPont
1938-1941	Serves as a research associate at the University of Cincinnati
1941-1943	Works on the synthesis of rubber at Esso Laboratories (now Exxon Laboratories)
1943-1948	Conducts research on rubber chemistry at Goodyear
1948	Named a professor of chemistry at Cornell University
1953	Publishes *Principles of Polymer Chemistry*
1957	Appointed executive director of research at Carnegie-Mellon Institute
1961-1975	Serves as a professor of chemistry at Stanford University
1969	Publishes *Statistical Mechanics of Chain Molecules*
1974	Awarded the Nobel Prize in Chemistry, the National Medal of Science, and the Priestley Medal of the American Chemical Society
Sept. 9, 1985	Dies in Big Sur, California

Early Life

Paul John Flory grew up in the small Illinois city of Sterling. His family had been farmers in the United States for six generations, and his parents were the first in their families to have attended college.

After high school, Flory enrolled at Manchester College in Indiana, which had only 600 students. He earned a degree in three years, explaining later that the college "hadn't much more than three years to offer at the time." Fortunately, his chemistry professor at Manchester persuaded him to pursue graduate studies in chemistry.

Flory entered Ohio State University and was awarded a Ph.D. in physical chemistry at the age of twenty-four. His thesis was on the photochemistry of nitric oxide.

Industrial Research

Graduating at the height of the Great Depression, Flory was fortunate to obtain a job with DuPont as a research chemist. He was assigned to work under Wallace Carothers, one of the great figures in the history of polymer chemistry. Carothers' group invented nylon, neoprene, and other important commercial plastics and rubbers, making DuPont the leading firm in these fields.

Flory's responsibility was to learn more about the physical structure of polymer macromolecules. By the early 1930s, chemists realized that polymers such as natural rubber consisted of combinations of simple molecules, or mers, joined over and over into very long chains. The number of mers that combined into a polymer molecule was variable, giving varying molecular weight distributions in real polymer samples, and seemed generally to be arranged in straight chains, with or without cross-links between chains. There was no direct way to measure molecular weights or their distributions, however, much less to control them in polymerization processes.

Flory's special approach to the problem of describing these structures quantitatively was to make use of thermodynamics and statistical mechanics to correlate measurable physical properties with a useful physical model of the molecular conformations of amorphous polymers. At this time, he also started work on theories of polymerization, culminating in his explanation of the four-step process of addition polymerization. These two activities were to engage most of his attention during the rest of his career.

World War II

After four years at DuPont studying polymerization kinetics, Flory began his teaching career with a three-year stint at the University of Cincinnati, where an important achievement was a theory to explain cross-linking of polymers to form gels.

When World War II began, Flory joined Esso (now Exxon) Laboratories to work on a crash program on synthetic rubber manufacture to replace endangered natural rubber supplies. One result of great import to his future research was his

Exploring the Conformation of Polymer Chains

Flory's contribution was to the quantitative description of the spatial conformations and to the effect of these conformations on polymer properties and polymerization kinetics.

Polymers are distinguished at the molecular level from other materials by being comprised of long chains of repeated chemical groups. Usually, the backbones of these chains are predominantly covalently bonded carbon atoms. The special properties of different polymers is attributable both to the types of chemical repeat groups and to the spatial relationships of the molecules.

Flory's critical insight was that analysts could not conveniently neglect the disturbance to the conformation caused by the exclusion of one chain segment from space already occupied by another segment. Effective chain volume and length must include excluded volume or free volume effects.

Once this was done, interpretation of solution properties of polymers confirmed previous models of random-coiled long chains in which bond rotation could freely occur but which were limited by excluded volume effects. Flory discovered that at high polymer concentrations, excluded volume tended toward zero; at this point, key structural parameters could be measured.

As a consequence of the new theories, molecular weight and molecular weight distributions could finally be measured. More recently, a convenient method of measuring these parameters on polymer solutions by gel permeation chromatography has become available to industry, but the older methods pioneered by Flory and his coworkers are still used to obtain calibration standards.

Bibliography

Modern Theory of Polymer Solutions.
  H. Yamakawa. New York: Harper & Row, 1971.
"Spatial Configuration of Macromolecular
  Chains." Paul J. Flory Nobel Prize lecture.
  December 11, 1974.

realization that viscosity and other properties of polymersolvent solutions of varying concentrations and temperatures might be correlated with polymer conformations.

Career in Academia

After two years at Exxon and five years at Goodyear, Flory joined the faculty at Cornell University where he stayed for nine years. There, he continued basic research on polymer structure. His most important work centered on the interpretation of the properties of polymer solutions. Using viscosity, osmotic pressure, and light-scattering measurements Flory derived verifiable physical models of the long chains. His classic book *Principles of Polymer Chemistry*, was published in 1953. At this time, he also began studies on liquid crystal polymers.

In 1957, Flory became director of a new effort to establish programs in basic research at the Carnegie-Mellon Institute, where applied research had been almost the sole activity. Flory made little progress there and after three years he returned to academic research, this time at Stanford. He remained there until the end of his career fourteen years later.

While at Stanford, he received numerous awards from scientific societies, including the Nobel Prize in Chemistry in 1974. In the same year, he was also awarded the National Medal of Science, and the Priestley Medal of the American Chemical Society. His second book, *Statistical Mechanics of Chain Molecules,* was published in 1969. In addition to his awards, he authored or coauthored about 400 scientific papers.

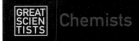

Flory had a tremendous influence on his profession as a teacher and a role model. His services as a consultant to industrial laboratories were avidly sought. After his retirement in 1975, he used the prestige of the Nobel Prize to work in support of human rights, especially in the Soviet Union, where he did his best to help dissident scientists.

Bibliography

By Flory
Principles of Polymer Chemistry, 1953.
Statistical Mechanics of Chain Molecules, 1969.
Selected Works of Paul J. Flory: Stanford,
    1985 (3 vols.).

About Flory
Seltzer, R. J. "Paul Flory: A Giant Who Excelled in Many Roles." *Chemical and Engineering News* (December, 1985).
Morton. M. "Paul John Flory, 1910–1985." *Rubber Chemistry and Technology* (May–June, 1987).

(Harold Belofsky)

Kenichi Fukui

Disciplines: Chemistry and physics
Contribution: In the early 1950s, Fukui proposed the frontier orbitals theory, which predicts the site and rate of a chemical reaction. He became the joint recipient of the 1981 Nobel Prize in Chemistry for this work.

Oct. 4, 1918	Born in Nara, Japan
1941	Graduates from Kyoto Imperial University, Japan
1941-1942	Engages in experimental research on synthetic fuel chemistry in the Army Fuel Laboratory
1943	Appointed a lecturer at Kyoto Imperial University
1951	Receives a promotion to professor in fuel chemistry at Kyoto University (formerly known as Kyoto Imperial University)
1952	Publishes his seminal paper on the correlation between frontier electron density and chemical reactivity in aromatic hydrocarbons
1962	Receives the Japan Academy Medal
1970	Publishes a paper on formulating the path of chemical reactions
1971	Works at the Illinois Institute of Technology in Chicago as a National Science Foundation Senior Foreign Scientist Fellow
1981	Becomes a foreign associate of the U.S. National Academy of Sciences
1981	Shares the Nobel Prize in Chemistry with Roald Hoffmann
Jan. 9, 1998	Dies in Kyoto, Japan

Following his graduation from Kyoto Imperial University in 1941, Fukui was engaged in the Army Fuel Laboratory of Japan during World War II. In 1943, he was appointed a lecturer in fuel chemistry at Kyoto Imperial University and began his career as an experimental organic chemist.

The Frontier Orbitals Theory

In 1952, Fukui with his collaborators T. Yoneza-wa and H. Shingu presented his molecular orbital theory of reactivity in aromatic hydrocarbons, which appeared in the *Journal of Chemical Physics*. At that time, his concept failed to garner adequate attention among chemists.

Fukui observed in his Nobel lecture in 1981 that his original paper "received a number of controversial comments. This was in a sense understandable because for lack of my experimental ability, the theoretical foundation for this conspicuous result was obscure or rather improperly given."

Early Life

Kenichi Fukui (pronounced "FOO-koo-ee") was the eldest of three sons of Ryokichi Fukui, a foreign trade merchant, and Chie Fukui. He was born in Nara, Japan. In his student days from 1938 and 1941, Fukui's interest was stimulated by quantum mechanics and Erwin Schrodinger's famous equation. He also had developed the belief that a breakthrough in science occurs through the unexpected fusion of remotely related fields.

In his autobiographical profile, published by the Nobel Foundation, Fukui reminisced, "In my high school years, chemistry was not my favorite subject, but the most decisive occurrence in my educational career came when my father asked the advice of Professor Genitsu Kita of the Kyoto Imperial University concerning the course I should take." On the advice of Kita, a personal friend of the elder Fukui, young Kenichi was directed to the Department of Industrial Chemistry, with which Kita was then affiliated.

Delayed Recognition

The frontier orbitals concept came to be recognized following the 1965 publication by Robert B. Woodward and Roald Hoffmann of the Wood-ward-Hoffmann stereoselection rules, which could predict the reaction rates between two reactants. These rules, depicted in diagrams, explain why some pairs react easily while other pairs do not. The basis for these rules lies in the symmetry properties of the molecules and especially in the disposition of their electrons.

Fukui himself noted in his Nobel lecture: "It is only after the remarkable appearance of the brilliant work by Woodward and Hoffmann that I have become fully aware that not only the density distribution but also the nodal property of the particular orbitals have significance in such a wide variety of chemical reactions."

What is striking in Fukui's significant contributions is that he developed his ideas before chemists had access to large computers for modeling.

Frontier Orbitals Theory

Fukui's contribution to molecular structure studies is now recognized as one of the important conceptual advances in chemistry of the second half of the twentieth century.

Fukui's theoretical contributions in chemistry were immensely influenced by the contributions of other chemistry Nobelists such as Robert Mulliken and Linus Pauling, who had contributed to the development of orbital theory. An orbital can be explained as an equation describing the motion and energy of individual electrons in a molecule.

In simpler terms, Fukui's frontier orbitals theory proposes that the electrons which are most loosely bound to one molecule are the ones most likely to be donated to another molecule in a reaction between the two reactants. The frontier orbitals that are responsible for determining the reaction path are labeled the highest occupied molecular orbital (HOMO) and the lowest unoccupied molecular orbital (LUMO).

In the early 1950s when Fukui and his collaborators proposed their frontier orbitals concept, it failed to capture the attention of fellow chemists. Two factors that worked against the early acceptance of this theory were noted by the information scientist Eugene Garfield. First, Fukui's mathematics were beyond the comprehension of most practicing chemists, who were accustomed to thinking in terms of ball-and-stick models rather than involved equations. Second, even those theoretical chemists who read Fukui's paper doubted that reactivity between two reactants could be reduced to such simple terms.

Following the publication of the Woodward-Hoffmann stereoselection rules for predicting the reactivity between two reactants, experimental chemists appreciated the value of the frontier orbitals concept, which bridged the gap between quantum theory and practical chemistry.

Bibliography

Streitwieser, Andrew Jr. The 1981 Nobel Prize in Chemistry." *Science* 214 (November 6, 1981).

Schwarzschild, B.M. "Nobel Prize for Chemistry to Fukui and Hoffmann." *Physics Today* 34 (1981).

Richards, G. "Rules for Chemical Reactions." *Nature* 294 (1981).

Apart from exploring the theory of chemical reactions, Fukui also contributed strongly to other areas, such as experimental organic chemistry, the statistical theory of gellation, organic synthesis by inorganic salts, and polymerization kinetics.

Bibliography

By Fukui

"A Molecular Orbital Theory of Reactivity in Aromatic Hydrocarbons," *Journal of Chemical Physics*, 1952 (with T. Yonezawa and H. Shingu).

"Recognition of Stereochemical Paths by Orbital Interaction," *Accounts of Chemical Research*, 1971.

"The Path of Chemical Reactions: The IRC Approach," *Accounts of Chemical Research*, 1981.

"Role of Frontier Orbitals in Chemical Reactions," *Science*, 1982.

Frontier Orbitals and Reaction Paths, 1997.

About Fukui

Garfield, Eugene. *Essays of an Information Scientist, 1981-1982.* Vol. 5. Philadelphia: ISI Press, 1983.

Fleming, I. *Frontier Orbitals and Organic Chemical Reactions.* New York: John Wiley & Sons, 1976.

Magill, Frank N. ed. "Kenichi Fukui." In *The Nobel Prize Winners: Chemistry*, Pasadena, Calif.: Salem Press, 1990.

(Sachi Sri Kantha)

Joseph-Louis Gay-Lussac

Disciplines: Chemistry and physics

Contribution: Gay-Lussac discovered the law of combining volumes, which played a key role in establishing that some gases exist as diatomic molecules. He also discovered boron and was the first to isolate sodium and potassium metals by chemical means.

Dec. 6, 1778	Born in St. Léonard-de-Noblat, France
1795-1800	Studies at the École Polytechnique in Paris
1800	Transfers to the École des Ponts et Chaussées
1804	Ascends to a record height of 23,040 feet in a balloon
1806	Elected to the French Académie des Sciences
1808	Presents a paper on the law of combining volumes to the Société Phiomatique
1808	Discovers the element boron
1809	Isolates sodium and potassium metals by chemical means
1810	Takes a position as professor of chemistry at the École Polytechnique
1831	Elected to the Chamber of Deputies
1832	Assumes the chair of general chemistry at the Muséum National d'Histoire Naturelle
May 9, 1850	Dies in Paris, France

Early Life

Joseph-Louis Gay-Lussac (pronounced "GEH-lyoo-SAK") was born on December 6, 1778, in St. Léonard-de-Noblat, France. His father was a judge who was imprisoned briefly during the French Revolution as a suspected royalist. By 1795, it was considered safe to send Joseph-Louis to Paris for schooling. He was admitted to the École Polytechnique at the age of nineteen and later transferred to the École des Ponts et Chaussées. There, he became an assistant to Claude Louis Berthollet, one of the leading chemists of his day.

Some of Gay-Lussac's earliest work was on the effect of temperature on the volume of gases. He found that equal volumes of different gases expand equally for the same increases in temperature. His careful measurements indicated that the gases showed an increase of $1/267$ of the original volume for each increase in temperature of one degree; this is very close to the modern figure of $1/273$.

Gay-Lussac never published these results when he learned that Jacques Alexandre César Charles had done work with similar results that was unpublished. Gay-Lussac formed a very productive association with Baron Alexander von Humboldt, another famous chemist of the time. They traveled through France, Italy, and Germany making measurements of the strength of Earth's magnetic field. In order to determine the effect of altitude on the magnetic field strength, Gay-Lussac ascended in a balloon to an altitude of 23,040 feet. In the process, he set an altitude record that stood for almost a half century.

The Reactions of Gases

Gay-Lussac and Humboldt also made careful measurements of the volumes of hydrogen and oxygen that react to form water. They found that two volumes of hydrogen react exactly with one volume of oxygen. Gay-Lussac did additional measurements

of the volumes of reactants in other gaseous reactions. In all cases, he observed small whole number ratios between the volumes of the reacting gases.

Gay-Lussac formulated these results in what is now known as Gay-Lussac's Law of Combining Volumes. This law was to become crucial in determining the chemical formula for water and in correcting John Dalton's atomic weight scale.

Discovering New Chemical Reactions

Gay-Lussac was an excellent experimentalist and a master at designing techniques for carrying out chemical reactions and analytical measurements. He and Louis Thénard isolated potassium and sodium metals by reduction of their salts with iron, the first large-scale isolation of these metals and the first by chemical means. Among the reactions of potassium carried out was one with boric acid that resulted in the isolation of the element boron.

The Law of Combining Volumes

Gay-Lussac discovered that reacting gases combine in ratios that can he expressed in small whole numbers, which is useful for determining atomic weights.

As part of his atomic theory, John Dalton determined the relative weights of atoms relative to hydrogen, the lightest element. Analysis indicates that the weight of oxygen (O) in water is eight times that of hydrogen (H), and Dalton assumed the formula for water to be HO. On that basis, he calculated the atomic weight of oxygen as eight, not sixteen as the correct formula of H_2O would have required. Gay-Lussac's law of combining volumes was crucial in establishing the correct formulas for water and other elements and solutions.

Amedeo Avogadro realized that this law required some relationship between the volume of a gas and the number of atoms that it contained. Therefore, Avogadro advanced his famous hypothesis that equal volumes of gases under the same conditions contain the same number of particles. Furthermore, he proposed

that the smallest particles of some gaseous elements can be diatomic molecules rather than single atoms. Under Avogadro's proposal, hydrogen could then be formulated as H_2 and oxygen as O_2. The combining volumes that Gay-Lussac determined for the reaction of hydrogen and oxygen to form water could not be rationalized when oxygen and hydrogen were treated as monatomic gases. They did make sense, however, when the reacting gases were treated as diatomic and the formula for water as H_2O. With the establishment of the correct formula for water, the atomic weight of oxygen was corrected.

Bibliography

Nash, Leonard K. *The Atomic Molecular Theory.* Cambridge, Mass.: Harvard University Press, 1965.

Boorse, Henry and Lloyd Motz. *The World of the Atom.* New York: Basic Books, 1966.

In the early nineteenth century, progress in the development of organic chemistry was hindered by the lack of effective methods for analysis of organic chemistry. The introduction by Gay-Lussac and Thenard of potassium chlorate and copper oxide as oxidizing agents for organic compounds led to much-improved analytical procedures.

Honors and Academic Positions

Gay-Lussac became a chemistry professor at the École Polytechnique in 1810 and, in 1832, was appointed to the chair of general chemistry at the Muséum National d'Histoire Naturelle. He was elected to the Chamber of Deputies in 1931, and he entered the House of Peers in 1839. Gay-Lussac died in Paris in 1850, at the age of seventy-one.

Bibliography

By Gay-Lussac

"Sur la dilatation des gaz et des vapeurs," *Annales de Chimie*, 1802.

"Sur la décomposition et recomposition de l'acide boracique," *Annales de Chimie*, 1808 (with Louis Thénard).

"Mémoire sur la combinasion des substances gazeuses, les unes avec les autres," *Mémoires de physique et de chimie de la Société d'Arcueil*, 1809.

Recherches physico-chimiques, faites sur la pile, sur la préparation chimique et les propriétés du potassium et du sodium, 1811 (2 vols.; with Louis Thénard).

About Gay-Lussac

Gillispie, Charles Coulston ed. *Dictionary of Scientific Biography.* Vol. 5. New York: Charles Scribner's Sons, 1972.

Crosland, Maurice. *Gay-Lussac, Scientist and Bourgeois.* Cambridge, England: Cambridge University Press, 1978.

(*Francis P. Mac Kay*)

William Francis Giauque

Disciplines: Chemistry and physics

Contribution: Giauque contributed significantly toward the establishment of the third law of thermodynamics. He also invented adiabatic demagnetization cooling, a new method of reaching very low temperatures.

May 12, 1895	Born in Niagara Falls, Canada
1915-1917	Works at the Hooker Electrochemical Company
1920	Earns a B.S. in chemistry from the University of California, Berkeley (UCB)
1922	Awarded a Ph.D. in chemistry from UCB
1922	Begins research on low-temperature entropy and the third law of thermodynamics
1929	With H. L. Johnston, discovers isotopes of atmospheric oxygen
1933	Demonstrates the first cooling to below 1 degree Kelvin by adiabatic demagnetization
1938	Invents a new thermometer for low-temperature measurement
1939-1944	Directs a program to build a mobile liquid oxygen-generating plant
1949	Awarded the Nobel Prize in Chemistry
1951	Receives J. Willard Gibbs Medal
Mar. 28, 1982	Dies in Oakland, California

Early Life

William Francis Giauque (pronounced "jee-OHK") was born in Niagara Falls, Ontario, Canada. He and his family soon moved to Michigan where his father, William Tecumseh Giauque, worked for the Michigan Central Railroad. Neither of his parents had completed high school, but put a strong emphasis on the value of education. Giauque's father died when Gaiuque was just thirteen, and the family had to move back to Niagara Falls.

Electrical engineering was Giauque's first choice of career, but, lacking finances and engineering experience, he began working for the Hooker Electrochemical Company in Niagara Falls, New York. The company's well-organized laboratory impressed Giauque greatly, and the two years that he spent there convinced him to study chemical engineering.

A family friend had moved to Berkeley, California, and encouraged Giauque to attend the University of California, Berkeley (UCB). Giauque graduated from UCB with the highest honors in 1920, receiving a B.S. degree in chemistry. After earning his Ph.D. in chemistry in 1922, Giauque remained at UCB for the rest of his life, conducting meticulous research and helping to produce chemists of first rank.

Cooling by Adiabatic Demagnetization

Giauque's earliest research dealt with low-temperature entropy and the third law of thermodynamics. His doctoral dissertation of 1922, in which he showed that the entropy of a perfect crystal is zero at absolute zero, demonstrated the correctness of Gilbert Lewis and G. E. Gibson's interpretation of this law in 1920.

Giauque's research into the third law continued in the 1920s and 1930s. In 1924 it led to his most significant accomplishment: the invention of cooling by adiabatic demagnetization. Giauque's new cooling method enabled scientists to better understand the principles and mechanisms of electrical and thermal conductivity, to determine heat capacities, and to investigate the behavior of superconductors at extremely low temperatures.

In 1933, Giauque successfully carried out the first adiabatic demagnetization cooling that produced temperatures below 1 degree Kelvin. By 1938, he had improved temperature measurement by inventing an extremely sensitive thermometer and had recorded temperatures as low as 0.004 degree Kelvin.

Other Awards and Accomplishments

In his nearly-sixty-year career at Berkeley, Giauque interrupted his research only once. During World War II, he directed a classified engineering program that designed and built a mobile liquid oxygen-generating plant.

Cooling by Adiabatic Demagnetization

Giauque's most significant accomplishment was adiabatic demagnetization, a new cooling method.

Giauque used magnetic susceptibility measurements of paramagnetic compounds such as gadolinium, cerium, and dysprosium salts at liquid helium temperatures (4.2 degrees Kelvin) to calculate the effect of a magnetic field on a compound's entropy. This enabled him to establish theoretically that the application and subsequent adiabatic (without the loss or gain of heat) removal of a magnetic field at liquid helium temperatures produced additional cooling.

Earlier thermodynamic relations, namely the Gibbs-Helmholtz equation and the Nernst heat theorem, showed that substances lost practically all their thermal entropy at temperatures below 10-15 degrees Kelvin. However, paramagnetic compounds—those that have a permanent magnetic moment because of one or more unpaired electrons and are attracted by a magnetic field—have both thermal and magnetic entropy and can still possess magnetic entropy at low temperatures because their atomic magnets have an irregular arrangement. Applying a powerful magnetic field forces the atomic magnets to line up with the field, reducing the magnetic entropy.

Giauque recognized that if he insulated the compound thermally and removed the magnetic field under adiabatic conditions, the total entropy must remain constant. Removing the field returned the atomic magnets to their random arrangement and increased their magnetic entropy. The accompanying decrease in thermal entropy, which corresponds to a decrease in motion, resulted in the lowering of the temperature.

In 1933, Giauque successfully produced temperatures below 1 degree Kelvin using adiabatic demagnetization cooling.

Bibliography

Giauque, William Francis. "Paramagnetism and the Third Law of Thermody-namics: Interpretation of the Low-Temperature Magnetic Susceptibility of Gadolinium Sulfate." *Journal of the American Chemical Society* 49 (1927).

Giauque, William Francis and G. E. Gibson. "The Third Law of Thermodynamics: Evidence from the Specific Heats of Glycerol That the Entropy of a Glass Exceeds That of a Crystal at the Absolute Zero." *Journal of the American Chemical Society* 45 (1923).

In addition to winning the 1949 Nobel Prize in Chemistry, Giauque earned many other honors. These included the American Chemical Society's J. Willard Gibbs Medal in 1951. The National Academy of Sciences elected him a member in 1936, and he became a member of the American Philosophical Society beginning in 1940.

A Long and Productive Career

In his long and productive career, Giauque published 183 papers and trained fifty-three graduate students. His invention of cooling by adiabatic demagnetization provided an experimental method for reaching temperatures closer to absolute zero than all earlier techniques. The result of Giauque's low-temperature entropy studies was that the third law of thermodynamics achieved the rank of a fundamental law of science.

In 1982, Giauque died of complications from a fall after riding an exercise bicycle; he was eighty-six years old.

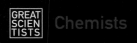

The Third Law of Thermodynamics

As a result of Giauque's low-temperature entropy studies, the third law of thermodynamics, as interpreted by Gilbert Lewis and G. E. Gibson in 1920, achieved the rank of a fundamental law of science.

Giauque showed experimentally from heat capacity and heat of fusion measurements that glycerol glass at 70 degrees Kelvin had considerably more entropy than crystalline glycerol, and he concluded that this difference remained even at absolute zero. His demonstrations of the third law of thermodynamics continued with investigations on diatomic gases in which he calculated their entropies from spectroscopic data and compared them with experimental entropies that he determined calorimetrically.

Giauque measured low-temperature heat capacities and changes of state to obtain the calorimetric entropies for molecules such as hydrogen chloride, hydrogen bromide, hydrogen iodide, oxygen, nitrogen, nitric oxide, and carbon monoxide. For the spectroscopic entropies, he used quantum-statistical equations recently developed from band spectra studies on gaseous molecules.

The close agreement of Giauque's spectroscopic and calorimetric entropy values clearly supported the third law of thermodynamics. So did the excellent agreement between his experimental entropies and those calculated from equations for the entropy of formation. His experiments also verified the use of quantum statistics and the partition function in calculating entropy.

Bibliography

Giauque, William Francis. "Paramagnetism and the Third Law of Thermodynamics: Interpretation of the Low-Temperature Magnetic Susceptibility of Gadolinium Sulfate." *Journal of the American Chemical Society* 49 (1927).

Giauque, William Francis and G. E. Gibson. "The Third Law of Thermodynamics: Evidence from the Specific Heats of Glycerol That the Entropy of a Glass Exceeds That of a Crystal at the Absolute Zero." *Journal of the American Chemical Society* 45 (1923).

Bibliography

By Giauque

"The Third Law of Thermodynamics: Evidence from the Specific Heats of Glycerol That the Entropy of a Glass Exceeds That of a Crystal at the Absolute Zero," *Journal of the American Chemical Society,* 1923 (with G. E. Gibson).

"Paramagnetism and the Third Law of Thermodynamics: Interpretation of the Low-Temperature Magnetic Susceptibility of Gadolinium Sulfate," *Journal of the American Chemical Society,* 1927.

"Some Consequences of Low Temperature Research in Chemical Thermodynamics" in *Nobel Lectures: Chemistry,* 1942-1962, 1964.

About Giauque

Jolly, William *From Retorts to Lasers.* Berkeley, Calif.: University of California Press, 1987.

Magill, Frank N. ed. "William Francis Giauque." In *The Nobel Prize Winners: Chemistry,* Pasadena, Calif.: Salem Press, 1990.

Stranges, Anthony N. "William Francis Giauque (1895-1982): An Adventure in Low-Temperature Research." *Journal of Chemical Education* 67 (1990).

(Anthony N. Stranges and Steve Kirkpatrick)

Otto Hahn

Disciplines: Chemistry and physics

Contribution: Hahn was a pioneer in the field of radiochemistry in the early twentieth century. His work with chemical separation of radioactive materials led to the unambiguous identification of barium produced from uranium, and established the concept of nuclear fission.

Mar. 8, 1879	Born in Frankfurt am Main, Germany
1897	Begins to study chemistry at the University of Marburg
1901	Receives a Ph.D. in organic chemistry
1904	Learns about radiochemistry at London and Montreal
1907	Begins a thirty-year association with Lise Meitner
1914	Works on chemical weapons under Fritz Haber
1917	Discovers radioactive protactinium
1928	Appointed director of the Kaiser Wilhelm Institute of Chemistry
1938	Finds experimental evidence for uranium fission
1946	Accepts the Nobel Prize in Chemistry (awarded in 1944)
1948	Begins a twelve-year presidency of the Max Planck Society
1955	Signs the Mainau Declaration against the misuse of nuclear energy
1957	Opposes the German acquisition of nuclear weapons
July 28, 1968	Dies in Göttingen, West Germany

Early Life

Otto Hahn was born in the city of Frankfurt am Main, in western Germany. His father had a business as a glasscutter, and his mother managed the household, while looking after their four sons. As a young boy, Hahn attended some evening lectures on chemistry and was fascinated by demonstrations showing color changes in chemical reactions.

Hahn entered the University of Marburg, Germany, in 1897 majoring in organic chemistry. He attended chemistry lectures regularly but frequently skipped classes in mathematics and physics. He passed his Ph.D. examination in 1901 and then went into the army for one year of obligatory military service.

From 1902 to 1904, Hahn was a chemistry assistant at Marburg, preparing demonstrations to accompany the lectures.

The Discovery of Uranium Fission

When Enrico Fermi irradiated uranium with neutrons, he reported finding four radioactive materials with distinctly different lifetimes. Hahn and Lise Meitner repeated Fermi's experiment to see if they could solve the mystery.

Hahn and Meitner's first step was to irradiate a sample of uranium with neutrons, which then was dissolved in acid. In order to see if the acid solution contained something besides uranium, chemicals were added that would selectively produce precipitates of various elements. Hahn and Meitner focused their attention on three induced activities, all of which acted chemically like the element radium.

In order to improve the yield obtained from chemical precipitations, a "carrier" technique had been developed in the early twentieth century. For example, radium could be separated from a solution by adding a barium carrier, because barium and radium are chemically very similar. The barium is not radioactive but carries the radium along with it through the chemical separation processes.

Over a period of four years, Hahn and Meitner studied the radioactive products of uranium irradiated by neutrons. Using other carriers, they were able to identify more than a dozen different activities.

In 1938, Hahn set himself the task of separating the supposed radium precipitate from its barium carrier using a method called fractional crystallization. When a solution containing both substances is cooled, the radium crystallizes first and the remaining liquid can be drained off. After repeating this procedure several times, the liquid still contains the barium but very little radium.

To his amazement, Hahn found that the barium solution, rather than the radium precipitate, retained the radioactivity. The experimental evidence seemed to show that neutron irradiation of uranium had created radioactive barium, not radium. Uranium is element 92, and barium is element 56. Past experience with nuclear reactions had never produced large changes in atomic number. Hahn could not bring himself to propose a nuclear reaction that would form barium from irradiated uranium. Nevertheless, he found the chemical evidence for barium convincing and unambiguous.

Meitner had fled to Sweden in 1938 to escape the Nazi persecution of people with Jewish heritage. When Hahn wrote to her about his identification of barium created from uranium, she and Otto Frisch proposed a mechanism by which such a nuclear conversion could occur.

Meitner and Frisch utilized the liquid drop model of the nucleus for their explanation. The nucleus can be visualized as a tiny drop of fluid consisting of many protons and neutrons. When an extra neutron enters, the droplet begins to vibrate until it becomes so elongated that it bursts into two pieces, which then fly apart as a result of electrical repulsion. They named this process "fission" because it was similar to cell division by fission in biology. Nuclear fission was later utilized both for weapons and for nuclear electric power plants.

Bibliography

"The Discovery of Fission." Otto Hahn. *Scientific American* (February, 1958).

The Discovery of Nuclear Fission. Hans G. Graetzer and David Anderson. New York: Arno Press, 1981.

"A Study of the Discovery of Fission." Esther B. Sparburg. *American Journal of Physics* (January, 1964).

Getting Started in Radiochemistry

Hahn's professor at Marburg suggested that he go to England for a year to improve his English because knowing another language would make him more employable in the chemical industry. He won a research appointment in London with William Ramsay, who was interested in the recently discovered phenomenon of radioactivity.

Hahn's first assignment was to separate radium and other radioactive material from a sample of barium. The procedure involved performing chemical separations and then using radiation detectors to determine which component contained the radioactive residue. Hahn succeeded in extracting the radium and also found a previously unknown radioactive material that he named "radiothorium."

Ramsay was impressed with Hahn's careful work and urged him to switch to the field of radiochemistry. He recommended him for an assistantship to Ernest Rutherford, the leading expert on natural radioactivity. Hahn joined Rutherford in 1905 for six months in Montreal, Canada.

Hahn returned to Berlin in 1906 to set up the first radiochemistry laboratory there. A year later, he was joined by Austrian physicist Lise Meitner, who became his friend and coworker for more than thirty years.

World War I

Fritz Haber, a well-known German chemist, recruited Hahn to work on poison gas research. He appealed to Hahn's patriotism and argued that gas warfare could save lives by ending the fighting more quickly.

Haber's chemical group developed chlorine, phosgene, and mustard gas for battlefield use. They also designed gas masks containing chemical absorbers. Hahn was sent to the front lines to train soldiers in the use of the masks. After one gas attack, he saw at first hand how soldiers died in agony. Later, he expressed shame about his role in the war.

Applications of Radiochemistry

After the war, Hahn returned to his research laboratory in Berlin. Hahn and Meitner showed how to extract radiothorium from thorium ore as a cheaper alternative to radium for medical radiation treatments. Another application utilized long-lived natural radioactivity as a geological clock for dating rock formations.

Neutron Irradiation of Uranium

In 1934, the Italian physicist Enrico Fermi pioneered the technique of neutron irradiation for creating artificial radioactivity. When uranium was exposed to neutrons, Fermi found products with several different half-lives. Hahn repeated Fermi's experiment and became convinced that one of the radioactive products from uranium irradiation was barium. Meitner suggested that the uranium nucleus had split into two pieces in a unique reaction that she named "fission."

During World War II, Germany did not have the resources to develop an atomic bomb, and Hahn refused to join the Nazi war effort. In 1945, after Germany fell to the Allies, he and nine other German scientists were taken to England for internment. There, they heard the news that the United States had used atomic bombs to destroy the Japanese cities of Hiroshima and Nagasaki.

Postwar Activities

When Hahn returned to Germany in early 1946, living conditions were chaotic and his laboratory facilities had been destroyed.

At the age of sixty-six, he was ready to retire. He believed, however, that it was his duty to help rebuild his country. In 1948, he helped to organize the Max Planck Society for the rejuvenation of German science. He was elected its president and retained that post for twelve years, until he reached the age of eighty.

In 1957, Hahn was instrumental in publicizing a petition against the placement of nuclear weapons

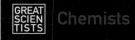

in Germany. This action brought him into political opposition to Chancellor Konrad Adenauer.

Hahn received several honorary degrees and shared in the Fermi Prize for 1966, given by the Atomic Energy Commission.

A personal tragedy was the loss of his only son and daughter-in-law in a car accident in 1960. Hahn died in 1968 at the age of eighty-nine.

Bibliography

By Hahn

Applied Radiochemistry, 1936.

New Atoms, Progress, and Some Memories, 1950.

"The Discovery of Fission," *Scientific American*, 1958.

Vom Radiothor zur Uranspaltung, 1962 (*Otto Hahn: A Scientific Autobiography*, 1966).

Mein Leben, 1968 (*Otto Hahn: My Life*, 1970).

About Hahn

Frisch, Otto R. *Atomic Physics Today*. New York: Basic Books, 1961.

Wasson, Tyler. ed. *Nobel Prize Winners: An H. W. Wilson Biographical Dictionary*. New York: H. W Wilson, 1987.

Shea, W. R. ed. *Otto Hahn and the Rise of Nuclear Physics*. Norwell, Mass.: Kluwer, 1983.

(Hans G. Graetzer)

Irène Joliot-Curie

Disciplines: Chemistry and physics

Contribution: Joliot-Curie and her husband created the world's first artificially produced radioactive elements. Their experiments in radioactivity enabled other scientists to discover the neutron and the positron. Her own experiments led to the discovery of nuclear fission.

Sept. 12, 1897	Born in Paris, France
1907-1909	Attends Marie Curie's private cooperative school
1914	Earns a baccalaureate degree from the Collège Sévigné
1914	Begins studies at the University of Paris
1914	Begins her service as an army nurse during World War I
1918	Becomes an assistant at the Radium Institute
1920	Passes licensing examinations in physics and mathematics
1925	Earns a doctorate from the University of Paris
1935	Shares the Nobel Prize for Chemistry with her husband
1936	Serves as France's Undersecretary of State for Scientific Research
1937	Named a professor at the University of Paris
1946	Named director of the Radium Institute
1946-1950	Serves on the board of directors of France's Atomic Energy Commission
Mar. 17, 1956	Dies in Paris, France

Early Life

Irène Joliot-Curie was born Irène Curie in Paris, France, on September 12, 1897. Her parents, Marie Sklodowska Curie and Pierre Curie, were known for their pioneering studies of radioactivity.

Irène received her earliest education at home. In 1907 she began attending a small private cooperative school organized by her mother. In 1909 she began studying at the Collège Sévigné, from which she graduated with a baccalaureate degree in 1914.

Curie began studying at the University of Paris in 1914, but her education was soon interrupted by the outbreak of World War I. While serving as an army nurse, she set up X-ray equipment in military hospitals near the front lines.

When the war ended in 1918, Curie became an assistant at the Radium Institute, directed by her mother. She passed licensing examinations in physics and mathematics in 1920. In 1921, she began studying the release of alpha radiation from polonium. For this research, she earned a doctorate from the University of Paris in 1925.

The Neutron and the Positron

In 1926, Irène Curie married Frédéric Joliot, who had joined the Radium Institute in 1925; they both changed their surname to "Joliot-Curie." The Joliot-Curies began studying a new kind of radiation produced by exposing light elements such as boron and beryllium to alpha radiation. When paraffin was exposed to this new radiation, protons were ejected at high velocity. The Joliot-Curies thought that the new radiation was a form of gamma radiation. In 1931, the British physicist Sir James Chadwick discovered that it consisted of previously unknown particles called neutrons.

Irène and Frédéric Joliot-Curie began using neutron radiation in their studies of cloud chambers. A cloud chamber contains a vapor that condenses into drops of liquid when particles pass through it. They discovered a trail of drops left by a strange new particle. The U.S. physicist Carl David Anderson discovered that this particle was identical to an electron, but with a positive charge rather than a negative charge. The new particle, now known as a positron, was the first known example of an antimatter particle.

Artificial Radioactivity and Fission

In 1933, the Joliot-Curies noted that when aluminum was exposed to alpha radiation, it emitted neutrons and positrons. When the source of alpha radiation was removed, the neutron radiation stopped but the positron radiation remained. This indicates that the aluminum had been transformed into a source of positrons. A chemical test proved that the nonradioactive aluminum atoms had been changed into radioactive phosphorus atoms. For their discovery of artificial radioactivity, the Joliot-Curies won the Nobel Prize for Chemistry in 1935. After this, Irène and Frédéric began separate careers.

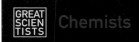

The Artificial Production of Radioactive Elements

Exposing nonradioactive elements to various forms of radiation can transform them into radioactive elements.

Radioactivity, or radioactive decay, was discovered near the end of the nineteenth century. It occurs when the nucleus of an atom is in an unstable state that causes it to release particles. The most common forms of radiation are known as alpha, beta, and gamma. Alpha radiation consists of helium nuclei, which contain two neutrons and two protons. Beta radiation consists of electrons or positrons. Gamma radiation consists of photons.

The first two elements studied as sources of natural radioactivity were uranium and thorium. Marie and Pierre Curie discovered the naturally occurring radioactive elements radium and polonium in 1898.

Irène and Frédéric Joliot-Curie created the first artificially produced radioactive elements in 1933. They placed a sample of aluminum next to a sample of polonium. The polonium released alpha particles. The aluminum atoms absorbed these particles and immediately released neutrons. After a few minutes, they released positrons. Chemical tests revealed the exact nature of the transformation taking place.

The nucleus of a normal, nonradioactive aluminum atom consists of thirteen protons and fourteen neutrons. When it absorbs an alpha particle, one of the two new neutrons is ejected immediately. The nucleus then has fifteen protons and fifteen neutrons. The added protons transform the aluminum atom into a phosphorus atom. Unlike an ordinary, nonradioactive phosphorous atom, which contains fifteen protons and sixteen neutrons, this atom is radioactive.

In a few minutes, the unstable nucleus releases a positron, which transforms one of the protons into a neutron. The nucleus then contains fourteen protons and sixteen neutrons. The loss of a proton transforms the radioactive phosphorus atom into a nonradioactive silicon atom. In a similar experiment, the Joliot-Curies transformed nonradioactive boron into radioactive nitrogen, which underwent radioactive decay into nonradioactive carbon.

The half-life of a radioactive element is the amount of time required for half of the atoms in a sample to undergo radioactive decay. Naturally occurring radioactive elements have long half-lives, up to billions of years or more. Artificially produced radioactive elements may have very short half-lives. The radioactive phosphorus produced by the Joliot-Curies, for example, had a half-life of about 3.5 minutes.

Certain artificially produced radioactive elements have important applications in medicine. Like ordinary iodine, artificially produced radioactive iodine is absorbed by the thyroid and is used to produce images of this gland. Artificially produced radioactive phosphorus, like ordinary phosphorus, is absorbed by cancer cells to a greater degree than by normal cells. It is used to produce images of cancerous tumors.

Bibliography

Satchler, G. R. *Introduction to Nuclear Reactions*. New York: John Wiley & Sons, 1980.

Gibson, W. M. *The Physics of Nuclear Reactions*. Oxford, England: Pergamon Press, 1980.

Trenn, Thaddeus J. *Transmutation, Natural and Artificial*. London: Heyden, 1981.

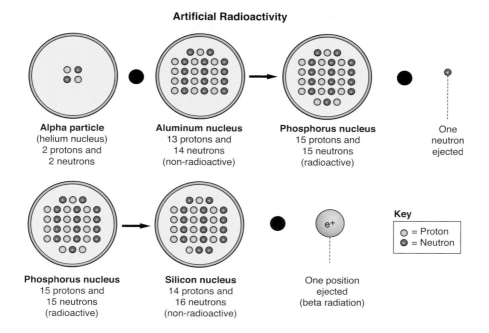

Artificial Radioactivity

Alpha particle
(helium nucleus)
2 protons and
2 neutrons

Aluminum nucleus
13 protons and
14 neutrons
(non-radioactive)

Phosphorus nucleus
15 protons and
15 neutrons
(radioactive)

One
neutron
ejected

Phosphorus nucleus
15 protons and
15 neutrons
(radioactive)

Silicon nucleus
14 protons and
16 neutrons
(non-radioactive)

One position
ejected
(beta radiation)

Key
○ = Proton
● = Neutron

Irène was appointed a professor at the University of Paris and continued to work at the Radium Institute. From June to September 1936, she served as Undersecretary of State for Scientific Research in the Popular Front government (a coalition of antifascist political parties). Then in 1938 she studied the effect of neutron radiation on uranium. She believed that the uranium would absorb neutrons and be transformed into a new, heavier element. Instead, she found that the lighter element lanthanum was present. Otto Hahn and Fritz Strassman repeated her experiments and discovered that the element barium was also present. German physicist Lise Meitner was able to explain these results when she realized that uranium atoms had split apart into lanthanum and barium atoms, a process known as nuclear fission.

World War II and Afterward

During the German occupation of France, the Joliot-Curies remained to continue their research. After the war, Frédéric was named high commissioner of France's Atomic Energy Commission. In 1946 Irène began serving on the board of directors of the Commission. The same year, she was named director of the Radium Institute. In 1950, the Joliot-Curies were removed from the Commission because of their leftist politics. Irène Joliot-Curie died of leukemia, probably caused by years of exposure to radiation, on March 17, 1956.

Bibliography

By Joliot-Curie

"Sur la vitesse d'émission des rayons alpha du polonium," *Comptes rendus hebdomadaires des séances de l'Académie des Sciences*, 1922.

"New Evidence for the Neutron," *Nature*, 1932 (with Frédéric Joliot-Curie).

"Production artificielle d'éléments radioactifs," *Journal de physique*, 1934 (with Joliot-Curie).

About Joliot-Curie

Bertsch McGrayne, Sharon. *Nobel Prize Women in Science*. New York: Carol, 1993.

Grinstein, Louise, Rose K. Rose, and Miriam H. Rafailovich, eds. *Women in Chemistry and Physics*. Westport, Conn.: Greenwood Press, 1993.

(Rose Secrest)

Percy Lavori Julian

Disciplines: Chemistry and invention
Contribution: A classical synthetic organic chemist, Julian combined a talent for creating complex molecular structures with a solid sense of how chemical transformations occur.

Sept. 12, 1897	Born in Montgomery, Alabama
1920	Earns a B.S. in chemistry from DePauw University, Indiana
1920-1922	Teaches chemistry at Fisk University, Tennessee
1923	Earns an M.S. in organic chemistry from Harvard University
1923-1929	Teaches at West Virginia State College
1923-1929	Serves as department head at Howard University
1929	Awarded a Rockefeller Foundation General Education Fellowship
1931	Awarded a Ph.D. in chemistry from the University of Vienna
1932-1936	Conducts research at DePauw
1936	Joins Glidden as chief chemist and director of research
1950	Elected "Chicagoan of the Year"
1954	Establishes Julian Laboratories
1956	Publishes a paper on the synthesis of cortisone derivatives
1968	Awarded the Chemical Pioneer Award of the American Institute of Chemistry
1973	Elected a member of the National Academy of Sciences
Apr. 19, 1975	Dies in Waukegan, Illinois

Early Life

When Percy Lavori Julian was born in 1899, an intellectual career was virtually impossible for African Americans in Montgomery, Alabama, as there was no secondary school for black children. Julian later told of pressing his nose against the window of the chemistry laboratory of the all-white high school.

Limited Opportunity

Julian's grandparents had been slaves. His grandfather's fingers were cut off as a punishment for learning to write. His grandmother sold produce on the streets so that his father could have more than the usual sixth-grade education. The dream of a college education for her son was realized by her grandchildren. All six children in the family obtained an education. Julian's brothers became doctors, and his sisters earned master's degrees. Julian always acknowledged his debt to his family. A private school for African Americans allowed

Julian to complete high school in 1916. Julian was admitted to DePauw University in Greencastle, Indiana, where his grandmother had dreamed of sending his father.

His secondary education had been so weak, however, that Julian was admitted on the condition that he complete two years of high school courses along with his college program. This requirement was in addition to his need to earn a portion of his expenses. These additional requirements failed to keep Julian down. He was graduated in 1920 as class valedictorian and Phi Beta Kappa.

Yet, this sterling record was insufficient to allow him to pursue a Ph.D. Several universities tried to soften their rejection, claiming that they were trying to help him because neither industry nor academia would hire an African American with a Ph.D. They suggested that he teach at a black school, where he did not need a further degree.

Two years later, Julian earned a fellowship to study chemistry at Harvard University with E. P. Kohler. Even there, discrimination was evident: he was denied an assistantship because he was told that white students would refuse to take instruction from a black man.

Foundation of a Career

In 1929, the Rockefeller Foundation awarded Julian a fellowship that allowed him to attend the University of Vienna. After teaching himself German, he worked with Ernst Späth and earned a doctorate in 1931. He found his lifelong interest in the synthesis of nature's complex molecules.

Julian returned to DePauw, where he made his greatest contribution to pure chemistry. He achieved the synthesis of physostigmine, an important drug for the treatment of the eye disease glaucoma. In 1935, he married Anna Johnson.

The Synthesis of Large Molecules

Julian spent his career synthesizing organic molecules, such as physostigine or cortisone, to be used as medications.

One of the most exciting competitions of twentieth century organic (or carbon) chemistry was the race to be the first person to synthesize a molecule of nature. Such a compound might have ten carbons, as in nicotine, or twenty-seven carbons, as in cholesterol. In most cases, a specific molecule was selected for synthesis because of its medicinal properties.

Although many types of molecules have been prepared in the laboratory, the alkaloids and steroids generally grab the spotlight. The distinctive features of these compounds include rings of atoms, carbon for the steroids and both carbon and nitrogen for the alkaloids. Thousands of such compounds have been prepared.

The synthetic process begins with a molecule in which the exact sequence of atoms is known. It might

be a small molecule consisting of a few atoms, but more often it is the large molecule related to the desired compound. In either case, the product is assembled step by step using chemical reactions that change the starting material in predictable ways.

At each step, it is essential to show that the new intermediate has the structure expected. The conclusion is reached when the synthetic material is shown to be identical to the natural substance in its chemical and physical properties.

Bibliography

Anand, Nitya, Jasjit S. Bindra, and Subramania Ranganathan. *Art in Organic Synthesis*. 2d ed. New York: John Wiley & Sons, 1988.

Fox, Marye Anne and James K. Whitesell. *Organic Chemistry*. Boston: Jones and Bartlett, 1997.

Bruice, Paula. *Organic Chemistry*. Upper Saddle River, N.J.: Prentice Hall, 1995.

In spite of his growing scientific reputation, Julian was denied faculty positions at several colleges. In 1936 he joined the Glidden Company, where he became director of research. From 1954 to 1961 he managed his own firm, Julian Laboratories, exploring the scientific and practical importance of soybeans and discovering an inexpensive synthesis of cortisone. Sadly, even this recognition was accompanied by continued threats and attacks on him and his family.

Julian died in 1975 just after his seventy-sixth birthday. In 1992, he was honored on a U.S. postage stamp.

Bibliography

By Julian

"Studies in the Indole Series: I, The Synthesis of Alpha-Benzylindoles," *Journal of the American Chemical Society*, 1933 (with Josef Pikl).

"Studies in the Indole Series: V, The Complete Synthesis of Physostigmine (Eserine)," *Journal of the American Chemical Society*, 1935 (with Pikl).

"Studies in the Indole Series: XII, Yohimbine (Part 3)—A Novel Synthesis of the Yohimbine Ring Structure," *Journal of the American Chemical Society*, 1949 (with Arthur Magnani).

About Julian

Brodie, James Michael. "Percy Julian, 1899-1975." In *Created Equal: The Lives and Ideas of Black American Innovators*. New York: William Morrow, 1993.

Witkop, Bernard. "Percy Lavon Julian: April 11, 1899–April 19, 1974." In *Biographical Memoirs of the National Academy of Sciences*. Vol. 52. Washington, D.C.: National Academy of Sciences, 1980.

Haber, Louis. "Percy Lavon Julian, 1899-)." In *Black Pioneers of Science and Invention*. New York: Harcourt, Brace & World, 1970.

(*K. Thomas Finley*)

Irving Langmuir

Disciplines: Chemistry, physics, and technology

Contribution: Langmuir preformed pioneering research in electrical technology, surface chemistry, the structure of matter, electrical discharge, thermionic emission, plasma physics, and weather modification.

Jan. 31, 1881	Born in Brooklyn, New York
1906	Earns a Ph.D. from the University of Göttingen, Germany
1906-1909	Works as an instructor at the Stevens Institute of Technology
1909	Joins the General Electric Research Laboratory
1918	Elected to the National Academy of Sciences
1929	Named president of the American Chemical Society
1932	Wins the Nobel Prize in Chemistry
1932-1950	Made associate director of the General Electric Research Laboratory
1938	Serves as Pilgrim Trust Lecturer for the Royal Society of London
1941	Becomes president of the American Association for the Advancement of Science
1943	Awarded the Faraday Medal
1946	Named Hitchcock Foundation Lecturer at the University of California
1948-1950	Serves on the Board of Trustees for the State University of New York
1950	Retires from General Electric
Aug. 16, 1957	Dies in Falmouth, Massachusetts

Early Life

Irving Langmuir was the third of four sons born to Charles and Sadie (Comings) Langmuir. He attended public school in Brooklyn until 1892, Parisian boarding schools from 1892 to 1895, and the Chestnut Hill Academy in Philadelphia from 1895 to 1896.

Langmuir graduated from the Pratt Institute's Manual Training High School of Brooklyn in 1899. He obtained a metallurgical engineering baccalaureate in 1903 from the Columbia School of Mines, and traveled to Germany to earn a Ph.D. in 1906 at the University of Göttingen under the physical chemist Walther Nernst. Langmuir then taught chemistry for three years at the Stevens Institute of Technology in Hoboken, New Jersey.

Joining General Electric

In 1909, Langmuir took a summer job under Willis Whitney at the Research Laboratory of the General Electric Company in Schenectady, New York, which became his lifelong employer. He established the international reputation of a celebrity and ultimately received fifteen honorary degrees and twenty-three scientific medals and prizes, including the Nobel Prize in Chemistry in 1932 for his surface chemistry work.

Industrial scientists at the General Electric Research Laboratory were free to pursue projects based on personal interest and scientific merit. Enormous long-term profits from practical applications of Langmuir's discoveries encouraged other corporations and governmental agencies to fund pure research.

A Prolific Scientist

Langmuir published more than 200 scientific papers, often arranged into the following interrelated categories: chemical reactions at high temperatures and low pressures (1906-1921); thermal effects in gases (1911-1936); atomic structure (1919-1921); thermionic emission and surfaces in vacuums (1913-1937); chemical forces in solids, liquids, and surface films (1916-1943); electrical discharges in gases (1923-1932); and atmospheric science (1938-1955).

The "octet rule" for "covalent" and "electrovalent" (ionic) chemical bonding were terms proposed by Langmuir to clarify the initial ideas of Gilbert Lewis. Langmuir also coined the word "plasma" and developed the field of magnetohydrodynamics to describe ionized gas as a fourth state of matter. This work provided fundamental concepts for understanding electrical discharges, thermonuclear fusion, and astrophysics. He offered a pioneering theory for thermionic emission from hot metals and the Child-Langmuir space-charge equation for the current between electrodes.

Langmuir's innovations, involving more than sixty patents, include the gas-filled incandescent lamp, atomic hydrogen welding, and the mercury-condensation pump used to produce high-vacuum power tubes for radio broadcasting.

Surface Chemistry

The surface of solids and liquids can be covered with a single layer of adsorbed molecules called a monolayer, whose presence influences interfacial phenomena and whose orderly structure is related to molecular properties.

Chemists of the early twentieth century lacked a comprehensive theory for the phenomenon of adsorption. Langmuir proposed that adsorption involves the formation of a single layer of molecules arranged evenly on a surface. The famous Langmuir isotherm expression was derived to measure the extent of surface coverage by this monolayer and confirmed its existence.

Langmuir's new concept of adsorption was applied to films of organic molecules spread onto the surface of water. The Langmuir film balance, developed at the General Electric Research Laboratory was used to measure the size, shape, surface orientation, packing, and intermolecular forces of molecules in organic monolayers ranging from simple fatty acids to proteins.

Monolayers provide models for biological membranes and are employed in the fabrication of sophisticated optical and electronic devices. The principles of surface chemistry summarized so clearly by Langmuir are applied in heterogeneous catalysis, lubrication, colloidal dispersion, and other interfacial phenomena.

Bibliography

Somorjai, Gabor A. *Introduction to Surface Chemistry and Catalysis*. New York: Wiley-Interscience, 1994.

Petty, Michael C. *Langmuir-Blodgett Films: An Introduction*. Cambridge, England: Cambridge University Press, 1996.

Birdi, K. S. *Lipid and Biopolymer Monolayers at Liquid Interfaces*. New York: Plenum Press, 1989.

Adamson, Arthur W. *Physical Chemistry of Surfaces*. 5th ed. New York: Wiley-Interscience, 1990.

Clint, John H. *Surfactant Aggregation*. New York: Chapman & Hall, 1992.

He worked on submarine detection during World War I and studied protective smoke screens and aircraft icing during World War II. He continued military research as the head of Project Cirrus, which led to the first artificial rain and snow produced by cloud seeding.

Langmuir died in 1957 at the age of seventy-six.

Bibliography

By Langmuir

"Atomic Hydrogen as an Aid to Industrial Research," *Science*, 1928.

"Surface Chemistry," *Chemical Reviews*, 1933.

"Science, Common Sense, and Decency," *Science*, 1943.

Phenomena, Atoms, and Molecules: An Attempt to Interpret Phenomena in Terms of Mechanisms or Atomic and Molecular Interactions, 1950.

About Langmuir

Kerker, Milton. "Classics and Classicists of Colloid and Interface Science: 9. Irving Langmuir." *Journal of Colloid and Interface Science* 133 (1989).

Suits, C. Guy and Miles J. Martin. "Irving Langmuir." *Biographical Memoirs of the National Academy of Sciences* 45 (1974).

Kohler, Robert E. "Irving Langmuir and the 'Octet' Theory of Valence." *Historical Studies in the Physical Sciences* 4 (1974).

Reich, Leonard S. "Irving Langmuir and the Pursuit of Science and Technology in the Corporate Environment." *Technology and Culture* 24 (1983).

Rosenfeld, Albert. *The Quintessence of Irving Langmuir*. Oxford, England: Pergamon Press, 1966.

(Martin V. Stewart)

Antoine-Laurent Lavoisier

Discipline: Chemistry

Contribution: Lavoisier's discoveries of oxygen and hydrogen established chemistry as a separate science. His laboratory methods and system for naming elements and compounds became standard in the field.

Aug. 26, 1743	Born in Paris, France
1754	Begins his formal education at Collège Mazarin
1763	Earns a law degree and enters the Order of Advocates
1764	Publishes a scientific paper on the properties of gypsum
1765	Awarded for his proposal for lighting the streets of Paris
1768	Becomes a member of the Académie Royale des Sciences
1772	Shows that phosphorus absorbs air while burning
1775	As Superintendent of the Arsenal, improves France's supply of gunpowder
1782-1783	Creates a calorimeter to measure the heat produced in chemical reactions
1783	Proves that water is composed of two gases
1787	Suggests a new method of naming chemical elements and compounds
1791	Proposes a tax reform plan to the revolutionary government
May 8, 1794	Dies in Paris, France

Early Life

Antoine-Laurent Lavoisier (pronounced "lah-vwah-ZYAY") was born in Paris, France, on August 26, 1743, to a comfortably middle-class family. He attended the Collège Mazarin, one of the best secondary schools, in order to prepare for a career in law, which was the profession of his father and grandfather. Lavoisier studied humanities for six years and won prizes in French, Latin, and Greek at the end of the sixth year. He then began a three-year program in mathematics and philosophy. After studying mathematics for a year, he left to study law.

Lavoisier earned his law degree in 1763 and was admitted to practice law at the *parlement*, the court of twelve judges in Paris. However, he was more interested in scientific research. He attended public lectures at the Jardin du Roi, the royal museum of natural history, botany, and zoology. There, Lavoisier heard lectures by prominent scientists and mathematicians.

The Chemical Revolution

Lavoisier brought great changes to chemistry by proving experimentally that elements can exist as gases, liquids, and solids, and that air and water are chemical compounds.

Combustion was the central problem in chemistry when Lavoisier began his experiments with phosphorus in 1772. Georg Ernst Stahl, a German chemist, had developed the generally accepted theory that combustion, or burning, involved the release of "phlogiston," leaving less material than existed before combustion. No chemist, however, had isolated phlogiston from other elements.

Stahl's theory of combustion explained many experiments, until Lavoisier noticed that iron weighs more after being burned. Lavoisier reasoned that if phlogiston was released during combustion, then iron should weigh less after combustion, not more. He also conducted experiments with phosphorus that convinced him that air combines with phosphorus during combustion. Lavoisier learned that the weight of the air lost during combustion equaled the weight gained by the phosphorus.

During these experiments, Lavoisier developed a new method of chemistry. With the most precise scales that could be made, he weighed all the instruments and all the materials before and after the experiments. He stored the materials carefully so that they would not be contaminated and he cleaned the instruments so that no foreign material would affect the experiment. He timed the experiments. His wife, Marie-Anne, kept precise records of everything that happened. He gave the name "oxygen" (meaning "acid-maker") to the air that had combined with the phosphorus. Thus, he began to write a new language for chemistry.

Lavoisier knew that the English chemists Joseph Black and Joseph Priestley had discovered several kinds of air because Marie-Anne had translated their reports into French. When he learned that dew appeared inside the glass vessel when Henry Cavendish, an English chemist, burned air, he knew that water was a chemical compound and air was part of it. Lavoisier replicated this experiment and was the first to understand what the result meant. He named the new air, or gas, "hydrogen" (meaning "water-maker").

In a decade, Lavoisier brought about a revolution in chemistry. He proved that elements can exist as gases, as liquids, and in solid states. He proved that air and water are not elements, as had been believed for thousands of years, but chemical compounds made of the same gases combined in different weights.

Bibliography

Guerlac, Henry. *Antoine-Laurent Lavoisier: Chemist and Revolutionary*. New York: Charles Scribner's Sons, 1975.

Crosland, Maurice. *Historical Studies in the Language of Chemistry*. Cambridge, Mass.: Harvard University Press, 1962.

Holmes, Frederic Lawrence. *Lavoisier and the Chemistry of Life*. Madison, Wis.: University of Wisconsin Press, 1985.

Lavoisier's maternal grandmother died in 1768, leaving him a large amount of money, which he used to buy a government position as a tax collector. This position did not require all his time and energy, so Lavoisier left the legal profession and began a new career in science.

Marriage and Early Success

The terms of his contract with the French government required Lavoisier to inspect the work of many tax collectors. He was away from Paris, traveling in the countryside, during 1769 and 1770. Lavoisier reported to Jacques Paulze, his future father-in-law.

Paulze's wife had died after giving birth to three sons and a daughter, Marie-Anne. The girl was reared in a convent according to the custom of the time, and Paulze introduced his daughter to Lavoisier. An older man, politically powerful but not wealthy, had asked to marry Marie-Anne, who had inherited a fortune from her mother and her mother's family. Instead, Lavoisier and Marie-Anne were married on December 16, 1771. The bride was not yet fourteen, and the groom was twenty-eight.

Before 1750, chemistry was the business of doctors and pharmacists. From the beginning, Lavoisier hoped that his experiments would be revolutionary: he wanted to make chemistry a separate science like physics or astronomy.

Lavoisier began his experiments on combustion in 1772. At that time, scientists accepted the theory of Aristotle, the ancient Greek philosopher, that there were four elements: earth, air, fire, and water. Lavoisier accomplished his revolution within ten years. He proved that air and water are chemical compounds. He also proved that many elements can exist in several states—as gases, as liquids, or as solids. Marie-Anne recorded all of his experiments, noting the time required and drawing illustrations of the arrangements of the laboratory equipment that Lavoisier used.

The French Revolution

Lavoisier continued to work on important government projects while conducting the research that made him the founder of modern chemistry. For years, he advocated the reform of the tax system. He kept his government position after the French Revolution began in 1789.

A new government, however, was formed in 1791. The leaders were suspicious of Lavoisier because of his success and fame as a scientist and as a public administrator under the old royal governments. When they ordered the imprisonment of tax collectors, Lavoisier and his father-in-law were among those arrested for conspiring against the people.

Although no evidence existed that he had broken any laws or deceived the public, Lavoisier was condemned to death. On May 8, 1794, he went to the guillotine. His widow, Marie-Anne, devoted the rest of her life to restoring his reputation.

Bibliography

By Lavoisier

Traité élémentaire de chimie, 1789 (*Elements of Chemistry in a New Systematic Order, Containing All the Modern Discoveries*, 1790).

Oeuvres de Lavoisier, 1862-1893 (6 vols.).

Fric, René. ed. *Oeuvres de Lavoisier: Correspondance*, 1955-1986.

About Lavoisier

Donovan, Arthur. *Antoine Lavoisier: Science, Administration, and Revolution*. Oxford, England: Blackwell, 1993.

Guerlac, Henry. *Lavoisier: The Crucial Year*. Ithaca, N.Y.: Cornell University Press, 1961.

(Hugh L. Guilderson)

Jean-Marie Lehn

Disciplines: Chemistry and technology

Contribution: Lehn was instrumental in the development of supramolecular chemistry. His work has improved the understanding of how molecules "recognize" one another, opening the door for the synthesis of artificial enzymes, cells, and molecular devices.

Sept. 30, 1939	Born in Rosheim, France
1960	Earns a B.S. in chemistry from the University of Strasbourg
1963	Earns a Ph.D. in organic chemistry at Strasbourg
1963	Awarded a Bronze Medal from the Centre National de la Recherche Scientifique
1964	Becomes a postdoctoral research associate at Harvard University
1965	Returns to Strasbourg as a lecturer
11970	Promoted to full professor at Strasbourg
1972	Awarded a Silver Medal from the Centre National de la Recherche Scientifique
1980	Elected to a chair at the Collège de France in Paris
1981	Awarded a Gold Medal from the Centre National de la Recherche Scientifique
1983	Named to the French Legion of Honor
1987	Awarded the Nobel Prize in Chemistry
1996	Awarded Commander of the Légion d'Honneur
2007	Receives the ISA Medal for Science

Early Life

Jean-Marie Lehn (pronounced "layn") was born in 1939, the first of Pierre and Marie Lehn's four sons. Entering high school in 1950, he studied classics, with an emphasis on philosophy but developed an interest in science, too. In 1957, he received his *baccalauréat* in philosophy and experimental sciences.

In the fall of 1957, Lehn entered the University of Strasbourg, where he intended to study philosophy, but he soon reconsidered. He was quite taken with the experimental power of organic chemistry, which was able to interconvert complicated substances following well-defined rules and routes.

After receiving his bachelor of science degree in chemistry in 1960, Lehn remained at Strasbourg to begin his graduate studies with Guy Ourisson. He received his Ph.D. in only three years, after which he spent a year at Harvard University as a postdoctoral research associate, working with Robert Burns Woodward on the total synthesis of vitamin B-12.

Supramolecular Chemistry

Certain large molecules can recognize and bind other molecules having a complementary shape. Such binding significantly alters the chemical and physical properties of the pair.

The Function of Enzymes

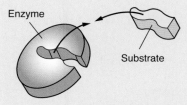

An enzyme combines with a substrate that has molecules of a complementary shape.

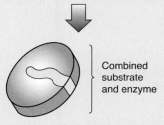

The interaction between the enzyme and substrate causes a chemical change in the substrate, splitting it in two.

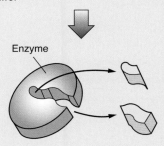

The enzyme is unchanged and can repeat the process with another substrate molecule.

The term "supramolecular chemistry" refers to interactions in which host molecules with cavities of precisely defined sizes and shapes recognize and bind to smaller guest molecules of a complementary size and shape, much in the same way that a key fits into a lock. The host-guest interaction is very specific; only guests of the appropriate structure can be accommodated by a particular host.

This sort of molecular recognition is vital to all life processes. For example, enzymes, substances that catalyze specific biochemical reactions, must be able to recognize and act on only the appropriate substrate molecules. A given enzyme might be able to break down the proteins in food, but it must not also break down the proteins in the body's own cells.

Lehn has described three functions as being characteristic of supramolecular species: recognition, transformation, and translocation. The earliest cryptands performed only the first of these three functions. To be truly useful, however, complexation must be followed either by a chemical reaction that would not occur otherwise or by the transport of the guest molecule across some barrier that it would not cross on its own.

Lehn and other researchers in this rapidly growing field soon succeeded in producing supramolecular compounds that could do so as artificial enzymes (transformation), and some others that could selectively transport drugs or other chemicals to and from specific tissues within the body (translocation). Other applications of supramolecular chemistry are under development, such as artificial cells and molecular-level circuit components. The principles of supramolecular chemistry guide the research efforts of many scientists.

Bibliography

Peterson, Ivars. "Cages, Cavities, and Clefts." *Science News* 132 (August 8, 1987).

Lehn, Jean Marie et al., eds. *Comprehensive Supramolecular Chemistry*. Tarrytown, N.Y.: Pergamon Press, 1996.

Vogtle, Fritz. *Supramolecular Chemistry: An Introduction*. New York: John Wiley & Sons, 1993.

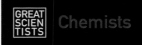

Early Academic Career

Lehn returned to Strasbourg in 1965 and was appointed assistant professor of chemistry in 1966. Initially, he worked in the area of physical organic chemistry: the relationship between the structure and shape of an organic (carbon-containing) molecule and its physical properties.

Lehn's interest in the physical and chemical processes occurring within the nervous system made him wonder if a chemist could contribute to their study. Nerve cells communicate, in part, by enforcing an imbalance in the concentration of certain positively charged atoms called cations—most notably sodium and potassium—inside and outside the cell. Noting that certain natural antibiotics were able to make cell membranes permeable to cations, Lehn reasoned that it should be possible to devise and synthesize chemical substances that could accomplish the same feat.

A New Direction

Lehn also took note of the recently discovered crown ethers: doughnut-shaped molecules having remarkable abilities to bind cations tightly, yet reversibly to form what was called a supramolecular complex. Crown ethers are essentially planar molecules. Shape determines function, Lehn reasoned, and if a two-dimensional crown ether can form a strong complex with specific cations, then a three-dimensional analog should do the job even better. This hypothesis turned out to be true.

Lehn chose the term "cryptand" to describe his new class of molecules, because their interior cavities resembled crypts in which some other molecule could be "entombed." Work on the synthesis of the first cryptand began in October, 1967, and was completed the following September. This molecule forms a complex with the potassium cation that is 10,000 times stronger than the strongest complex formed between potassium and any crown ether.

Amazingly, by altering the structure of the simplest cryptand only slightly, Lehn and his co-workers succeeded in synthesizing molecules that could act as artificial enzymes. Similarly, they synthesized molecules that can selectively separate toxic from nontoxic metal cations.

In recognition of his pioneering efforts in the field of supramolecular chemistry, Lehn was awarded the 1987 Nobel Prize in Chemistry, jointly with Donald J. Cram and Charles J. Pedersen. He continues to work at the Université Louis Pasteur in Strasbourg.

Bibliography

By Lehn

"Design of Organic Complexing Agents: Strategies Toward Properties," *Structure and Bonding*, 1973.

"Cryptâtes: Inclusion Complexes of Macropolycyclic Receptor Molecules," *Pure and Applied Chemistry*, 1978.

"Macrocyclic Receptor Molecules—Aspects of Chemical Reactivity: Investigations into Molecular Catalysis and Transport Processes," *Pure and Applied Chemistry*, 1979.

"Supramolecular Chemistry: Receptors, Catalysts, and Carriers," *Science*, 1985.

Balzani, V. ed. "Photophysical and Photochemical Aspects of Supramolecular Chemistry" in *Supramolecular Photochemistry*, 1987.

About Lehn

Magill, Frank N. ed. "Jean-Marie Lehn." In *The Nobel Prize Winners: Chemistry*. Pasadena, Calif.: Salem Press, 1990.

"Jean-Marie Lehn," Superstars of Science, http://superstarsofscience.com/scientist/jean-marie-lehn

James, Laylin K. ed. *Nobel Laureates in Chemistry, 1901-1992*. Washington, D.C.: American Chemical Society, 1993.

(Thomas H. Eberlein)

Gilbert N. Lewis

Discipline: Chemistry

Contribution: Lewis, a leader in chemical thermodynamics and an early exponent of relativity theory, laid the foundation for the electron theory of valence, extended the concept of acids and bases, and was the first to isolate heavy hydrogen.

Oct. 25, 1875	Born in Weymouth, Massachusetts
1899	Earns a Ph.D. in chemistry at Harvard under T. W. Richards
1900	Studies under Wilhelm Ostwald at the University of Leipzig and Walther Nernst at the University of Göttingen
1901-1904	Teaches at Harvard
1904	Serves as Superintendent of Weights and Measures and as a chemist in the Bureau of Science in the Philippines
1905	Conducts research at the Massachusetts Institute of Technology with Arthur A. Noyes
1912	Named dean of the college of chemistry and chair of the chemistry department at the University of California, Berkeley
1922	Awarded the Distinguished Service Medal
1923	Begins to study the theory of radiation and relativity
1933-1938	Conducts research on isotopes and their preparation
1938	Performs theoretical and experimental studies in photochemistry
Mar. 23, 1946	Dies in Berkeley, California

Early Life

Gilbert Newton Lewis was born near Boston in 1875. He received his primary education at home from his father who was a lawyer, and his mother. Lewis' formal education began in 1889 at the University of Nebraska Preparatory School.

Lewis transferred to Harvard in 1893 and graduated with a B.S. in 1896. After teaching for a year at Phillips Academy at Andover, he returned to Harvard for an M.A. in 1898 and a Ph.D. in 1899. He taught chemistry at Harvard for one year before going abroad on a traveling fellowship to study under Wilhelm Ostwald at the University of Leipzig and Walther Nernst at the University of Göttingen.

Lewis returned to Harvard in 1901 and taught thermodynamics and electrochemistry there until 1904. Several of his long-time interests date from this early period, the most important of which were thermodynamics, valence theory, and photochemistry.

He spent 1904 as Superintendent of Weights and Measures in the Philippines and as a chemist in the Bureau of Science in Manila. He returned to the United States in 1905 and joined the group of physical chemists assembled by Arthur A. Noyes at the Massachusetts Institute of Technology (MIT). Noyes's laboratory became the first center for physical chemists in the United States.

Thermodynamics and MIT

Lewis remained at MIT for seven years, publishing more than thirty papers, including "Outlines of a New System of Thermodynamic Chemistry" in 1907 and "The Free Energy of Chemical Substances" in 1913. They were among the most important in a long series of papers on the experimental determination of free energy, and led in 1923 to the publication of Lewis' monumental work *Thermodynamics and the Free Energy of Chemical Substances*.

During his years at MIT, Lewis met Albert Einstein and became a supporter of the then-unpopular theory of relativity. This move into a new field of investigation resulted in his publications on relativity with R. C. Tolman and E. B. Wilson.

Chemical Education and Atomic Studies

In 1912, Lewis left MIT to become dean of the college of chemistry and chair of the chemistry department at the University of California, Berkeley (UCB). His recruitment of an exceptional faculty and curricular reforms made UCB the model for U.S. chemical education. Berkeley's production of first-rate chemists soon rivaled that of the leading German universities.

Lewis' work on thermodynamics became more intense at UCB, as he transformed an essentially theoretical science into a practical tool for chemists. His other interests, such as atomic structure and valence, continued to develop, and

in 1916 he published "The Atom and the Molecule." In this paper, he defined the chemical bond as a shared pair of electrons, and introduced the electron dot formulas, or Lewis formulas, to represent a chemical bond. His most extensive treatment of valence appeared in 1923 as *Valence and the Structure of Atoms and Molecules*.

World War I Service

World War I and his commission as a major in the Chemical Warfare Service interrupted Lewis' work at UCB. As chief of the service's defense division, he instructed U.S. army officers on the effects of poison gas and how to defend against poison gas attacks. Lewis received the Distinguished Service Medal in 1922 for his valuable contribution.

Other Interests

Lewis returned to UCB after World War I and concluded his work in thermodynamics and chemical valence with major publications in both areas in 1923. He devoted the next decade to the theories of quantum radiation and relativity, before turning in 1933 to research on the separation of deuterium from ordinary water.

Lewis was the first to concentrate nearly pure deuterium in quantities sufficient for experimentation, and spent two years focused on the chemistry and physics of deuterium, heavy water, and other deuterium compounds.

In the late 1930s, Lewis resumed his earlier studies on photochemistry, particularly the relation of electron structure to phosphorescence, fluorescence, and color in compounds. His last publications dealt with the relation between phosphorescence and the triplet electronic state of organic molecules.

Lewis died suddenly of heart failure on March 23, 1946, while performing an experiment on phosphorescence; he was seventy years old.

Atomic Structure

Lewis made significant contributions to the study of atomic structure with his theories of the cubic atom and shared-pair electron bond.

Lewis developed the idea of electrons in an atom arranged in concentric cubes in 1902 while trying to explain the periodic law to an elementary chemistry class. He proposed that a polar (ionic) compound results whenever two or more atoms complete their outermost cubes by gaining or losing electrons and form a stable octet (group of eight). Electrostatic attraction produces the polar bond between them.

Despite the cubic atom's success in accounting for the formulas of simple polar compounds of inorganic chemistry, Lewis' model left unexplained the vast number of nonpolar or organic compounds that do not consist of ions. He solved this problem in 1916 by postulating that the cubes or atomic shells are interpenetrable. Because of shell interpenetrability, an electron or electrons from one atom can form part of another atom's shell but not belong exclusively to either atom. Hence, neither atom has lost or gained electrons. This arrangement is the mechanism for electron pair sharing or chemical bond formation. Only in purely polar compounds is the electron transfer complete.

In order to represent clearly the shared electron pair bond, Lewis in 1916 introduced electron dot formulas. Each pair of dots or colon (:) symbolizes the electron pair constituting the chemical bond. Although the cubic atom became obsolete—in his 1916 paper, Lewis replaced the eight electrons at the cube's corners with four pairs at the corners of a tetrahedron—his shared electron pair bond became the starting point for the new quantum chemistry.

Bibliography

Electrons and Valence: Development of the Theory, 1900-1925. Anthony N. Stranges. College Station: Texas A&M University Press, 1982.

Polar Bonds

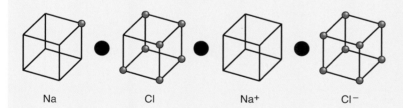

Na   Cl   Na⁺   Cl⁻

**The circles represent bonds.
Na is sodium and Cl is chorine.**

Nonpolar Bonds

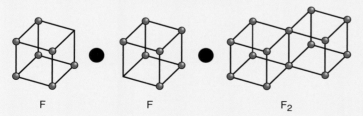

F   F   F₂

**The circles represent bonds.
F is fluorine**

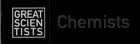

Thermodynamics

Lewis' rationalization of and contributions to chemical thermodynamics transformed it from an abstract science into a valuable tool for chemists.

Lewis' earliest paper of 1900-1901 attempted to establish a fundamental principle from which chemists could derive all thermodynamic relations. He proposed the idea of an "escaping tendency" or "fugacity" to express the tendency of a substance to pass from one chemical phase to another and thereby provide information on the extent and direction of the chemical reaction.

Lewis never found a fundamental fugacity, but he did demonstrate that measurements of free energy and entropy provide an exact chemical thermodynamics. Previously, chemists had relied on calorimetrie measurements of enthalpy (a body's internal energy added to the product of its volume and the pressure) and heat of formation to calculate chemical affinity (attraction) and thereby predict the direction of any chemical reaction. By 1907, he had made clear that a system's free energy and entropy (unavailable energy) were key concepts, and he and his coworkers began free energy calculations from measurements of equilibria, electromotive force, and entropy.

Lewis summarized and brought up to date the theory and methods for calculating free energy in 1913 and in 1923 published his classic book on thermodynamics. This work made the techniques and fruits of thermodynamics, once the luxury of specialists, available to every chemist. Lewis' main contribution to thermodynamics was not in his elaboration of theory but in his expansion of its practical applications.

Bibliography

Mahan, Bruce H. *Elementary Chemical Thermodynamics*. New York: W. A. Benjamin, 1964.

"Gilbert N. Lewis and the Thermodynamics of Strong Electrolytes." *Journal of Chemical Education* 61 (1984).

Bibliography

By Lewis

"Outlines of a New System of Thermodynamic Chemistry," *Proceedings of the American Academy of Arts and Sciences*, 1907.

"The Space-Time Manifold of Relativity: The Non-Euclidean Geometry of Mechanics and Electromagnetics," *Proceedings of the American Academy of Arts and Sciences*, 1912 (with E. B. Wilson).

"The Free Energy of Chemical Substances," *Journal of the American Chemical Society*, 1913.

Valence and the Structure of Atoms and Molecules, 1923.

"The Quantum Laws and the Uncertainty Principle of Heisenberg," *Proceedings of the National Academy of Sciences*, 1929 (with Joseph E. Mayer.)

About Lewis

Lachman, Arthur. *Borderland of the Unknown*. New York: Pageant Press, 1995.

Jolly, William. *From Retorts to Lasers*. Berkeley, Calif.: University of California Press, 1987.

Hildebrand, Joel H. "Gilbert Newton Lewis." *National Academy of Sciences Biographical Memoirs* 31 (1958).

Gillispie, Charles Coulston. ed. "Lewis, Gilbert Newton." In *Dictionary of Scientific Biography*. New York: Charles Scribner's Sons, 1973.

Stranges, Anthony N. "Reflections on the Electron Theory of the Chemical Bond: 1900-1925." *Journal of Chemical Education* 61 (1984).

(Anthony N. Stranges and Steve Kirkpatrick)

William N. Lipscomb

Discipline: Chemistry

Contribution: An authority on chemical physics, X-ray crystallography, and chemical biology, Lipscomb won the Nobel Prize in Chemistry for his studies of chemical bonding.

Jul. 16, 1919	Born in Cleveland, Ohio
1941	Earns a B.S. in chemistry from the University of Kentucky
1946	Earns a Ph.D. in chemistry from the California Institute of Technology (Caltech)
1946-1959	Serves on the faculty of the University of Minnesota
1947	Conducts X-ray studies of single crystals at low temperatures
1954-1955	Becomes Guggenheim Fellow at Oxford University
1955	President of the American Crystallographic Association
1959-1971	Professor of chemistry at Harvard University
1961	Elected to the National Academy of Sciences
1962-1965	Chair of the chemistry department at Harvard
1971-1990	Named Abbott and James Lawrence Professor of Chemistry at Harvard
1973	Guggenheim Fellow at the University of Cambridge, England
1976	Awarded the Nobel Prize in Chemistry
1986-1996	Given the National Institutes of Health's MERIT Award
Apr. 14, 2011	Dies in Massachusetts

Early Life

William Nunn Lipscomb, Jr., whose father was a physician and whose mother was a music voice teacher, grew up near Lexington, Kentucky. Beginning with a chemistry set at the age of eleven, he acquired enough chemicals and apparatus to equip a home laboratory. At his father's request, the high school instituted a chemistry course for him.

At the University of Kentucky, which he attended on a music scholarship, Lipscomb majored in chemistry and physics and also studied quantum mechanics. After receiving a B.S. in chemistry in 1941, he went to the California Institute of Technology (Caltech) to study physics.

Influenced by future Nobel chemistry laureate Linus Pauling, Lipscomb switched to chemistry and earned a Ph.D. under Pauling's supervision. During World War II and for more than three of his five years at Caltech, he worked as a physical chemist for the Office of Scientific Research and Development on war-related projects.

Bonding in Boranes

The chemical bonding displayed in boranes (binary compounds of boron and hydrogen) has posed challenging problems in both experimental and theoretical chemistry.

Because the lighter boranes are volatile, sensitive to air and moisture, toxic, and pyrophoric (burning spontaneously in air), their preparation and characterization are very difficult, requiring complicated equipment and time-consuming techniques. Therefore, they remained laboratory curiosities until World War II, when the US government supported research to find volatile uranium compounds (borohydrides) for isotope separation in the Manhattan Project to build the atomic bomb, and the 1950s, when it supported programs to develop high-energy fuels for rockets and jet aircraft. Their study, in which Lipscomb served as a leading participant, soon became one of the most rapidly expanding areas of inorganic chemistry.

Aside from these practical applications, chemists have been interested in boranes because they possess structures different from any other class of compounds. Because boron has only three valence electrons rather than four valence electrons like carbon and because ordinary covalent bonds between two atoms usually involve a pair of electrons, boranes have been called electron-deficient compounds.

Through skillful calculations involving electron pair multicenter bonds, Lipscomb clarified their structures and developed rules permitting the prediction of stability of new compounds and the conditions for their synthesis.

Bibliography

"Boranes and Carboranes." George B. Kauffman. In *Encyclopædia Britannica*. Vol. 15. Chicago: Encyclopaedia Britannica, 1995.

Hydrides of Boron and Silicon. Alfred Stock. Ithaca, N.Y: Cornell University Press, 1957.

Inorganic Chemistry. Keith E Purcell and John C. Kotz. Philadelphia: W. B. Saunders, 1977.

"The 1976 Nobel Prize for Chemistry." Russell N. Grimes. *Science* 194 (1976).

The University of Minnesota

From 1946 to 1959, Lipscomb was a faculty member at the University of Minnesota, serving as assistant professor, associate professor, and professor of physical chemistry, as well as acting chief and chief of the physical chemistry division. There he developed techniques to grow single crystals at low temperatures for use in X-ray diffraction methods.

After several studies of problems of residual entropy (the measure of disorder of a system), Lipscomb began a series of studies of the structures of the lower boron hydrides (boranes) B_5H_9, B_4H_{10}, B_5H_{11}, and B_6H_{10}. These surprisingly compact structures required the postulation of electron pair bonds that sometimes joined together three or more atoms. Numerous further studies supported the bonding descriptions in these boranes as well as in larger, more complex boranes, carboranes (cage compounds of boron, carbon, and hydrogen), and related molecules.

Harvard University

At Harvard, Lipscomb expanded his theoretical and experimental studies of boranes. Advances in computing led him to a systematic general method to obtain molecular orbitals that were even more delocalized (with electron density regarded as spread out over several atoms or the entire molecule) as a description of bonding. He also introduced L. L. Lohr, Jr., and future Nobel chemistry laureate Roald Hoffmann to the general three-dimensional extended Hückel molecular orbitals method.

Lipscomb extended his X-ray crystallographic studies to proteins, highlighting structures of enzymes such as those containing zinc and allosteric enzymes (aspartate trans-carbamylase, fructose-l, 6-bisphosphatase, and chorismate mutase). He emphasized the mechanism at the active site, and, in the case of allosteric enzymes, the transformation of conformational information from regulatory sites to the active sites of an allosteric enzyme with several subunits.

As an associate editor of two journals and the recipient of numerous awards, including many honorary degrees, by the mid-1990s Lipscomb had delivered more than 250 lectures and published more than 600 articles. He expressed his interest in reading and tennis, and he played the clarinet in classical chamber music concerts.

Bibliography

By Lipscomb

"The Valence Structure of the Boron Hydrides,"
Journal of Chemical Physics, 1954 (with W. H. Eberhardt and Bryce Crawford, Jr.).
The Boron Hydrides, 1963.
NMR Studies of Boron Hydrides and Related Compounds, 1969 (with Gareth Eaton).
"Structure and Mechanism in the Enzymatic Activity of Carboxypeptidase A and Relations to Chemical Sequence," *Accounts of Chemical Research*, 1970.
"The Boranes and Their Relatives" *Science*, 1977.

About Lipscomb

Hargittai, István. "Interview: William N. Lipscomb." *The Chemical Intelligencer 2*, no. 3 (July, 1996).
Bonnesen, Peter V. "William N. Lipscomb, Jr." in *Nobel Laureates in Chemistry, 1901-1992*, edited by Laylin K. James. Washington, D.C.: American Chemical Society, 1993.

(George B. Kauffman)

Edwin Mattison McMillan

Disciplines: Chemistry, physics, and technology
Contribution: McMillan discovered the element neptunium and made major contributions to understanding the transuranic elements. He also developed synchrotron particle accelerators that attained higher energies than cyclotrons.

Sept. 18, 1907	Born in Redondo Beach, California
1932	Earns a Ph.D. from Princeton University
1940	Discovers neptunium
1941-1942	Conducts radar research at the Massachusetts Institute of Technology (MIT)
1942-1945	Conducts research on the atomic bomb at Los Alamos, New Mexico
1946-1973	While a professor at UCB, develops a proton synchrotron accelerator
1951	Shares the Nobel Prize in Chemistry with Glenn Seaborg
1958	Appointed director of the Lawrence Berkeley Laboratory
1963	Shares the Atoms for Peace Prize with V. I. Veksler for developing the synchrocyclotron
1990	Awarded the National Medal of Science
Sept. 7, 1991	Dies in El Cerrito, California

Early Life

Edwin Mattison McMillan was born in Redondo Beach, California, but grew up in Pasadena, where his father established a medical practice. He had an interest in physics as far back as he could remember, and started building electronic gadgets and attending public lectures at the California Institute of Technology (Caltech) when he was quite young.

After receiving his bachelor's and master's degrees from Caltech, he moved to Princeton University, where he received his Ph.D. in 1932.

Following his doctorate, McMillan spent two years on a National Research Council fellowship and was then asked by Ernest Orlando Lawrence to join his newly established Radiation Laboratory at the University of California, Berkeley. The laboratory was built around Lawrence's high-energy cyclotrons: particle accelerators that were beginning to be applied to the study of the radioactive isotopes produced by nuclear disintegration.

Transuranic Elements

In 1940, McMillan, like many other scientists in the world, was studying the fission process that had been discovered the year before by Otto Hahn and Fritz Strassman in Germany. He found that after uranium was bombarded with neutrons, an element remained with a half-life of 2.3 days that could not be identified as one of the fission products. After chemically separating this element, he discovered that it had been produced by the attachment of a neutron to the uranium and subsequent radioactive decay to a new element. Since uranium was named for the planet Uranus, McMillan decided to call the new element neptunium after the planet Neptune, the next planet out in the solar system.

The Development of the Atomic Bomb

After working on radar at the beginning of World War II, McMillan was asked to join the highly secret atomic bomb project at Los Alamos. He organized a series of lectures on nuclear physics so that all the scientists at that laboratory would have the latest information. His main task was the development of the guntype bomb that fired a subcritical piece of uranium 235 into another mass of the same element in order to produce a chain reaction and a nuclear explosion. This bomb was exploded over the city of Hiroshima, Japan, on August 6, 1945.

High-Energy Accelerator Research

The cyclotron, which had been invented in 1932 by Lawrence, was limited in the energy that it could impart to a proton by the increase in mass caused by relativity. As the mass increases, the proton loses its synchronization with the electrical impulses provided by the cyclotron.

McMillan found a way to keep the accelerating impulses in step with the bunches of particles being accelerated. This made it possible to accelerate the protons to much higher energies, and it

The Discovery of Element 93

McMillan discovered neptunium, the first transuranic element and the first artificially created one.

When a uranium nucleus is struck by a neutron, either it will split into two fragments, with an accompanying release of energy, or the neutron will attach to the nucleus to form a radioactive isotope. The fission fragments fly apart in opposite directions, sharing the fission energy of 200 million electronvolts, while any new isotope of uranium will remain near its original position.

McMillan used a thin target of uranium so that most of the fission fragments would leave the target and any activity remaining would be attributable to new isotopes of uranium. Two new radioactive species were found in the target after neutron bombardment—one decaying quickly, with a half-life of about 23 minutes, and the other decaying more slowly, with a half-life slightly longer than two days.

The shorter-lived activity had been identified earlier as uranium 239, and McMillan guessed that the longer-lived activity might be a new element formed by beta decay of the excited nucleus. Since each element has unique chemical properties, any new element should be separable by chemical processes.

McMillan, using chemical techniques, successfully separated the longer-lived activity from the shorter one and thus proved that he had found element 93, which he called neptunium.

Bibliography

Heilbron, J. L. and Robert W. Seidel. *Lawrence and His Laboratory*. Berkeley, Calif.: University of California Press, 1989.

McMillan, Edwin Mattison and P. H. Abelson. "Radioactive Element 93." *Physical Review* 97 (1940).

is this process that is used in most high-energy accelerators, or synchrocyclotrons, today.

McMillan was given many awards in his career. Most notably, he received the Nobel Prize in Chemistry in 1951, the Atoms for Peace Prize in 1963, and the National Medal of Science in 1990.

McMillan died on September 7, 1991.

Bibliography

By McMillan

"Radioactive Element 93," *Physical Review*, 1940 (with P. H. Abelson).

"The Synchrotron: A Proposed High-Energy Particle Accelerator," *Physical Review*, 1945.

Lecture Series in Nuclear Physics, 1947.

"The Transuranium Elements: Early History" *Les Prix Nobel en 1951*, 1952.

Experimental Nuclear Physics, vol. 3, 1959 (with E. Segrè, G. C. Hanna, M. Deutsch, and O. Kofoed-Hansen).

"The History of the Cyclotron," *Physics Today*, 1959.

About McMillan

Rothe, Anna. ed. *Current Biography Yearbook*. New York: H. W. Wilson, 1952.

Magill, Frank N. "Edwin Mattison McMillan." in *The Nobel Prize Winners: Chemistry*, Pasadena, Calif.: Salem Press, 1990.

(*Raymond D. Cooper*)

Dmitry Ivanovich Mendeleev

Discipline: Chemistry

Contribution: Mendeleev recognized the regular variation in the chemical and physical properties of the elements. This periodic law aided in the discovery of new elements and in the prediction of their properties.

Feb. 8, 1834	Born in Tobolsk, Siberia
1849	Travels to the University of Moscow but is denied entry
1850	Begins training as a teacher at the Institute of Pedagogy, St. Petersburg
1855	Receives a teaching diploma
1859	Travels on a government grant throughout Europe
1863	Appointed a professor of chemistry at the Technological Institute of St. Petersburg
1866	Appointed a professor of chemistry at the University of St. Petersburg
1868-1871	Publishes the chemistry textbook *Osnovy khimii* (1890; *The Principles of Chemistry*)
1871	Predicts that the vacant spaces in the periodic table will be filled by yet-to-be-discovered elements
1876	Visits the United States
1890	Resigns his university position in protest
1893	Becomes the director of the Bureau of Weights and Measures
Feb. 2, 1907	Dies in St. Petersburg, Russia

Early Life

Dmitry Ivanovich Mendeleev (pronounced "mehn-deh-LAY-ehf") was born in Siberia in 1834. Shortly after his birth, his father went blind and had to resign as director of the local high school. Consequently, his mother was forced to seek work in a glass factory to support the family of fourteen children.

In 1849, his father died and in the same year, the glass factory was destroyed by fire. Mendeleev and his mother hitchhiked to Moscow, so that fifteen-year-old Dmitry could finish his education at the university there. Being Siberian, however, he was not permitted entrance, and again mother and son traveled across country to St. Petersburg.

The Fascination Begins

At the St. Petersburg Institute of Pedagogy, while training to be a teacher, Mendeleev was instructed by the notable chemist Alexander Woskressensky. Woskressensky's work on inorganic chemistry fascinated Mendeleev, who was struck by the similarities in the chemical and physical properties of various groups of elements. Mendeleev's interest in classification was also aroused by classes in zoology, genetics, and mineralogy.

A Career in Academia

After spending a few years as a science teacher in Odessa, Mendeleev returned to the University of St. Petersburg to obtain a higher degree in chemistry. In 1859, a government grant enabled him to travel through Europe and participate in chemical conferences. As a result, his thoughts once more turned to chemical classification. He recognized the need for classifying the chemical and physical properties of the elements.

After receiving his doctorate, Mendeleev was appointed a professor of chemistry at the Technological Institute of St. Petersburg in 1863. Three years later, he took a similar position at the University of St. Petersburg.

Mendeleev was required to teach classes in inorganic chemistry, and he soon realized that no suitable textbook existed for this field of study. Therefore, he began to write his own, a comprehensive text that eventually was published as *Osnovy khimii* between 1868 and 1871. The book was translated into English as *The Principles of Chemistry* in 1890, as well as into French and German, and it brought Mendeleev recognition throughout Europe.

As a result of his liberal views and sympathies with student grievances, Mendeleev often found himself battling university administrators and government bureaucracy. Perhaps because of this he was never elected to the Imperial Academy of Sciences. In 1890 he resigned his university position in protest after another such battle. Three years later, he became the director of the Bureau of Weights and Measures.

The Periodic Law

Mendeleev's attempt to organize his chemistry textbook in a logical manner led him to the discovery of the periodic law. Unlike the recent successes at classifying carbon compounds, no systematic classification of the other elements and their compounds was then available.

Using a series of cards, Mendeleev wrote down the properties and atomic weights of the elements (about seventy were known at the time). By arranging and rearranging the cards, he recognized a repeating or periodic relationship between the properties of the elements and their atomic weights: When arranged in order of increasing atomic weights, the properties of the elements were repeated every so often.

While other chemists had noticed the periodicity of the elements with little interest, it was Mendeleev who recognized the fundamental significance of this arrangement. Elements with similar properties fell into vertical columns (groups) and horizontal rows (periods), which formed a chart that is known today as the periodic table. Elements within the groups have similar valences (degrees of combining power, according to atomic weights).

Mendeleev left spaces in his periodic table, and, in 1871, he predicted that they would be filled by elements unknown at that time. He also predicted the properties of these undiscovered elements. Between 1875 and 1886, the elements gallium, scandium, and germanium were discovered, and each fitted into its position as predicted by Mendeleev. As a result, the concept of the periodic law gained universal acceptance.

Mendeleev died in St. Petersburg in 1907 just before his seventy-third birthday, of influenza.

Mendeleev's legacy lives on: the crater Mendeleev on the moon, as well as element number 101, the radioactive mendelevium, are named after him.

The Periodic Table of the Elements

IA	IIA	IIIB	IVB	VB	VIB	VIIB	VIII	VIII	VIII	IB	IIB	IIIA	IVA	VA	VIA	VIIA	0
1 H																	2 He
3 Li	4 Be											5 B	6 C	7 N	8 O	9 F	10 Ne
11 Na	12 Mg				Transition elements →							13 Al	14 Si	15 P	16 S	17 Cl	18 Ar
19 K	20 Ca	21 Sc	22 Ti	23 V	24 Cr	25 Mn	26 Fe	27 Co	28 Ni	29 Cu	30 Zn	31 Ga	32 Ge	33 As	34 Se	35 Br	36 Kr
37 Rb	38 Sr	39 Y	40 Zr	41 Nb	42 Mo	43 Tc*	44 Ru	45 Rh	46 Pd	47 Ag	48 Cd	49 In	50 Sn	51 Sb	52 Te	53 I	54 Xe
55 Cs	56 Ba	57* La	72 Hf	73 Ta	74 W	75 Re	76 Os	77 Ir	78 Pt	79 Au	80 Hg	81 Tl	82 Pb	83 Bi	84 Po	85 At	86 Rn
87 Fr	88 Ra	89† Ac	104 Unq	105 Unp	106 Unh	107 Uns	108 Uno	109 Une									

*Lanthanoids	57 La	58 Ce	59 Pr	60 Nd	61 Pm	62 Sm	63 Eu	64 Gd	65 Tb	66 Dy	67 Ho	68 Er	69 Tm	70 Yb	71 Lu
†Actinoids	89 Ac	90 Th	91 Pa	92 U	93 Np	94 Pu	95 Am	96 Cm	97 Bk	98 Cf	99 Es	100 Fm	101 Md	102 No	103 Lr

Bibliography

By Mendeleev

"Die periodische Gesetzmässigkeit der chemisch-en Elemente," *Justus Liebigs Annalen der Chemie*, Supplementband VIII, 1871.

"Remarques a propos de la découverte du gallium," *Comptes Rendus*, 1875.

"The Periodic Law of the Chemical Elements," *Journal of the Chemical Society*, 1889.

Osnovy khimii, 1868–1871 (*The Principles of Chemistry*, 1890).

An Attempt Towards a Chemical Conception of the Ether, 1904.

About Mendeleev

Farber, E. ed. *Great Chemists*. New York: Inter-science, 1961.

"Mendeleev's Periodic System of Chemical Elements." Bernadette Bensaude-Vincent. *British Journal for the History of Science* 19 (1986).

Brown, Don C. "The Process of Discovery: Mendeleev and the Periodic Law." *Annals of Science* 31 (1974).

(*Nicholas C. Thomas*)

The Periodic Law

Mendeleev noticed that, when the chemical elements were arranged in order of increasing atomic weights, their properties were repeated in a predictable manner, forming a table of vertical columns (groups) and horizontal rows (periods).

Mendeleev's early versions of the periodic table were not without their problems, and the table was modified over the years as new research into the fundamental nature of matter was uncovered. When Mendeleev first formulated his periodic table, the existence of protons, electrons, and neutrons was not known. Consequently, the periodicity of the elements was based on atomic weight, which was a measurable and variable quantity for each element.

One major problem with Mendeleev's periodic table was that some elements fell into groups in which they obviously did not belong. For example, if arranged in order of increasing atomic weight, iodine did not fall into the same group as bromine and chlorine, elements with which it shared many common properties. Periodicity was eventually found to depend on atomic number, rather than atomic weight as Mendeleev had thought, and the revised periodic law states that the properties of the elements are a periodic function of their atomic numbers. Switching iodine and tellurium places both elements in their correct groups.

Early in the twentieth century, it was shown that the atomic weight of an element is roughly equal to the sum of protons and neutrons in one of its atoms. The atomic number was shown to be equal to the number of protons. For the lighter elements (the first two dozen or so), the ratio of protons to neutrons is about 1:1. For these elements, either the atomic weight or atomic number can be used to demonstrate the periodicity of the elements. Mendeleev's periodic table worked quite well for these lighter elements but not as well for the heavier elements, which have more neutrons in proportion to their protons.

Elements in the same group have the same number of electrons in their outer (valence) shells. The number of valence electrons is also related to the group number. Lithium, sodium, and potassium, which all have one valence electron, are found in group 1 and have similar properties. For this reason, they generally show similar chemical and physical properties to one another but quite different properties to many other groups of elements.

Mendeleev knew nothing about electrons when he first predicted that new elements would be discovered one day to fill the spaces in his periodic table. He recognized, however, that each new element would be found to have similar properties to the other elements in the same group.

Bibliography

Sanderson, R. T. *Chemical Periodicity*. New York: Reinhold, 1960.

van Sprosen, J. *The Periodic System of the Chemical Elements*. Amsterdam: Elsevier, 1969.

Puddephatt, R. J. and P. K. Monaghan. *The Periodic Table of the Elements*. Oxford, England: Oxford University Press, 1986.

Robert S. Mulliken

Disciplines: Chemistry and physics

Contribution: One of the first scientists to apply quantum physics to the study of chemical bonds in molecules, Mulliken won the Nobel Prize in Chemistry for his development of the molecular orbital method.

June 7, 1896	Born in Newburyport, Massachusetts
1921	Earns a Ph.D. in chemistry from the University of Chicago
1921	National Research Fellow at the University of Chicago
1923	National Research Fellow at Harvard University
1926	Joins the faculty of the physics department at New York University
1928	Professor of physics at the University of Chicago
1930	Visits Europe on a Guggenheim Fellowship
1932-1935	Publishes a series of papers on the electronic structures of polyatomic molecules and valence
1936	Elected to the National Academy of Sciences
1942-1945	Directs the information division of the Manhattan Project at the University of Chicago
1952-1954	Fulbright Scholar at Oxford University.
1955	Named science attaché to the U.S. embassy in London, England
1966	Wins the Nobel Prize in Chemistry
Oct. 31, 1986	Dies in Arlington, Virginia

Early Life

Robert Sanderson Mulliken, the son of a chemist, was reared in the colonial seaport town of Newburyport, Massachusetts. He expressed an early interest in science and chemistry in particular. With a scholarship from the Wheelwright Fund, he studied chemistry at the Massachusetts Institute of Technology (MIT), graduating in 1917.

Mulliken took a wartime job at the American University in Washington, D.C., studying poison gases under the supervision of James B. Conant, but a laboratory accident cut short this work. Following the war, he was employed briefly at the New Jersey Zinc Company.

Mulliken began graduate studies in chemistry at the University of Chicago in 1919. He worked with William Harkins on problems of isotope separation and, after receiving his Ph.D. in 1921, continued this investigation with a National Research Council Fellowship. In order to study isotope effects in the spectra of molecules, Mulliken went to Harvard University in 1923. There, he became proficient in the experimental techniques of spectroscopy and in the new theoretical advances in quantum physics.

In 1925, he made his first trip to Europe, where he met many of the leading physicists and chemists of the day. He made another trip to Europe in the summer of 1927 and returned twice as a Guggenheim Fellow in the early 1930s. This exposure to the newest advances in quantum science helped Mulliken to develop his own important ideas about the nature of molecular bonding.

Research and Professional Activities

From 1926 to 1928, Mulliken was an assistant professor of physics at New York University. In 1928, he returned to the University of Chicago as a member of the physics department. Mulliken's movement from chemistry to physics and back again reflects the special nature of his research interests, which used physical techniques to investigate chemical problems.

Mulliken's study of the behavior of electrons in molecules produced a particularly important series of papers published from 1932 to 1935. They set out Mulliken's major contribution to the development of the molecular orbital theory. This theory, along with a rival model known as the Valence Bond Theory, attempted to use quantum mechanics to explain molecular structure.

During World War II, Mulliken suspended his scientific research to assume the post of director of the information division for the Manhattan Project, a group of scientists trying to develop an atomic bomb. In this role, Mulliken was involved in some of the earliest evaluations by scientists of the prospects for the future uses of nuclear weapons and nuclear power.

Mulliken continued to work in the field of molecular science into the 1980s, publishing more than 200 papers during his career.

Molecular Orbitals

The molecular orbital model helps to explain the behavior of electrons in molecules.

Mulliken was one of several scientists to advance the molecular orbital model, which tries to explain the behavior of electrons and atoms in molecules using the methods of quantum physics. A rival theory, advanced about the same time by Linus Pauling and others, was called the valence bond theory.

The valence bond theory treated molecules as made of interacting but individual atoms, each maintaining its own electrons. The molecular orbital theory treats the electrons of a molecule as spread out in wave functions, or orbitals, over all the atoms in the chemical bonds of a molecule.

In molecular orbital theory, each state of the molecule is characterized by an electron configuration giving the number and kind of molecular orbitals and how many electrons are in each one. Molecular orbitals each have a particular mathematical form, which can be classified according to the symmetries of a molecule.

The molecular orbital theory became increasingly valuable to scientists as computers made the solution of its complex mathematical equations possible.

Bibliography

The Modern Structural Theory of Organic Chemistry. Lloyd N. Ferguson. Englewood Cliffs, N.J.: Prentice Hall, 1963.

"Molecular Orbitals." Robert S. Mulliken. *Encyclopedic Dictionary of Physics* 4 (1962).

"Spectroscopy, Molecular Orbitals, and Chemical Bonding." Robert S. Mulliken. *Science* (1967).

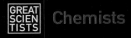

He received most of the major awards in his field, including the Nobel Prize in Chemistry in 1966.

Personal Activities

Mulliken married Mary Helen Von Noé in 1929. They had two daughters, Lucia Maria and Valerie Noé. He maintained a strong interest in the role of science in society, demonstrated by his active participation in the American Association of Scientific Workers during the 1930s and his role as the science attaché to the U.S. embassy in London in 1955.

Mulliken died in 1986 in Virginia at the age of ninety.

Bibliography

By Mulliken

"Electronic Structures of Polyatomic Molecules and Valence," *Physical Review*, 1932-1933 (parts 1-4).

"Electronic Structures of Polyatomic Molecules and Valence," *Journal of Chemical Physics*, 1933-1935 (parts 5-14).

Ramsay, D. A. and J. Hinzel. eds. Selected Papers of R. S. Mulliken, 1975.

Ransil, Bernard J., ed. *Life of a Scientist: An Autobiographical Account of the Development of Molecular Orbital Theory*, 1989).

About Mulliken

James, Laylin K., ed. *Nobel Laureates in Chemistry, 1901-1992.* Washington, D.C.: American Chemical Society 1993.

Magill, Frank N., ed "Robert S. Mulliken." in *The Nobel Prize Winners: Chemistry*, Pasadena, Calif.: Salem Press, 1990.

(Loren Butler Feffer)

Walther Hermann Nernst

Disciplines: Astronomy, chemistry, physics, and technology

Contribution: Nernst made fundamental contributions to electrochemistry, thermodynamics, and photochemistry, which form the foundation of modern physical chemistry.

June 25, 1864	Born in Briesen, West Prussia
1887	Works as assistant to Wilhelm Ostwald at Leipzig University
1887	Establishes the field of physical chemistry with Ostwald, Jacobus van't Hoff, and Svante Arrhenius
1889	Explains the theory of galvanic cells
1890	Joins the physics department of the University of Göttingen
1894	Becomes the first professor of physical chemistry
1905	Joins the Physicochemical Laboratory, University of Berlin
1906	Presents his heat theorem
1912	Erroneously uses the second law of thermodynamics to "prove" the unattainability of absolute zero
1918	Announces his photochemical atom chain reaction theory
1920	Wins the Nobel Prize in Chemistry
1924	Directs the Institute for Experimental Physics at Berlin
1932	Elected to the Royal Society of London
Nov. 18, 1941	Dies in Bad Muskau, Prussia

Early Life

Walther Hermann Nernst, the son of a Gustav Nernst and Ottilie Nerger Nernst, was born in Briesen, West Prussia, in 1864. His father was a district judge. During his rigorous secondary education, he had ambitions of being a poet, but he also carried out scientific experiments in his basement.

Nernst was educated at universities in Zurich, Graz, and Würzburg, where he obtained his doctorate. He conducted work at Graz under the direction of A. von Ettinghausen in the study of the electrification of heated metals placed in a magnetic field.

Later, he discovered an electric lamp made of zirconium oxide. His lamp had widespread use, replacing the carbon fiber filament, but it was soon replaced by the use of tungsten filaments. Nernst "glowers" are still used today, however, in infrared spectrophotometers.

Contributions to Electrochemistry

Nernst became an assistant to Wilhelm Ostwald at Leipzig University in 1887. While there, he also worked with Jacobus van't Hoff and Svante Arrhenius to establish the independent field of modern physical chemistry.

In 1889, Nernst presented his theory of galvanic cells based on the new dissociation theory of ions proposed by Arrhenius. The voltage of electrochemical cells is calculated using the Nernst equation. In this same year, Nernst derived equations for the solubility products of ionic materials. These equations predict the conditions under which materials will precipitate from solutions.

The Third Law of Thermodynamics

In 1907, Nernst set forth the third law of thermodynamics, which shows that the maximum amount of work in a process can be calculated by the heat given off by the process at temperatures near absolute zero. Nernst erroneously used the second law of thermodynamics to "prove" the unattainability of absolute zero in 1912. Albert Einstein later pointed out the fallacy of Nernst's argument.

Photochemical Atom Chain Reaction

In 1918, Nernst explained his photochemical atom chain reaction theory. He theorized that the energy of a photon produces free radicals that can, in turn, react with other molecules to produce other free radicals. These reactions can continue to occur even after the source of light is removed. This theory explained previous observations that had been unexplained.

Nernst won the 1920 Nobel Prize in Chemistry for his heat theorem. He retired from his position as director of the Institute for Experimental Physics at the University of Berlin in 1933. He died in 1941, at the age of seventy-seven.

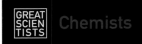
Heat Theorem

Nernst's heat theorem, known as the Third Law of Thermodynamics, shows that the maximum amount of work obtained from a process can be calculated from the heat given off at temperatures near absolute zero.

In 1900, Theodore William Richards studied the Gibbs free energy of reactions as a function of temperature. Nernst remarked that this data showed that the slope of the change in the Gibbs free energy as a function of temperature of a chemical reaction, approaches zero as the temperature approaches absolute zero.

In 1907, Nernst postulated that, at constant pressure, the change in the Gibbs free energy of a reaction is zero at absolute zero. This means that the entropy of a reaction is zero at absolute zero. While Nernst believed this to be valid for any process, it was later shown to be valid only for reactions involving pure substances in internal equilibrium. For example, this theorem does not apply to supercooled liquids.

Older work had ignored the effect of temperature when calculating equilibrium conditions. Nernst's work added a higher level of refinement to earlier work and allowed precise calculations of equilibrium conditions.

Bibliography

Hill, Eric Brian. *Basic Chemical Thermodynamics.* 3d ed. Oxford, England: Clarendon Press, 1982.

Farber, Eduard. *The Evolution of Chemistry: A History of Its Ideas, Methods, and Materials.* 2d ed. New York: Ronald Press, 1969.

Callen, Herbert. *Thermodynamics: An Introduction to the Physical Theories of Equilibrium Thermostatics and Irreversible Thermodynamics.* New York: John Wiley & Sons, 1960.

Bibliography

By Nernst

Theoretische Chemie vom Standpunkte der Avogadroschen Regel und der Thermodynamik, 1893 (*Theoretical Chemistry from the Standpoint of Avogadro's Rule and Thermodynamics,* 1895).

Experimental and Theoretical Applications of Thermodynamics to Chemistry, 1907.

Die theoretischen und experimentellen Grundlagen des neuen Wärmasatzes, 1918 (*The New Heat Theorem: Its Foundations in Theory and Experiment,* 1918).

About Nernst

Farber, Eduard. *Great Chemists.* New York: Interscience, 1961.

Partington, James Riddick. "Nernst Memorial Lecture." *Journal of the Chemical Society* 3 (1953).

Magill, Frank N., ed. "Walther Hermann Nernst." in *The Nobel Prize Winners: Chemistry,* Pasadena, Calif.: Salem Press, 1990.

Mendelssohn, Kurt. *The World of Walther Nernst: The Rise and Fall of German Science.* Pittsburgh, P. A.: University of Pittsburgh Press, 1973.

(Christopher J. Biermann)

George A. Olah

Discipline: Chemistry

Contribution: Olah was an organic chemist who developed synthetic methods. He shaped the modern concept of carbocations and pioneered super-acid chemistry.

May 22, 1927	Born in Budapest, Hungary
1949	Earns a Ph.D. from the Technical University of Budapest
1949-1954	Professor at the Technical University of Budapest
1954-1956	Associate scientific director of the Central Chemical Research Institute of the Hungarian Academy of Sciences
1957-1965	Works as a research scientist with the Dow Chemical Company
1964	Wins the American Chemical Society Award in Petroleum Chemistry
1965-1977	Chair and Mabery Professor at Case Western Reserve University
1976	Elected to the U.S. National Academy of Sciences
1977	Loker Professor at the University of Southern California
1977	Recieves Centenary Lectureship from the British Chemical Society
1991-present	Director of Loker Hydrocarbon Research Institute
1992	Receives the Richard C. Tolman Award and the Mendeléev Medal
1993	Wins the Pioneer of Chemistry Award from the American Institute of Chemists
1994	Awarded the Nobel Prize in Chemistry
2011	Receives Szechenyi Grand Prize of Hungary

Early Life

George Andrew Olah was born in 1927 to Julius and Magda (Krasznai) Olah in Budapest, Hungary. His passion for science began during under-graduate and graduate work at the Technical University of Budapest. He received a doctorate in organic chemistry under Geza Zemplén in 1949.

In 1954, he joined the Central Chemical Research Institute of the Hungarian Academy of Sciences as associate scientific director and head of the organic chemistry department. Following the abortive Hungarian uprising against Soviet rule in October, 1956, Olah, his wife Judith Lengyel, their young son, and much of their research group fled Hungary for London, England, subsequently moving to Canada by the spring of 1957.

Immigrating to America

Olah was employed by Dow Chemical Company first at its subsidiary Dow Chemical Canada Ltd., Ontario, where a second son was born.

Later he worked at Dow's Eastern Research Laboratory in Framingham, Massachusetts.

In 1965, Olah became chair of the chemistry department of Western Reserve University in Cleveland, Ohio, and continued as chair after its merger with Case Institute until 1969, when he was appointed Charles F. Mabery Distinguished Research Professor.

In 1977, he settled in Los Angeles as the Donald P. and Katherine B. Loker Distinguished Professor of Organic Chemistry and director of the Loker Hydrocarbon Research Institute at the University of Southern California (USC).

Olah obtained naturalized U.S. citizenship in 1970.

Research

Some organic chemists are mainly concerned with chemical synthesis. Others are physical organic chemists who study how chemical reactions work. Olah applied physical organic concepts to develop new synthetic methods and reagents. This research includes hydrocarbon chemistry superacids, ionic intermediates and complexes, and organic fluorine and phosphorous compounds.

His early work on aromatic alkylations and other electrophilic reactions contributed to later discoveries of previously unknown substitution reactions under superacid conditions for the controlled functionalization of alkanes and related chemical processes such as high-octane gasoline

Superacids Stabilize Carbocations

Superacids provide a medium in which unstable carbocations are prepared and preserved long enough for their structure and other properties to be studied.

Many chemical reactions of organic compounds proceed through transient intermediates called carbocations, which are the positive ions of carbon compounds. Carbocations are electrophilic (electron-deficient) species that ordinarily are too fleeting for direct observation. Kinetic, stereochemical, and product studies since the 1920s, however, support their presence.

Highly polar solvents that are chemically inert toward electrophiles ("electron-loving" substances) were needed for carbocations to become stable, long-lived species. Olah first used the Lewis acid antimony pentafluoride (SbF_5) for this purpose in 1962 and later employed fluoroantimonic acid ($HF-SbF_5$) magic acid (FSO_3H-SbF_5), and other mixtures to confirm the existence of alkyl carbocations with nuclear magnetic resonance (NMR) and other spectroscopic methods. Such media are referred to as superacids because they are more acidic than 100 percent sulfuric acid. Superacid solutions promote a variety of acidcatalyzed reactions that have potential importance for industrial chemistry. Olah also developed solid superacids for use as heterogeneous catalysts.

Bibliography

Vogel, Pierre. *Carbocation Chemistry*. Amsterdam, the Netherlands: Elsevier, 1985.

Thomas, Barry. "George Olah and the Chemistry of Carbocations." *Chemistry Review* 5 (November, 1995).

Olah, George A. "My Search for Carbocations and Their Role in Chemistry." *Angewandte Chemie International Edition in English* 34 (1995).

Olah, George A. and Charles U. Pittman. "Spectroscopic Observation of Alkylcarbonium Ions in Strong Acid Solutions." *Advances in Physical Organic Chemistry* 4 (1966).

O'Donnell, Thomas A. *Superacids and Acidic Melts as Inorganic Chemical Reaction Media*. New York: VCH, 1993.

production, the condensation of methane to yield liquid hydrocarbons, and the depolymerization of heavy oils and coal.

By the late 1990s Olah had published more than 1,000 scientific papers and monograph chapters, had written or co-authored at least fourteen books, and held more than 100 patents. This was in addition to his role as general editor for the Wiley-Interscience series "Reactive Intermediates in Organic Chemistry" and "Monographs in Organic Chemistry." He also held positions on the editorial boards of the *Journal of Organic Chemistry*, *Index Chemicus*, and *Current Abstracts*.

Olah was awarded the Nobel Prize in Chemistry in 1994. He continues his research at the University of Southern California, studying synthetic and mechanistic organic chemistry, focusing on hydrocarbon chemistry.

Bibliography

By Olah
Carbocations and Electrophilic Reactions, 1973.
Halonium Ions, 1975.
Superacids, 1985 (with G. K. Surya Prakash and Jean Sommer).
Hydrocarbon Chemistry, 2nd Edition, 2003 (with Árpád Molnár).
"After Oil and Gas: Methanol Economy," *Catalysis Letters*, 2004.

About Olah
Garmon, Linda. "The Disputed Charge Account." *Science News* 124 (August 13, 1983).
"George A. Olah," Department of Chemistry, http://chem.usc.edu/faculty/Olah.html
Magill, Frank N., ed. "George A. Olah." in *The Nobel Prize Winners: Chemistry*, Pasadena, Calif.: Salem Press, 1990.
Baum, Rudy "George Olah Reflects on Chemical Research." *Chemical and Engineering News* 73 (February 27, 1995).

(Martin V. Stewart)

Linus Pauling

Disciplines: Biology, chemistry, immunology, medicine, and physics

Contribution: Pauling, one of the greatest chemists of the twentieth century, made the structure of molecules a principal theme of his work in structural chemistry, molecular biology, and molecular medicine. His theory of the chemical bond dominated science for several decades.

Feb. 28, 1901	Born in Portland, Oregon
1917-1922	Majors in chemical engineering at Oregon Agricultural College
1922-1926	Conducts graduate and post-doctoral work at the California Institute of Technology (Caltech)
1926-1927	Named a Guggenheim Fellow
1937	Appointed director of the Gates Laboratory and chair of the Division of Chemistry and Chemical Engineering
1947	Publishes *General Chemistry*
1949	Announces that sickle-cell anemia is a molecular disease
1951	Publishes a series of papers on protein structure
1954	Wins the Nobel Prize in Chemistry
1958	With Ava Helen Pauling, presents a petition to the United Nations to halt nuclear bomb tests
1963	Receives the Nobel Peace Prize for his campaign against nuclear testing
Aug. 19, 1994	Dies in Big Sur, California

Early Life

Linus Carl Pauling was born in Oregon in 1901. His father, a pharmacist, guided the reading of his inquisitive young son, but his death in 1909 left the family economically and emotionally devastated. Linus studied mathematics and chemistry at Washington High School in Portland, but what convinced him to become a chemist was a dramatic experiment performed by a classmate in his bedroom laboratory.

Pauling's educational career at Oregon Agricultural College was interrupted by financial difficulties, but through persistence and hard work, he managed to graduate with highest honors in 1922. During his graduate studies at the California Institute of Technology (Caltech), he married Ava Helen Miller; their marriage resulted in three sons and a daughter. Pauling received his Ph.D. in 1925.

Following a period of postdoctoral studies, he accepted a Guggenheim Fellowship in 1926 to study the application of the new quantum mechanics to chemical problems. He spent most of his time at Arnold Sommerfeld's Institute for Theoretical Physics in Munich, Germany. In 1927 he returned to California as a teacher and researcher at Caltech. He was prodigiously successful, becoming a full professor in 1931 and head of the Division of Chemistry and Chemical Engineering in 1937.

Structural Chemistry

Structure was the main theme of Pauling's scientific work. In his early research, he used the X-ray-diffraction technique to determine the structures of such crystals as molybdenite and various silicates and sulfides. In 1930, he began using the electron-diffraction technique for exploring the structures of such molecules as benzene and cyclohexane.

As X-ray and electron diffraction gave Pauling experimental tools for discovering the structures of molecules, so quantum mechanics provided him with a theoretical tool. In 1931, he used quantum mechanics to account for the equivalency of the four bonds around the carbon atom by introducing the idea of hybrid orbitals. In 1939, he integrated many of his structural discoveries into *The Nature of the Chemical Bond*, one of the most influential scientific books of the twentieth century.

In the mid-1930s, Pauling's interest began to shift to molecules contained in living things. His studies of the hemoglobin molecule led to his general studies of protein structure. While at Oxford University, he used a paper on which he had drawn a chain of linked amino acids to discover a cylindrical coil-like configuration, later called the alpha helix. The most significant element of Pauling's structure was its nonintegral number of amino acids per turn of the helix.

Following an initial announcement of his discovery in 1950, Pauling and his collaborators published a series of eight articles on the alpha helix, the pleated sheet, and the structure of hair, muscle, collagen, hemoglobin, and other proteins.

Pauling's Discoveries on the Nature of the Chemical Bond

Pauling's work on the chemical bond helped establish the modern science of molecular structure. By using the tools of X-ray and electron diffraction, he was able to determine the detailed architecture of minerals and metals, and he used the ideas of quantum mechanics to understand these structures through a new theory of the chemical bond.

When Pauling first studied chemistry in high school, valence (the combining power of atoms) was crudely represented by a model of hooks and eyelets. For example, the valence 2 oxygen atom had two eyelets, and the valence 1 hydrogen atom had a single hook. When the two hydrogens were hooked to the oxygen, the formula of water, H_2O, was made reasonable in terms of the two hydrogen-to-oxygen bonds.

In college, Pauling came across the scientific papers of Gilbert Newton Lewis, who became his inspiration and later his friend. Lewis described the chemical bond as a shared pair of electrons. For example, in the hydrogen molecule, made up of two hydrogen atoms, each with a proton and an electron, Lewis depicted the configuration as H:H, where the H's represent the positively charged protons and the dots represent the two negative electrons that are shared between them. These electrons are the "glue" holding together the molecule.

Pauling used X-rays to probe inside crystals to discover precisely where atoms are located in relation to neighboring atoms in the substance. For example, in the mineral molybdenite, he found that each molybdenum atom is surrounded by six sulfur atoms arranged in a trigonal prism. He naturally wondered why atoms arranged themselves in these characteristic structures. He discovered the answer in quantum mechanics, which explained how electrons behaved. According to this new theory, electrons in atoms can only exist in certain specific energy states. Furthermore, electrons in and between atoms have to be understood not as particles but as waves.

Instead of orbits of electron particles around nuclei, quantum mechanics uses "orbitals" to describe specific regions where electrons are most likely to be found.

Before Pauling's work, physicists could not explain how a carbon atom could form four equivalent bonds, since quantum mechanics describes carbon as having two kinds of outer electron orbitals: an *s* orbital, which is spherically shaped, and *p* orbitals, which have a two-lobed shape able to be oriented up and down, side to side, and back to front (that is, in the *x*, *y*, and *z* directions). Pauling showed how the interchange (or resonance) energy of two electrons could lead to the mixing or hybridizing of the two pure s and p orbitals into new ones. In the case of certain compounds of carbon, the carbon atom can form four equivalent tetrahedral bond orbitals, each a hybrid of one s and three *p* orbitals. This idea of hybridization allowed Pauling to explain not only the structural and chemical properties of carbon compounds but also the magnetic properties of certain complex inorganic substances.

A central idea in Pauling's theoretical treatment of the chemical bond was resonance, in which the true state of a chemical system is neither of the component quantum states but some intermediate one, caused by an interaction that lowers the energy. This idea was a major factor in Pauling's development of the Valence Bond Theory, in which he proposed that a molecule could be described by an intermediate structure that was a resonance combination or hybrid of other structures. His paper *The Nature of the Chemical Bond* (1939) was responsible for the dominance of Valence Bond theory in chemistry in the 1940s and 1950s.

Bibliography

Pauling, Linus. *The Chemical Bond: A Brief Introduction to Modern Structural Chemistry*. Ithaca, N.Y.: Cornell University Press, 1967.

Salem, L. *The Marvels of the Molecule*. New York: VCH, 1987.

Molecular Medicine

In the late 1930s, Pauling's work centered increasingly on molecules of medical interest. In 1940, he published his first paper on the structure of antibodies, and, during World War II, he worked on various immunological problems. By the end of the war, he had become involved with sickle-cell anemia research, which, in 1949 he showed to be a molecular disease caused by an abnormal hemoglobin molecule.

Capitalizing on his reputation as a great scientist—he won the Nobel Prize in Chemistry in 1954—Pauling, in the 1950s, began to devote his attention to humanitarian issues connected with science. For example, he became involved in the debate over radioactive fallout from nuclear bomb tests. In 1958, he and his wife presented a petition against nuclear testing signed by more than 11,000 scientists from around the world to Dag Hammarskjöld at the United Nations. In that same year, he wrote a book, *No More War!*, in which he tried to make people aware of the horrifying dangers of nuclear weapons. He received the 1962 Nobel Peace Prize in 1963, when the Partial Nuclear Test Ban Treaty went into effect.

Pauling's later career centered on a particular molecule: ascorbic acid (vitamin C). From published evidence, he concluded that vitamin C, provided it is taken in large enough quantities has a beneficial effect in helping the body fight off colds and other diseases. The outcome of this work was a pair of books, *Vitamin C and the Common Cold* (1970) and *Cancer and Vitamin C* (1979).

These books and the many papers and speeches that Pauling gave initiated a controversy about the relative benefits and dangers of treating illnesses with large doses of vitamin C (megavitamin therapy). Large amounts of vitamin C did not prevent his wife from getting cancer, although Pauling claimed that these megadoses helped prolong her life for five years; she died on December 7, 1981.

Philosophy of Science

Pauling's basic approach to science was interdisciplinary, and he made many of his greatest discoveries in fields where scientific disciplines overlap: between chemistry and physics, chemistry and biology, chemistry and medicine.

As an atheist and reductionist, he deeply believed that the universe comprises solely matter and energy and that the structures of moleculars can explain all physical, biological, and even psychological phenomena. He interpreted the death of his wife in this way, as he did the prostate cancer that progressed to his colon and finally to his liver, causing his death on August 19, 1994.

Bibliography

By Pauling

Introduction to Quantum Mechanics, with Applications to Chemistry, 1935 (with E. Bright Wilson, Jr.).

The Architecture of Molecules, 1964 (with Roger Hayward).

The Chemical Bond, 1967.

Cancer and Vitamin C, 1979 (with Ewan Cameron).

About Pauling

Hager, Thomas. *Force of Nature: The Life of Linus Pauling*. New York: Simon & Schuster, 1995.

Goertzel, Ted and Ben Goertzel. *Linus Pauling: A Life in Science and Politics*. New York: Basic Books, 1995.

Marinacci, Barbara, ed. *Linus Pauling in His Own Words*. New York: Simon & Schuster, 1995.

Newton, David E. *Linus Pauling: Scientist and Advocate*. New York: Facts on File, 1994.

White, Florence Meiman. *Linus Pauling: Scientist and Crusader*. New York: Walker, 1980.

(Robert J. Paradowski)

Vladimir Prelog

Discipline: Chemistry

Contribution: Prelog worked productively on a wide variety of chemical problems, ranging from simple carbon rings to protein enzymes. All of his studies emphasize the significance of molecular geometry.

July 23, 1906	Born in Sarajevo, Bosnia
1924-1929	Studies at the Czech Institute of Technology, Prague
1929-1935	Employed by G. J. Dríza in Prague
1935-1941	Joins the faculty of the University of Zagreb as a lecturer and advances to professor of organic chemistry
1941	Starts work as an assistant at Eidgenössiche Technische Hochschule (ETH) in Zurich, Switzerland
1957	Becomes head of Organic Chemistry Laboratory at ETH
1959	Becomes Swiss citizen
1975	Awarded the Nobel Prize in Chemistry, jointly with John Warcup Cornforth
1976	Retires from teaching
July 23, 1998	Dies in Zurich, Switzerland

Early Life

Born in Sarajevo in 1906, Vladimir Prelog (pronounced "PREH-lohg") was interested in science at an early age. As a boy, he imagined three noted chemists—Sir Robert Robinson, Christopher Ingold, and Leopold Ruzicka—to be his teachers and, surprisingly, went on to work with them in later years.

Prelog was educated at the Gymnasium in Zagreb and the Technological Institute in Prague, but his career plans were abruptly terminated by the worldwide economic catastrophe of 1929. Instead of pursuing a degree, he was forced to accept an industrial position. until the economic situation improved.

Chemical Variety

Prelog was to exercise his creativity in the study of carbon compounds, those found in organic or living organisms. His early work centered on the synthesis of cyclic compounds. While conceptually simple, their successful preparation is difficult. Numerous open-chain molecules with reactive atoms are found at either end, and it would seem easy to bring the ends together and cause them to react within the same molecule. That is precisely the problem, however, for the reactive atoms may instead react with the ends of different molecules. This undesirable reaction was the only product in rings of certain sizes until Prelog's work. Prelog worked with Ruzicka on this problem, and the method they developed remains the only practical preparation. It involves carrying out the reaction with an extremely low concentration of starting material. Under these conditions, the chance of ring formation becomes greater than that of polymer formation because of a change in the relative probability of collision. A second factor in Prelog's method is his use of a reactive metal surface as the reaction site.

Where the Paths May Lead

Prelog and Ruzicka had discovered more than a method for a particular synthesis. Further experimentation proved the existence of a number of paths that one could take and that would reveal new molecular architecture. Never content simply to make new compounds, no matter how elegant the method, Prelog thought deeply about these other possibilities. He was especially interested in the so-called medium rings, those with eight to eleven atoms, which are very difficult to form.

Naming Chiral Compounds

In collaboration with two British chemists, Prelog developed the now universally accepted method of designating right-handed and left-handed molecules.

The basic method of naming stereochemical molecules developed by Prelog, in collaboration with R. S. Cahn and C. K. Ingold, depends on two basic conventions: an unambiguous sequence of the groups or atoms attached to the chiral atom and a specific point in space from which to view the molecule under consideration. The rules that allow clear communication among scientists are illustrated here using the most common type of chiral arrangement.

When four different atoms or groups of atoms are attached to one carbon atom, the molecule exists in two nonidentical structures related as object and mirror image. Consider the following generalized models:

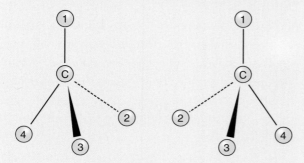

The numbers refer to the priority of the atoms as assigned largely on the basis of atomic numbers.

The viewing convention is from the chiral atom along the bond to the group of lowest priority.

These structures are turned in space so that the three groups of highest priority are arranged as the spokes of a wheel.

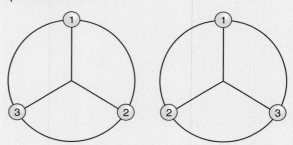

The first structure has a clockwise sequence of decreasing priority and the second is counterclockwise. The name of the first compound contains *R* (from the Latin *rectus*, "right"), and the second contains *S* (*sinister*, "left").

Bibliography

Carey, Francis A. and Richard J. Sundberg. *Advanced Organic Chemistry*. 3d ed. New York: Plenum Press, 1990.

Ramsay, Bertrand O. *Stereochemistry*. London: Heyden, 1981.

By studying accurate models, he concluded that a structure in some remote site on the ring might influence the chemistry being studied in another part of the ring. Prelog's description of such transannular (across-the-ring) chemistry has become important in several fields, including protein chemistry.

His interest in these fine details of chemical structure also involved questions of stereochemistry. This term is applied to molecules that differ only in their arrangement of atoms in space. To study such small differences, it is necessary to separate the forms. One of Prelog's contributions involved the use of columns of a single form found in nature to purify selectively the mixtures usually found in the laboratory.

Prelog shared the 1975 Nobel Prize in Chemistry with John Warcup Cornforth for his work on chemical reactions.

Bibliography

By Prelog

"Newer Developments of the Chemistry of Many-Membered Ring Compounds," *Journal of the Chemical Society*, 1950.

"Conformation and Reactivity of Medium Sized Ring Compounds," *Pure Applied Chemistry*, 1963.

"Problems in Chemical Topology," *Chemistry in Britain*, 1968.

"Chirality in Chemistry" *Les Prix Nobel*, 1975.

About Prelog

Eliel, Ernest L. and Harry S. Mosher. "The 1975 Nobel Prize for Chemistry." *Science* 190 (1975).

Encyclopædia Britannica Online, s. v. "Vladimir Prelog," http://www.britannica.com/

Greene, Jay E., ed "Vladimir Prelog." in *McGraw-Hill Modern Scientists and Engineers*, Vol. 3. New York: McGraw-Hill, 1980.

(K. Thomas Finley)

Joseph Priestley

Disciplines: Chemistry and physics
Contribution: Priestley is credited with the discovery of oxygen, which helped overthrow the phlogiston theory.

Mar. 13, 1733	Born in Yorkshire, England
1762	Ordained as a minister of the Congregational Church
1765	Receives an L.L.D. degree from the University of Edinburgh
1766	Named a Fellow of the Royal Society of London
1767	Becomes a pastor of the Mill Hill Chapel in Leeds
1767	Publishes *The History and Present State of Electricity*
1772	Accepts a position as librarian to Lord Shelburne
1772	Shows that a gas necessary for animal life is produced by plants
1772	Discovers nitrogen monoxide and isolates gaseous ammonia
1773	Receives the Copley Medal from the Royal Society of London
1774	Discovers oxygen by heating mercuric oxide
1774	Isolates sulfur dioxide from sulfuric acid
1780	Becomes a minister of the New Meeting Chapel
1791	His chapel, home, and laboratory are destroyed by a mob
1794	Immigrates to the United States and settles in Northumberland, Pennsylvania
Feb. 6, 1804	Dies in Northumberland

Early Life

Joseph Priestley's father was a clothmaker who lived in Birstal Fieldhead near Leeds, England. Joseph's mother died in childbirth when he was six years old. Religion was a strong, lifelong influence on Priestley. His grandfather was a Calvinist dissenter and raised Priestly as a Calvinist. As Joseph grew older, he developed independent ideas about religion that led to his rejection of the strict Calvinist doctrines.

Since only members of the Church of England were allowed to enter English universities at the time, Priestley entered the dissenting academy at Daventry. In 1755 he left Daventry to take a position as assistant minister to a congregation in Needham Market, Suffolk. His unorthodox religious views were not well received there, and his congregation and income dwindled.

Priestley was much more successful at a position in Nantwich in Cheshire, where he started a school. Its success led to the offer of a position at the Warrington Academy. His primary duty was to teach languages, but while there he attended some lectures in chemistry.

Although Priestley himself had no formal science training, he believed that science should be an important part of a school's curriculum. His initial scientific interest in electricity was aroused when he met Benjamin Franklin in London in 1766. Franklin's work with electricity was well known. Priestley planned to write a detailed history of science, the first volume of which was to be devoted to electricity. Franklin encouraged Priestley to proceed with his history and gave him ideas for new experiments.

Work with Electricity

Priestley's work on his history of electricity proceeded quickly, and *The History and Present State of Electricity* was published in the Fall of 1767.

The most notable of his original observations was that charcoal and coke are good conductors of electricity. Up to this time, it was thought that only metals and water were electrical conductors. Priestley also proposed the inverse square law for the attraction between oppositely charged bodies. This law was experimentally demonstrated by Charles-Augustin Coulomb in 1784 and now bears his name.

Initial Work with Gases

In 1767, at the age of thirty-four, Priestley assumed the position of pastor of the Mill Hill Chapel at Leeds.

It is now known that air consists mainly of nitrogen and oxygen. At the time that Priestley began his work at Leeds, however, it was thought to be a single, pure substance. The word "air" was used as a general term for what is now called a gas. Common air was thought to be the only gas until Joseph Black isolated carbon dioxide, which he called "fixed air." Soon after arriving at Leeds, Priestley began experimenting with carbon dioxide.

Oxygen and the Overthrow of the Phlogiston Theory

Priestley's discovery of oxygen was crucial to the overthrow of the phlogiston theory, which proposed that a substance was lost in all combustion reactions.

The work for which Priestley is best known was done in 1774. He had obtained a 12-inch lens that he used to focus the rays of the sun in order to achieve high temperatures. He used the lens to heat various chemicals to see if they would give off a gas. On August 1, he used his lens to heat "mercurius calcinatus" (mercuric oxide) and then collected and tested the emitted gas. It was not soluble in water, and a candle placed in it burned more brightly than in air. He also determined that mice would live longer in the gas than in an equal volume of air. Two months later, Priestley went to Paris and visited chemist Antoine-Laurent Lavoisier. He told Lavoisier of his discovery of this new gas, which is now known as oxygen.

This discovery helped discredit the phlogiston theory, chemistry's first comprehensive theory. It offered an explanation for a number of well-known chemical reactions. Its origin is attributed to the German chemist Georg Stahl in 1714. In the most familiar combustion reactions, something appears to be lost. For example, when wood is burned, only ash remains. Stahl proposed that a substance, which he called "phlogiston," is lost in all combustion reactions. Something burned until it had given off all of its phlogiston. If the burning was done in a closed vessel, it stopped when the air in the vessel was saturated with phlogiston.

The theory was extended beyond ordinary combustion reactions. When a metal was burned in air, it was thought to give up phlogiston, producing a product called a "calx." When the calx was heated with charcoal, it took up phlogiston from the charcoal and regenerated the original metal. Oxide is the modern name for a calx. Priestley was a lifelong believer in the phlogiston theory, but Lavoisier disproved it using some of Priestley's own work.

In 1772, Lavoisier determined that when burned, sulfur and phosphorus, rather than losing a substance, actually gained weight. His explanation for the increase in weight was that the phosphorus and sulfur combined with air. With Priestley's discovery of oxygen, Lavoisier was able to demonstrate that it was only the oxygen in air that combined with the material being burned. He did so by repeating Priestley's oxygen experiment using quantitative measurements.

Lavoisier weighed a sample of mercuric oxide, heated it to drive off the oxygen, and weighed the mercury produced. The weight of the collected oxygen was close to the difference between those of the mercury and the oxide. This demonstrated that when mercury was burned, oxygen must have combined with it, instead of "phlogiston" being removed.

Bibliography

Conant, James., ed. *Harvard Case Histories in Experimental Science.* Cambridge, Mass.: Harvard University Press, 1957.

Brock, William H. *The Norton History of Chemistry.* New York: W. W. Norton, 1992.

Stillman, John. *The Story of Alchemy and Early Chemistry.* New York: Dover, 1960.

His work produced no startling results, but it did gain for him some recognition from the prestigious Royal Society of London.

At the time, gases were routinely collected by the pneumatic method. In this method, the gas is bubbled into a jar containing water, which is forced out by the gas. Priestley improved this gas-collecting technique by using both water and mercury as the displaced liquid. Displacement of water cannot be used to collect water-soluble gases, as the gases will dissolve in the water rather than displace it.

Using his technique, Priestley isolated the water-soluble hydrogen chloride gas. He did so by heating sodium chloride and sulfuric acid.

Solutions of ammonia in water had been prepared previously, but ammonia gas had never been isolated. Priestley accomplished this task by heating ammonia water and collecting the ammonia gas driven off by mercury displacement. He knew that solutions of hydrogen chloride are acidic and that ammonia solutions are basic. He wondered if a neutral gas would be formed if they reacted together.

When he brought the two gases together, he observed the formation of a white cloud that gradually settled to form a fine powder. He identified the powder as "sal ammoniac," now called ammonium chloride. This work was done in 1772 and 1773.

In 1791, Priestley's unpopular religious and political views led to the destruction of his chapel, home, and laboratory by a mob. Three years later, he moved to the United States, where he died in 1804.

Bibliography

By Priestley

The History and Present State of Electricity, 1767.

Experiments and Observations on Different Kinds of Air, 1774 (6 vols) revised 1790 (3 vols.).

Considerations on the Doctrine of Phlogiston and the Decomposition of Water, 1796.

Memoirs of Dr. Joseph Priestley, to the Year 1795.

About Priestley

Partington, J. R. *A History of Chemistry*. Vol. B. New York: St. Martin's Press, 1962.

Gibbs, F. W. *Joseph Priestley*. London: Thomas Nelson, 1965.

Schofield, Robert. *A Scientific Autobiography of Joseph Priestley, Selected Scientific Correspondence Edited with Commentary*. Cambridge, Mass.: MIT Press, 1966.

(*Francis P. Mac Kay*)

Ellen Swallow Richards

Discipline: Chemistry

Contribution: A major contributor to the application of chemistry to practical concerns, Richards launched the fields of environmental, domestic, and sanitation chemistry.

Dec. 3, 1842	Born in Dunstable, Massachusetts
1870	Earns an A.B. from Vassar College
1871	Admitted to the Massachusetts Institute of Technology (MIT)
1873	Becomes the first U.S. woman to earn a B.S. from MIT
1873	Awarded an M.A. by Vassar
1873-1875	Conducts work in water chemistry for the Massachusetts State Board of Health
1876	Establishes the Woman's Laboratory at MIT
1879	Becomes an assistant instructor, without pay, at MIT
1882	First woman elected to the American Institute of Mining and Metallurgical Engineers
1882	Publishes *The Chemistry of Cooking and Cleaning*
1883	Appointed Instructor in Sanitary Chemistry at MIT
1887-1897	Works as a State Board of Health water analyst
1908	Elected president of the American Home Economics Association
Mar. 30, 1911	Dies in Jamaica Plain, Boston

Early Life

Ellen Henrietta Swallow, the only child of Peter and Fanny Swallow, was born in December 1842 in rural Massachusetts and reared there and in New Hampshire. Her parents, who had both been teachers, placed an unusual emphasis on education and taught Ellen at home until she was sixteen. This early education, coupled with much hard, out-of-doors work, set important patterns for her lifelong interest in the practical application of chemistry.

Through her growing years, Ellen showed talent in both academic and practical areas. She helped her parents with their farms and stores, and tutored other students. While working seriously at her studies and achieving high marks, Swallow also managed the home during her mother's frequent illnesses. She saved every available cent to reach her dreams of further education and never lost sight of her goals.

Education and Opportunity

Vassar College, Matthew Vassar's experiment in higher education for women, had only been open in Poughkeepsie for three years when Swallow entered as a special student at the advanced age of twenty-five. In 1869, only one year later, she was admitted to the senior class. Her talents in teaching, especially mathematics and Latin, provided the the money necessary for minimal support.

During those two years at Vassar, Swallow discovered her love of science. The famous astronomer Maria Mitchell greatly impressed Swallow, but it was a forward-thinking male chemist, Charles A. Farrar, who captured her imagination. Farrar was well ahead of his times, not only in supporting education for women but also in seeing the opportunities for chemistry to solve practical problems.

The Technology Establishment

The newly opened Massachusetts Institute of Technology (MIT) in Boston had a firm policy of refusing women, but, when Swallow presented Mitchell and Farrar as references, she became "the Swallow Experiment." Her admission, as a special student, was to be without charge. While this tuition waiver appeared magnanimous, she later learned that MIT had made the offer in order to be free of any serious involvement if she were unable to compete in an all-male environment.

She did not fail. Throughout her life, Swallow—who would change her name to Ellen Swallow Richards upon her marriage to Robert Hallowell Richards in 1875—contributed her talents to the institute, her profession, and other women looking for opportunities to make use of their intellect. In making educational opportunities available at MIT, she opened doors to scientific education and employment to succeeding generations of women. At the same time, Richards established the bases for the analytical chemistry of water, sanitation, air, and food.

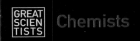

Pioneering Work and Belated Recognition

Richards never doubted that women deserved an opportunity to participate in scientific work or that social problems could be solved only through sound analysis. The homes of the U.S. demanded clean water and air for a healthy environment. Pure food, properly prepared, would lead to healthy families. Richards believed that home management by women who were scientifically trained gave hope of eliminating the worst aspects of poverty.

It was nearly seventy years after her death in 1911 before MIT finally recognized the achievements of their first female faculty member by creating the Ellen Swallow Richards Professorship.

Applied Analytical Chemistry

Richards sought to apply the principles and methods of chemistry to sanitation in order to promote a clean, healthy environment.

Few scientific activities have received as much attention as ecology, the study of humankind's relationship to the environment. The demand for pure water, air, and food at once raises the questions "what makes these vital substances impure?" and "how much impurity is allowable?" The unspoken assumption about what is present in pure materials is not as self-evident as might be first thought. For example, one drink of pure water is enough for those who prefer mineral water, with its dissolved gases and salts.

More scientific questions concern purity itself. What does it mean when a substance is pure? Are there no atoms or molecules of another substance present? How does one know? The best one can say is that the level of impurity in a "pure" substance is less than a given method can detect.

The development of more precise analytical methods constantly engages the analytical chemist. Not only must the method determine the specific impurity, but it must also function in the presence of other materials in the sample. These materials may be known or not, but the chemist must avoid false results. Even the known materials may be present in amounts and render the results unreliable.

This notion of interfering substances introduces a second important area of analytical chemistry: separation. Often, a precise analysis demands that matter be removed selectively. In dealing with the complex mixtures of the environment, analysis and separation must be studied together, with each aspect playing a role in the study of the other.

Above all, the analyst's intellectual and technical skills must be maintained at a high level. Only careful attention to detail yields reliable results. Amazingly small amounts of impurities are known to influence health. A level of 1 percent represents only one impurity in one hundred, but parts per million (ppm) or one ten-thousandth of a percent are routinely sought.

Powerful methods for such fine analyses involve electronics. The human hand and eye are replaced by an electrical signal. Such methods have revolutionized analytical chemistry, but they ultimately depend on the scientific knowledge and the technical skill of the person designing, testing, and using them.

Bibliography

Hill, John W. Stuart J. Baum, and Dorothy M. Feigl. *Chemistry and Life*. 5th ed. Upper Saddle River, N.J.: Prentice Hall, 1997.

Hill, John W. and Doris K. Kolb. *Chemistry for Changing Times*. 7th ed. Englewood Cliffs, N.J.: Prentice Hall, 1995.

Selinger, Ben. *Chemistry in the Marketplace*. 4th ed. Sydney: Harcourt Brace Jovanovich, 1989.

Snyder, Carl H. *The Extraordinary Chemistry of Ordinary Things*. 2d ed. New York: John Wiley & Sons, 1995.

Bibliography

By Richards

The Chemistry of Cooking and Cleaning: A Manual for Housekeepers, 1882.
Food Materials and Their Adulterations, 1886.
Sanitation in Daily Life, 1907.
Euthenics, the Science of Controllable Environment, 1910.
Conservation by Sanitation, 1911.

About Richards

Creese, Mary and Thomas M. Creese. "Ellen Henrietta Swallow Richards (1842-1911)." in *Women in Chemistry and Physics*, edited by Louise S. Grinstein, Rose K. Rose, and Miriam H. Rafailovich. Westport, Conn.: Greenwood Press, 1993.
Clarke, Robert. *Ellen Swallow: The Woman Who Founded Ecology.* Chicago: Follett, 1973.
Hunt, Caroline L. *The Life of Ellen H. Richards.* Boston: M. Barrows, 1925.

(K. Thomas Finley)

Sir Robert Robinson

Discipline: Chemistry

Contribution: Robinson contributed to the modern electronic theory of organic reactions. He is best known for the structure determination and chemical synthesis of natural products, especially alkaloids, plant pigments, and steroids.

Sept. 13, 1886	Born in Derbyshire, England
1912-1930	Works as an organic chemistry professor at several universities
1920	Elected a Fellow of the Royal Society of London
1930-1955	Named Waynflete Professor of Chemistry at Oxford University
1939-1941	Elected president of the Chemical Society
1942	Receives the Copley Medal of the Royal Society of London
1945-1950	President of the Royal Society of London
1947	Wins the Nobel Prize in Chemistry and the U.S. Medal of Freedom
1953	Receives the Priestley Medal from the American Chemical Society
1955	Elected president of the British Association for the Advancement of Science
1955	Becomes director and consultant for Shell Chemical Company
1958-1959	Elected president of the Society of Chemical Industry
Feb. 8, 1975	Dies in Buckinghamshire, England

Early Life

Robert Robinson was born in England at Rufford Farm near Chesterfield, Derbyshire. He was the eldest of William Bradbury and Jane (Davenport) Robinson's five children. The family also included the seven surviving children from William's previous marriage to Elizabeth Lowe, who died in 1871. When Robert was three, the family moved to Field House in nearby New Brampton, where his father was a prominent Congregationalist and manufacturer of surgical dressings and boxes for ointments and pills.

Robinson's early education was in Chesterfield until the age of twelve, when he was enrolled in Fulneck School, run by the Moravian Church, at Pudsey Greenside near Leeds.

He entered Manchester University in 1902 to study chemistry, earning a B.Sc. degree with first-class honors in 1905 and remaining as a University Fellow (1906) and 1851 Exhibition Scholar (1907-1909) to acquire a doctor of science degree in 1910

under William H. Perkin, Jr., who, together with Arthur Lapworth, greatly influenced Robinson's lifelong research interests.

A Diverse Academic Career

Robinson was an assistant lecturer and demonstrator while at Manchester from 1909 to 1912. He then traveled to Australia to become the first professor of organic chemistry at the University of Sydney. In 1915, he returned to England to accept the newly created Heath Harrison Chair of Organic Chemistry at the University of Liverpool, which he left in 1920 to serve as the research director of British Dye-stuffs Corporation.

Robinson subsequently held chairs of organic chemistry at St. Andrews University in Scotland, Manchester University, and University College of London. He succeeded his mentor Perkin as the Waynflete Professor of Chemistry at Magdalen College of Oxford University in 1930 and remained there until his retirement in 1955.

Robinson founded the international journal of organic chemistry *Tetrahedron* in 1957. Until his death in 1975 he continued his research on alkaloids and the composition and origins of petroleum in a small laboratory at Egham, where he was a consultant for the Shell group of chemical companies.

The Foremost Natural Products Chemist

Robinson studied the chemical constituents from natural sources as diverse as the royal jelly of bees, the dyes from brazilwood (brazilin and brazilein) and logwood (hematoxylin), and numerous plant alkaloids. He was fascinated by flowers and investigated the chemical basis for genetic variations in flower color. He alsodevised small-scale tests to establish which pigments give a flower petal a particular hue, and synthesized the group of anthocyanin (blue-red) pigments and anthoxanthin (yellow) pigments.

The Natural Products Chemistry of Alkaloids

Robinson investigated the chemical structure and synthesis of alkaloids.

The traditional definition of an alkaloid as a basic, pharmacologically active and nitrogen-containing heterocyclic organic compound from plants has been broadened to include about 10,000 naturally occurring nitrogenous secondary metabolites of vegetable, microbial, or even animal origin. Many exhibit pronounced physiological activity on humans and animals as medicines, cardiac and respiratory stimulants, tranquilizers and muscle relaxants, analgesics, psychedelics, or poisons.

Alkaloidal natural products are designated by the ending "-ine" in their chemical name. The nitrogen of most alkaloids resides in a heterocyclic ring. Examples include caffeine from coffee beans, nicotine from tobacco, morphine from the opium poppy, cocaine from coca leaves, quinine from cinchona bark, atropine from deadly nightshade, coniine from poison hemlock, and strychnine from *Strychnos nux-vomica*. Alkaloids with exocyclic nitrogen include ephedrine from several *Ephedra* species, mescaline from peyotyl cactus, and other biogenic amines.

The natural products chemist isolates a pure alkaloid using extraction, crystallization, and chromatography; then determines its structural formula with chemical reactions, spectroscopy, or X-ray diffraction. Total chemical synthesis provides ultimate proof of the molecular structure and is often an incentive to discover new chemical reactions in organic chemistry.

Bibliography

Dalton, David R. "Alkaloids." in *Kirk-Othmer Encyclopedia of Chemical Technology*. Vol. 1. 4th ed. New York: Wiley-Interscience, 1991.

Colegate, Steven M. and Russell J. Molyneux. *Bioactive Natural Products: Detection, Isolation, and Structure Determination*. S Boca Raton, Fla.: CRS Press, 1993.

Pelletier, S. W. ed. *Chemistry of the Alkaloids*. New York: Van Nostrand Reinhold, 1970.

Southon, I. W. and J. Buckingham, eds. *Dictionary of Alkaloids*. 2 vols. London: Chapman and Hall, 1989.

Cordell, Geoffrey A. *Introduction to Alkaloids: A Biogenic Approach*. New York: Wiley-Interscience, 1981.

Robinson also made major contributions to establishing the molecular structure of penicillin and to the synthesis of the female hormone estrone and more powerful artificial steroid hormones (stilbestrol, hexestrol, and dienestrol) used for oral contraception and cancer therapy.

Many of Robinson's synthetic procedures, such as his annulation to close five- and six-membered rings, were reported in more than 700 publications. His chemical syntheses and biosynthetic speculations were aided by his development of a qualitative electronic theory for organic reactions, from which the modern concepts of mechanistic "curly arrows" and aromatic sextet are derived.

Bibliography

By Robinson

A Theory of the Mechanism of the Phyto-chemical Synthesis of Certain Alkaloids," *Journal of the Chemical Society*, 1917.

An Outline of an Electrochemical (Electronic) Theory of the Course of Organic Reactions, 1932.

"Synthesis in Biochemistry," *Journal of the Chemical Society*, 1936.

The Building of Molecules, 1937.

"The Red and Blue Colouring Matters of Plants," *Endeavour*, 1942.

"The Origins of Petroleum," *Nature*, 1966.

About Robinson

"A Centenary Tribute to Sir Robert Robinson." Special issue of *Natural Product Reports* 4 (February, 1987).

Lord Todd and J. W. Cornforth. "Robert Robinson." *Biographical Memoirs of Fellows of the Royal Society* 22 (1976).

Saltzman, Martin D. "Robert Robinson." in *Nobel Laureates in Chemistry: 1901-1992*, edited by Laylin K. James. Washington, D.C.: American Chemical Society, 1993.

Williams, Trevor I. *Robert Robinson: Chemist Extraordinary*. Oxford, England: Clarendon Press, 1990.

Birch, A. J. "Sir Robert Robinson: A Contemporary Historical Assessment and a Personal Memoir." *Journal and Proceedings of the Royal Society of New South Wales* 109 (1976).

(Martin V. Stewart)

Ernest Rutherford

Disciplines: Chemistry and physics
Contribution: Rutherford identified radioactivity as a process in which the emanation of radioactive particles results in the transmutation of the element. He also discovered the nucleus of the atom.

Aug. 30, 1871	Born in Spring Grove (later Brightwater), near Nelson, New Zealand
1887	Enters Canterbury College in Christchurch, New Zealand
1895	Receives a scholarship to Trinity College, the University of Cambridge
1897	Distinguishes alpha and beta radiation from uranium
1898	Becomes a professor of physics at McGill University, Canada
1902	Becomes a Fellow of the Royal Society of London
1904	Receives the Rumford Medal of the Royal Society of London
1907	Named a professor of physics at the University of Manchester
1908	Wins the Nobel Prize in Chemistry
1911	Discovers the atomic nucleus
1914	Knighted
1919	Becomes Cavendish Professor of Physics at the University of Cambridge
1919	Detects protons in the nucleus
1931	Named Baron Rutherford of Nelson
Oct. 19, 1937	Dies in Cambridge, England

Early Life

Ernest Rutherford was born in a rural area near Nelson, New Zealand. When he was fifteen, his family moved to Pungarehu, where his father raised flax and ran a mill. Rutherford won a scholarship to Canterbury College in New Zealand and then another to the Cavendish Laboratories at the University of Cambridge, England. The director of the laboratories was the great physicist Sir J. J. Thomson, the discoverer of the electron. Rutherford was twenty-four when he arrived at Cambridge in 1895.

The Transformation of Elements

At around that same time, two discoveries were made on the continent of Europe that determined the course of Rutherford's research at Cambridge. Wilhelm Röntgen discovered X-rays in 1895, and Antoine-Henri Becquerel discovered radioactivity in 1896. Thomson invited Rutherford to join him in studying these two new phenomena. In his experiments with uranium, Rutherford observed

two different kinds of radioactive emanation, which he called alpha radiation and beta radiation. Paul Villard, a French scientist, is credited with the discovery of the third kind of radioactive emanation, gamma radiation. Work by others showed that beta rays are electrons and gamma rays are electromagnetic radiation.

The nature of alpha particles was determined later by Rutherford. In working with the radioactive element thorium, he observed that it gave off a gaseous, radioactive substance, which he called thorium emanation. He enlisted the aid of the chemist, Frederick Soddy, to isolate and identify it.

Soddy was able to demonstrate that thorium emanation was a gas that was chemically unreactive, just like the recently discovered family of inert gases. The gas that was called thoron is now known to be an isotope of radon with a mass of 220. In giving off its radiation, thorium is converted into a different element, radon. In radioactive disintegration, nature does spontaneously what chemists had thought impossible.

Rutherford then set out to determine the nature of alpha particles. The charge-mass ratio of the alpha particle had led him to suspect that it was a double positively charged helium atom. He confirmed this hypothesis by collecting alpha particles and condensing the resulting gas. The atomic spectrum of the gas confirmed that it was helium.

The Structure of the Atom

Rutherford's next two discoveries involved the use of alpha particles. When a beam of alpha particles was passed through a thin gold foil, the image of the beam on a detection screen appeared to be fuzzy. This result seemed to indicate that something was producing deflections of the alpha particles as they passed through the atoms in the foil. Follow-up work by Hans Geiger and Ernest Marsden showed that for one in every 8,000 alpha particles, the deflections were not small but exceeded ninety degrees.

The Nucleus and the Structure of the Atom

Rutherford's discovery of the nucleus prompted the suggestion of a planetary model for atomic structure.

At the time that Ernest Marsden and Hans Geiger did their experiment bombarding a gold foil with alpha particles, Sir J. J. Thomson's theory of the structure of the atom was dominant. The proton had not yet been discovered, so there was no reason to believe that the atom contained positive particles. Thomson proposed that the atom consisted of a jellylike mass of positively charged material, with the electrons embedded in it in a definite arrangement.

Rutherford followed his discovery of the nucleus with a planetary model for the atom, in which electrons orbit the nucleus just as the planets orbit the sun. Even those who advanced the model, however, recognized that it had a serious flaw. The laws of electrodynamics state that a moving electric charge must constantly give off energy. As the electron orbited the nucleus, its energy would steadily decrease. This means that it should spiral down into the nucleus as it lost energy, resulting in the collapse of the atom.

Niels Bohr spent the first half of 1912 in Rutherford's laboratory in Manchester, so he was quite familiar with Rutherford's model. He was also familiar with the ideas of Max Planck on the quantization of energy. Bohr was able to combine the two to solve the problem of the collapse that would occur with the Rutherford model.

Bohr applied the quantization hypothesis to the atom by proposing that the electron could occupy only certain orbits around the nucleus. Each orbit would have a definite energy depending on its distance from the nucleus. Since the electron can have only certain energies, it could not steadily lose energy as it orbits. It could only change its energy by single jumps between orbits.

Using concepts of classical Newtonian physics and the quantum hypothesis, Bohr was able to calculate the energies of the orbits in the hydrogen atom. These energies correlated very well with the experimentally determined atomic spectrum of hydrogen that had previously been determined. With this verification of its validity, the Bohr-Rutherford model for the atom gained quick acceptance.

Since its development in 1869, chemists had been using the concept of the periodic table developed independently by Dmitry Mendeleev and Julius Lothar Meyer to systematize and predict the reactivity of the chemical elements. No basic understanding existed, however, of why the elements in groups in the periodic table had similar properties and chemical reactivities. When the electrons in elements were assigned to the energy levels in the Rutherford-Bohr model, it was found that the outer electrons were in parallel energy levels. It then became apparent that the reactivities of the elements were determined by their outer electron configurations.

This focus on the electrons as the determinants of chemical reactivity led to enormous growth in the field of mechanistic studies of chemical reactions. The greater understanding of how chemical reactions occur has facilitated the development of materials such as polymers and pharmaceuticals that are so important in modern life.

Bibliography

Hecht, Selig. *Explaining the Atom.* New York: Viking Press, 1964.

Boorse, Henry and Lloyd Motz, eds. *The World of the Atom.* 2 vols. New York: Basic Books, 1966.

Rutherford calculated that a charge greater than one hundred times that of the electron would be needed to produce so great a deflection of the charged alpha particles. It took him two years to arrive at a model that explained this unexpected result. The atom had to have a very tiny nucleus that contained all of its positive charge.

At this time, the nature of the positive charge in the atom was not known. No positive particle corresponding to the electron had been discovered. Additional experiments using alpha particles led to Rutherford's last great achievement: the discovery of the proton.

When he passed alpha particles through nitrogen gas, he was able to detect the presence of protons, positively charged hydrogen atoms. Since there was no hydrogen gas present to account for the production of the protons, Rutherford concluded that the nucleus of the nitrogen atom contained protons. The collision of the alpha particle with the nitrogen nucleus resulted in the expulsion of a proton. Rutherford realized that this nuclear reaction resulted in the conversion of nitrogen to oxygen. He was therefore the first to carry out the artificial transmutation of an element. This was the last work that he did at the University of Manchester.

In 1919, he succeeded Thomson as Cavendish Professor of Physics at Cambridge. Rutherford died on October 19, 1937.

Bibliography

By Rutherford
Radioactivity, 1904.
Radioactive Substances and Their Radiations, 1913.
The Newer Alchemy, 1937.

About Rutherford
Feather, Norman. *Lord Rutherford*. London: Priory Press, 1973.
Wilson, David. *Rutherford*. Cambridge, Mass.: MIT Press, 1983.

(*K. Thomas Finley*)

Glenn Theodore Seaborg

Discipline: Chemistry
Contribution: Seaborg received the Nobel Prize in Chemistry for his discovery of "not less than four more transuranium elements." He also discovered, in collaboration with other chemists, the elements 94 through 102 on the periodic table.

Apr. 19, 1912	Born in Ishpeming, Michigan
1934	Earns a B.A. in chemistry from the University of California, Los Angeles (UCLA)
1937	Receives a Ph.D. in chemistry from the University of California, Berkeley (UCB)
1939-1982	Teaches chemistry at UCB
1942-1946	Takes wartime leave to work on the Manhattan Project
1948-1950	Serves on the Atomic Energy Commission's General Advisory Committee
1951	Awarded the Nobel Prize in Chemistry
1954	Named associate director of the Lawrence Radiation Laboratory
1958-1961	Acts as chancellor of UCB
1959	Receives the Enrico Fermi Award
1961-1971	Serves as chair of the Atomic Energy Commission
1976	Named a decorated officer by the French Legion of Honor
1982	Retires from UCB
1982-1999	Serves as Associate Director At Large at the Lawrence Berkeley National Laboratory
1999	Dies in Lafayette, California

Early Life

Glenn Theodore Seaborg began life in a small mining community on Michigan's upper peninsula, where he was born to Herman Theodore Seaborg, a machinist, and his wife, Selma, on April 19, 1912. The family moved to Southern California when Seaborg was ten.

When he entered the University of California, Los Angeles (UCLA), in 1929, the Westwood campus consisted of four buildings.

Excelling in chemistry, Seaborg received a B.A. degree in 1934. He continued his studies at the University of California, Berkeley (UCB), receiving a Ph.D. in chemistry UCB in 1937.

Although he knew early that he wanted to study chemistry, Seaborg's initial studies in that subject were unfocused. It was not until he was well along in graduate school that he began to concentrate on isotopes of the elements on the periodic table.

At this time, the heavier elements of the periodic table remained undiscovered, although scien-

tific evidence suggested their existence. Seaborg ultimately focused his research on these undiscovered transuranium elements. He spent two postdoctoral years at UCB as a research chemist, continuing his doctoral research on how isotopes of lead are altered by bombardments of fast neutrons. In time, he discovered a number of new isotopes.

Seaborg's work with Enrico Fermi, which began in 1934, led him toward the discovery of new elements in the periodic table, for which he would receive the Nobel Prize in Chemistry in 1951.

The Manhattan Project

When the United States entered World War II in 1941, the nation embarked on an accelerated program of scientific research that led to the eventual development of nuclear energy and to the building of the first atomic bombs. Seaborg, on leave from UCB, became a member of the blue-ribbon staff of the Manhattan Project.

It was there, where he focused on developing chemical means of separating plutonium from uranium in sufficient quantities to use in building weaponry, that his work on the transuranium elements moved toward its fullest development. By 1944, Seaborg's group achieved its aim of separating plutonium from uranium on a scale large enough to build the "superbomb" that a nation at war required.

By 1945, the group had produced enough plutonium to build the atomic bombs that the United States would use against Japan. It was the dropping of these bombs on the Japanese cities of Nagasaki and Hiroshima that ended World War II.

After War

From 1939 until he retired in 1982 Seaborg was a member of the UCB faculty. He served as chancellor of the Berkeley campus of the University of California for three years before President Kennedy recruited him in 1961 to become chairman of the Atomic Energy Commission, the precursor of the Department of Energy. For the next ten years Seaborg was instrumental in negotiations of nuclear testing and supported the use of nuclear energy. Later he became an advocate for science and mathematics education as a member of President Reagan's National Commission on Excellence in Education, and made waves with his influential report "A Nation at Risk."

Later Years

In 1971 Seaborg returned to Berkeley as full professor of chemistry. There he taught classes until 1979 and served as associate director at large of Berkeley Nation Laboratory.

Throughout his career Seaborg achieved many honors. His most beloved, however, was the 1997 renaming of element 106 to seaborgium, a tribute to his lasting impact on the periodic table. Seaborg died on February 25, 1999.

Discovering Transuranium Elements

Seaborg's most significant contribution to the field of chemistry was his discovery, with colleagues, of ten new elements and three new nuclear energy isotopes.

In the course of his distinguished career, Seaborg discovered a number of new isotopes—forms of the same element that have an identical number of protons but differ in the number of their neutrons—for many common elements on the periodic table.

By 1934, Enrico Fermi was convinced of the existence of elements heavier than uranium, which was at that time the heaviest element on the periodic table. Fermi, and other researchers working independently in Germany, added neutrons to the nuclei of uranium atoms, but this act did not produce heavier atoms. Rather, atoms of the uranium nuclei split, resulting in the release of incredible energy.

Knowledge of these experiments drew Seaborg into his extensive research on the transuranium elements, as the new elements were called. The result was a scientific exploration that led to the discovery by Seaborg and his colleagues of elements 94 through 102 on the periodic table, as well as element 106.

Some of Seaborg's colleagues at the University of California, Berkeley, observed that when neutrons are aimed at uranium atoms, some of the atomic nuclei that the neutrons hit do not split. Rather, they decay, emitting an electron that increases their atomic number by one, thereby creating a new element. Edwin Mattison McMillan named the resulting element "neptunium."

Seaborg and his fellow researchers found that as neptunium decays, it emits beta waves as electrons increasing its atomic weight by one, resulting in another element that Seaborg named "plutonium." Before they were done, Seaborg and his colleagues had discovered ten new elements (plutonium, americium, curium, berkelium, californium, einsteinium, fermium, mendelevium, nobelium, and element 106), three new nuclear energy isotopes (plutonium 239, uranium 233, and neptunium 237), and such other isotopes as iodine 131, iron 59, tellurium 99m, and cobalt 60.

It is for this pioneering work that Seaborg and McMillan were awarded the Nobel Prize in Chemistry in 1951, a year short of Seaborg's fortieth birthday. These discoveries paved the way for the nuclear age, which began shortly before the end of World War II.

Bibliography

Loveland, Walter D. and Glenn Seaborg. *The Elements Beyond Uranium.* New York: John Wiley & Sons, 1990.

Katz, Joseph J., Winston M. Manning, and Glenn Seaborg, eds. *The Transuranium Elements.* New York: McGraw-Hill, 1949.

Bibliography

By Seaborg

Comprehensive Inorganic Chemistry, 1953.
The Chemistry of Actinide Elements, 1957.
Man-Made Transuranium Elements, 1963.
Man and Atom: Shaping a New World Through Technology, 1971 (with W. R. Corliss).
Primary Papers in Physical Chemistry and Chemical Physics, 1978.

About Seaborg

Magill, Frank N., ed. "Glenn Theodore Seaborg." in *The Nobel Prize Winners: Chemistry*. Pasadena, Calif.: Salem Press, 1990.

Olsson, Nils William and Christopher Olssen, eds. *Great Swedish Heritage Awards Night.* Minneapolis, Minn.: Swedish Council of America, 1984.

Hoffman, Darleane C., "Glenn Theodore Seaborg," The National Academies Press, http://www.nap.edu/readingroom/books/biomems/gseaborg.html

Wasson, Tyler, ed. *Nobel Prize Winners: An H. W. Wilson Biographical Dictionary.* New York: H. W. Wilson, 1987.

Madden, Charles F., ed. *Talks with Social Scientists.* Carbondale, Ill: Southern Illinois University Press, 1968.

Stone, Irvine, ed. *There Was a Light: An Autobiography of a University—Berkeley, 1868-1968.* Berkeley, Calif.: University of California Press, 1970.

Yarris, Lynn, "Seaborg: An Educating Man" Sciencebeat, March 5, 1999, http://www.lbl.gov/Science-Articles/Archive/seaborg-edu-legacy.html

House, Peggy, "Glenn T. Seaborg, Citizen-Scholar," Northern Michigan University, April 1999, http://www.nmu.edu/seaborg/node/9

(R. Baird Shuman)

Nikolai Semenov

Disciplines: Chemistry and physics

Contribution: Semenov won the Nobel Prize in Chemistry for his work on branched chain chemical reactions in combustion processes, which was important in the development of internal combustion engines and plastic polymerization processes.

Apr. 15, 1896	Born in Saratov, Russia
1914-1917	Studies chemistry at Petrograd University
1917-1920	Lectures at Tomsk University
1920-1928	Serves as a lecturer at Petrograd Polytechnical Institute
1920	Appointed director of the Electron Phenomenon Laboratory of Petrograd Physical-Technical Institute
1924	Begins work on combustion processes
1928	Publishes a paper on a theory of combustion processes
1928	Appointed a full professor at Petrograd Polytechnical Institute
1932	Becomes a member of the Soviet Academy of Sciences
1934	Publishes *Tsepnye reaktsii (Chemical Kinetics and Chain Reactions, 1935)*
1939	Appointed director of the Institute of Chemical Physics of the Soviet Academy of Sciences
1956	Wins the Nobel Prize in Chemistry
Sept. 25, 1986	Dies in Moscow, Soviet Union

Early Life

Nikolai Nikolayevich Semenov (pronounced "sih-MYOH-nuhf"), the son of Elena Dmitrieva and Nikolai Alex Semyonov, was born in Saratov, Russia, on April 15, 1896. He completed his secondary education there and then enrolled at Petrograd University, where he studied chemistry from 1914 to 1917, completing his degree on the eve of the Bolshevik Revolution.

Semenov taught chemistry in Tomsk, western Siberia, during the troubled civil war period and in 1920 he returned to Petrograd (which was later St. Petersburg, then Leningrad, and then St. Petersburg again). He taught chemistry at the Petrograd Polytechnical Institute and conducted research at the Petrograd Physical-Technical Institute, where he was director of the Electron Phenomenon Laboratory.

In 1924, he married Natalia Burtseva and the couple had two children (a son and daughter).

Scientific Career

In 1924, Semenov became involved in the research of Yuri Khariton and Z. Val'ta, who were investigating the oxidation of phosphorus vapor. This explosive reaction displayed a number of anomalous features that could not be explained by the simple kinetic model (Arrhenius' Law) in use at the time. Semenov was able to formulate a model that explained these anomalous features by postulating that a chain reaction was involved. He published his results in 1928 in the landmark paper "K teorii protsessov goreniyaa, Soobsch. i" (toward a theory of combustion processes, part 1).

The chain reaction model proved to be useful in explaining many combustion processes and it had immense practical importance. Understanding that the burning of gasoline is a chemical chain reaction led directly to improvements in the efficiency of internal combustion engines.

Semenov became a member of the Soviet Academy of Sciences in 1932 and director of its Institute of Chemical Physics in 1939. In 1943, while Leningrad was being besieged by German troops, the institute was permanently moved to Moscow. Association with the Academy of Sciences is a high honor that brought Semenov a substantial increase in salary, preferential access to funding and publication, and the opportunity to travel abroad.

Awards and Honors

Semenov's accomplishments were honored in the Soviet Union and in other countries around the world well before he received the Nobel Prize for Chemistry.

He received the prestigious Stalin Prize and held honorary doctorates from the Universities of Oxford, England and Brussels, Belgium. Semenov was also a foreign member of the Royal Society of London and of the U.S., Indian, German, and Hungarian academies of sciences.

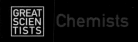
Chain Reactions and the Theory of Combustion

Combustion involves a collision between two molecules, breaking the chemical bonds between atoms and recombining them.

Some energy must be supplied to break the initial bonds between atoms. This may be in the form of heat, causing the molecules to move more rapidly and collide with greater force. If the reaction releases heat, then an increasing number of collisions will occur and combustion will increase in intensity until so many of the original molecules are used up that the frequency of collisions between them declines. This is the simple linear model of combustion.

In a branched chain reaction, the initial collision between reacting products creates not only the stable end product but also an unstable intermediary product capable of initiating a chemical reaction at a lower velocity.

Chemical chain reaction theory depends on the role of free radicals in chemical reactions. A free radical is an atom or fragment of a molecule that has an unpaired electron in its outer electron shell. Free radicals are more reactive than stable molecules, which have complete outer electron shells, so lower collision energies are required for reactions involving them. In the case that Semenov investigated initially, the explosive combination of oxygen and phosphorus vapor, each collision between a free radical and a molecule produces a stable end product plus three free radicals, and a chain reaction occurs.

Chemical chain reactions have many of the characteristics of atomic chain reactions: they require a high initiation energy, are violently explosive, and can be controlled by introducing a substance that removes free radicals. The octane in gasoline that removes free radicals from burning fuel mixtures is analogous to the graphite rods in a nuclear reactor, which efficiently absorb alpha particles.

Bibliography

Kondratev, V. N. and E. E. Nikitin. *Gas Phase Reactions: Kinetics and Mechanisms.* New York: Springer-Verlag, 1981.

Zelkovich, Ya. B. *The Mathematical Theory of Combustion and Explosions.* New York: Consultant's Bureau, 1985.

Semenov shared the 1956 Nobel Prize in Chemistry with Sir Cyril Hinshelwood of Great Britain, who had also made discoveries in chemical kinetics. Semenov was the first citizen of the Soviet Union to receive a Nobel Prize in any field. He died in 1986 in Moscow.

Bibliography

By Semenov
"K teorii protsessov goreniyaa, Soobsch. i," *Zhurnal fizicheskoy khimii,* 1928.

O nekotorykh problemakh khimicheskoi kinetiki i reaktsionnoi sposobnosti, 1954 (*Some Problems in Chemical Kinetics and Reactivity,* 1958, 2 vols.)

Heterogeneous Catalysis in the Chemical Industry, 1955 (with V. V. Voevodskii).

Nauka i obshchestvo, 1973.

About Semenov
Kondrat'ev, V. N., "Nikolai Nikolaevich Semenov, on His Seventieth Birthday." *Soviet Physics Uspekhi* 9 (1966).

Semenov, N. N. "The Road into Science." *Soviet Physics Uspekhi* 29 (1986).

(*Martha A. Sherwood*)

Richard E. Smalley

Discipline: Chemistry

Contribution: With Robert F. Curl, Jr., and Sir Harold W. Kroto, Smalley won the Nobel Prize in Chemistry for the discovery of fullerenes.

June 6, 1943	Born in Akron, Ohio
1961-1963	Attends Hope College in Holland, Michigan
1969-1973	Earns an M.A. and a Ph.D. from Princeton University
1973-1976	Works as a graduate research assistant at the James Franck Institute at the University of Chicago
1976-1982	Promoted to full professor of chemistry at Rice University
1978-1980	Named an Alfred P. Sloan Fellow
1982	Named Gene & Norman Hackerman Professor of Chemistry
1986-1996	Serves as chair of the Rice Quantum Institute
1990	Elected to the National Academy of Sciences
1990	Appointed a professor of physics at Rice
1992	Wins the Robert A. Welch Award in Chemistry
1993	Founds Center for Nanoscale Science and Technology
1996	Awarded the Franklin Medal
1996	Named director of the Center for Nanoscale Science and Technology
1996	Wins the Nobel Prize in Chemistry
2002	Receives the Glenn T. Seaborg Medal
Oct. 28, 2005	Dies in Houston, Texas

Early Life

Richard Errett Smalley grew up in Kansas City, Missouri. A quiet child, he spent most of his time in his father's basement workshop, where he achieved one of his first successes: he kept the family collie out of the rose garden by rigging it so that any intruder would set off fireworks.

An erratic student, Smalley did not become interested in chemistry until he took the subject in his junior year in high school, the first time that he did well academically. After an engineer-scientist spoke at his school, Smalley was motivated to pursue those fields.

Studies

On the recommendation of his aunt, a professor of organic chemistry, Smalley attended Hope College in Holland, Michigan. After his favorite professor died and the chair of the organic chemistry department retired, he transferred to the University of Michigan, where he received only mediocre grades.

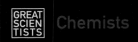

Fullerenes: A New Form of Carbon

The fullerenes, a family of highly symmetrical carbon cage molecules whose atoms are arranged in the shape of a soccer ball, opened up a new branch of chemistry with numerous possible applications.

Several widely diverse scientific areas coincided in the serendipitous discovery of the fullerenes, a third allotropic form of carbon (the first two being graphite and diamond).

During the 1980s, Sir Harold W. Kroto, a professor of chemistry at the University of Sussex in England, used microwave spectroscopy to analyze gas in space and found that the spectral lines in the atmospheres of carbon-rich giant stars could be attributed to cyanopolyenes (long-chain molecules composed of carbon and nitrogen). Desiring to study the formation of these substances more closely, he contacted an acquaintance, Robert F. Curl, Jr., a professor of chemistry at Rice University and an authority on microwave and infrared spectroscopy.

Smalley, an authority on a branch of chemical physics called cluster chemistry, had designed and built a laser supersonic cluster beam apparatus capable of vaporizing almost any known material into a plasma of atoms. When atoms in a gas phase condense into clusters (aggregates of atoms or molecules between microscopic and macroscopic particles in size), they form a series in which the size of the clusters varies from a few to hundreds of atoms.

Often, certain cluster sizes may predominate. The number of atoms in these clusters is called a "magic number," a term borrowed from nuclear physics. These dominant cluster sizes are assumed to possess high stability or high symmetry.

Through Curl, Kroto arranged to use Smalley's apparatus to study the vaporization and cluster formation of carbon, which might provide evidence that cyanopolyenes could have been formed in hot regions of stellar atmospheres. The crucial experiments, carried out in September, 1985, by Curl, Kroto, and Smalley

with graduate students James R. Heath and Sean C. O'Brien, detected the formation of clusters of sixty and seventy atoms, especially the former.

Abandoning the idea of long chains, they proposed that C_{60} could have the highly symmetrical structure of a truncated (cut off) icosahedral cage, the shape of a soccer ball or U.S. architect R. Buckminster Fuller's geodesic dome. Therefore, they named the substance buckminsterfullerene (or fullerene or buckyball).

Their article on this unique structure in the November 14, 1985, issue of *Nature* aroused wide interest and a mixed reception—both criticism and acceptance. The discovery remained of primarily theoretical significance, however, until 1990, with the work of physicists Wolfgang Krätschmer of the Max Planck Institute for Nuclear Physics in Heidelberg, Germany, and Donald R. Huffman of the University of Arizona, Tucson. They developed a method for preparing fullerenes in macroscopic amounts, leading to a tremendous amount of research on this new family of molecules, with the potential for numerous practical applications.

Bibliography

Fowler, P. W. and D. E. Manolopoulos. *An Atlas of Fullerenes*. New York: Oxford University Press, 1995.

Billups, W. Edward and Marco A. Ciufolini, eds. *Buckminsterfullerenes*. New York: VCH, 1993.

Kroto, Harold W. and D. R. M. Walton, eds. *The Fullerenes: New Horizons for the Chemistry, Physics, and Astrophysics of Carbon*. Cambridge, England: Cambridge University Press, 1993.

Aldersey-Williams, Hugh. *The Most Beautiful Molecule: The Discovery of the Buckyball*. New York: John Wiley & Sons, 1995.

Baggott, Jim. *Perfect Symmetry: The Accidental Discovery of Buckminsterfullerene*. New York: Oxford University Press, 1995.

After earning his B.S. in chemistry, he worked as a research chemist with the Shell Oil Company, receiving an industrial deferment that kept him out of the Vietnam War and at the same time, developed his scientific skills.

In 1969, Smalley entered Princeton University to become a quantum chemist. He studied condensed-matter spectroscopy under Elliot R. Bernstein and earned an M.A. in 1971 and a Ph.D. in 1973. At the University of Chicago he pioneered supersonic beam laser spectroscopy, which has become a powerful technique in chemical physics.

In 1976, Smalley joined the faculty of Rice University, rising rapidly through the ranks to become Gene & Norman Hackerman Professor of Chemistry in 1982, professor of physics in 1990, chair of the Rice Quantum Institute from 1986 to 1996, director of the Center for Nanoscale Science and Technology from 1996 to 2001, and finally the director of the Carbon Nanotechnology Laboratory in 2003. Considered the grandfather of nanotechnology, Smalley developed many new techniques—such as supercold pulsed beams, ultrasensitive laser detection, and laser-driven sources of free radicals, triplets, metals, and both metal and semiconductor cluster beams—and applied them to a wide range of problems in chemical physics. He discovered and characterized buckminsterfullerene (C_{60}), a soccer ball-shaped molecule. He was the first to prepare fullerenes with metals trapped inside, and he produced continuous carbon fibers, which are essentially giant single-fullerene molecules.

Awards and Honors

The recipient of honorary degrees and an editorial board member of several journals, Smalley received many awards and honors, including the Langmuir Prize in Chemical Physics in 1991, the American Physical Society International Prize for New Materials in 1992, the William H. Nichols Medal in 1993, and the Madison Marshall Award in 1995.

For his work with fullerenes, Smalley shared the 1996 Nobel Prize in Chemistry with Robert F. Curl, Jr., and Sir Harold W. Kroto. Unfortunately, Smalley's talented life was cut short, and he died in 2005, after a long battle with leukemia.

Bibliography
By Smalley
"C_{60}: Buckminsterfullerene," *Nature*, 1985 (with Harold W. Kroto et al).

"Probing C_{60}," *Science*, 1988 (with Curl).

"Great Balls of Carbon: The Story of Buckminsterfullerene," *Sciences*, 1991.

"Fullerenes," *Scientific American*, 1991 (with Curl).

"Ultrathin 'Bed-Of-Nails' Membranes of Wingle-Wall Carbon Nanotubes" *Journal of the American Chemical Society*, 2004 (with Y. H. Wang et al).

"A model for nucleation and growth of single wall carbon nanotubes via the HiPco process: A catalyst concentration study." *Journal of Nanoscience and Nanotechnology*, 2005 (with R. L. Carver et al).

About Smalley
"About Our Founder – Richard E. Smalley," Smalley Institute, http://smalley.rice.edu/founder/?ekmensel=c580fa7b_26_28_214_8

Yam, Philip. "The All-Star of Buckyball." *Scientific American* 269, no. 3 (September, 1993).

Baum, Rudy. "Fullerenes Gain Nobel Stature." *Chemical & Engineering News* 75, no. 1 (January 6, 1997).

Adams, W. Wade and Ray H. Baughman, "Richard E. Smalley" *Science* 23 (2005) 1916, doi: 10.1126/science.1122120.

(George B. Kauffman)

Frederick Soddy

Discipline: Chemistry

Contribution: In collaboration with Ernest Rutherford, Soddy developed the disintegration theory of radioactive transformation. He also explored other concepts crucial to the subsequent understanding of radioactivity.

Sept. 2, 1877	Born in Sussex, England
1898	Graduates from Oxford University
1900	Travels to Canada and collaborates with Ernest Rutherford at McGill University
1903	Returns to England to work with Sir William Ramsay at University College in London
1903	Shows that helium is produced in the disintegration of radium
1904	Lectures about physical chemistry and radioactivity at Glasgow University, Scotland
1910	Fellow of the Royal Society of London
1913	Awarded the Cannizzaro Prize in Rome
1913	Proposes the term "isotope"
1914	Teaches physical chemistry at the University of Aberdeen
1919	Becomes Lee Professor of Chemistry at Oxford
1921	Wins the Nobel Prize in Chemistry
1934	Given an honorary L.L.D. degree by Glasgow University
1936	Retires from Oxford
Sept. 22, 1956	Dies in Sussex, England

Early Life

Frederick Soddy was the last of seven children born to Benjamin Soddy, a successful London corn merchant, and Hannah (Green) Soddy. Frederick's mother died less than two years after his birth, and he was reared by an older sister. The family held strong Calvinist beliefs that, even though rejected by Soddy as an adult, seem to have shaped his attitudes about getting at the truth.

Soddy showed no interest in science until he came under the influence of the science master at Eastbourne College. Together with his mentor, Soddy published his first scientific paper at the age of seventeen. He entered Merton College at Oxford University in 1896 and graduated with first-class honors in chemistry two years later.

Research into Radioactivity

After two more years of study at Oxford, Soddy applied for the post of professor of chemistry at the University of Toronto in Canada.

Without waiting for a response, traveled there to further his application in person. When he found no chance of success, he set out for home but stopped on the way at McGill University in Montreal.

There, in May 1900 he accepted the position of junior demonstrator in chemistry. By September, he had met Ernest Rutherford, a professor of physics at McGill. With their combined knowledge of chemistry and physics, they embarked on a joint study of thorium and other recently discovered radioactive elements.

After this successful collaboration, Soddy returned to London in 1903 to work with Sir William Ramsay. They showed that helium is produced in the radioactive disintegration of radium. The following year, Soddy accepted a position as a lecturer in physical chemistry at Glasgow University, Scotland.

At Glasgow, Soddy continued his research into radioactivity. His major accomplishments include the development of the concept of isotopes, two or more forms of the same chemical element with different masses, and the displacement law, which traces the products of radioactive disintegration through their positions in the periodic table as a result of the emission of either alpha particles (helium nuclei) or beta particles (electrons).

In 1914, Soddy became a professor of chemistry at the University of Aberdeen, Scotland. The outbreak of World War I interrupted his research into radioactivity, and he undertook technical work in chemistry for the war effort. The war also caused him to become more concerned about the connections of science with society at large, and he wondered "why so far the progress of science has proved as much a curse as a blessing to humanity."

The Disintegration Theory

In collaboration with Ernest Rutherford, Soddy proposed the idea that radioactive transformation occurs through the spontaneous disintegration of one radioactive element with the simultaneous production of another element, which may or may not be radioactive itself This theory led to a radical change in scientific thinking about the stability of matter.

The element thorium was known to give off a radioactive gas, or emanation, which quickly loses its radioactivity. Rutherford and Soddy found that when thorium is precipitated out of a solution, it does not initially produce any emanation, while the material remaining in solution—termed thorium-X—does. After a month, the thorium regains its previous ability to produce the emanation, but the thorium-X loses its ability. Thus, Rutherford and Soddy demonstrated that the radioactive gas is given off by thorium-X rather than by thorium itself.

Their disintegration theory proposed that the transformation of thorium occurs through the spontaneous disintegration of some of its atoms to produce thorium-X, which in turn undergoes the disintegration of some of its atoms with the simultaneous production of the emanation, which is now known to be radon gas. Rutherford and Soddy also found that the rate of this radioactive disintegration follows a well-known law: The number of atoms that disintegrate at a particular time is directly proportional to the total number of such atoms present.

Bibliography

Atkins, P. W. and J. A. Beran. *General Chemistry.* 2d ed. New York: Scientific American Books, 1992.

Romer, Alfred, ed. *Radiochemistry and the Discovery of Isotopes.* New York: Dover, 1970.

Soddy, Frederick. "Some Recent Advances in Radioactivity." *Contemporary Review* 83 (1903).

Milne, Lorus J. and Margery Milne. *Understanding Radioactivity.* New York: Atheneum, 1989.

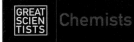
When the war ended in 1918, Soddy became Lee Professor of Chemistry at Oxford University, but he did little further scientific work, turning instead to problems of economics and monetary policy.

When his wife of twenty-eight years, Winifred Moller Beilby, died suddenly in 1936, he retired from teaching and spent the rest of his life writing on economic questions, trying to solve social problems, and traveling to out-of-the-way places. He died in Brighton, Sussex in 1956 at the age of seventy-nine.

Bibliography

By Soddy

"Some Recent Advances in Radioactivity," *Contemporary Review*, 1903.

The Interpretation of Radium, 1909.

The Chemistry of the Radio-Elements, 1911.

"The Origins of the Conception of Isotopes," *Nature*, 1923.

The Interpretation of the Atom, 1932.

The Story of Atomic Energy, 1949.

About Soddy

Howorth, Muriel, ed. *Atomic Transformation: The Greatest Discovery Ever Made, from Memoirs of Frederick Soddy*. London: New World, 1953.

Fleck, Alexander. "Frederick Soddy." *Biographical Memoirs of Fellows of the Royal Society* 3 (1957).

Howorth, Muriel. *Pioneer Research on the Atom*. London: New World, 1958.

Trenn, Thaddeus J. *The Self-Splitting Atom: The History of the Rutherford-Soddy Collaboration*. London: Taylor & Francis, 1977.

(Richard E. Rice)

Henry Taube

Discipline: Chemistry

Contribution: Universally recognized as the founder of the modern study of inorganic mechanisms, Taube won the Nobel Prize in Chemistry for his work on electron transfer reactions.

Nov. 30, 1915	Born in Neudorf, Canada
1935	Earns a B.S. in chemistry from the University of Saskatchewan
1937	Receives an M.S. in chemistry from Saskatchewan
1940-1941	Earns a Ph.D. in chemistry from the University of California, Berkeley, and works as an instructor there
1941-1946	Works as an instructor and assistant professor of chemistry at Cornell University
1946-1962	Professor of chemistry at the University of Chicago
1956-1959	Serves as chair of the chemistry department at Chicago
1962-1976	Works as professor of chemistry, Stanford University
1976-1986	Named Marguerite Blake Wilbur Professor of Chemistry at Stanford
1976	Wins the National Medal of Science
1983	Awarded the Nobel Prize in Chemistry
1985	Given the Priestley Medal by the American Chemical Society
1986	Emeritus professor at Stanford and becomes a consultant for Catalytica Associates
2005	Dies in Stanford, California

Early Life

Henry Taube was the youngest of four brothers whose parents were German peasant emigrants from Ukraine. He spent his first two years in a rented sod hut. His father was a farm hand, and his mother cleaned houses. When he was four, his father rented a farm, and the family moved to a two-room shack. Taube attended a one-room school until the age of thirteen, when he left home to study for the ministry at Luther College in the provincial capital of Regina.

Because his father lost the little that he had saved in the stock market crash of 1929, Taube helped in the school chemistry laboratory to pay for his stay. Although he planned to major in English literature, hoping to become a writer, he registered at the University of Saskatchewan for a chemistry course because all the other courses had long registration lines.

After earning B.S. and M.S. degrees in chemistry he pursued graduate work at the University of California, Berkeley (UCB), where he became deeply interested in chemistry. He earned a Ph.D. with a study of the oxidation-reduction (redox) reactions of oxygen- and halogen-containing oxidizing agents. Teaching jobs were scarce during the Great Depression, so he remained at UCB as an instructor and became a US citizen while he sought a permanent position.

Mechanistic Coordination Chemistry

Taube continued to work on the subject of his Ph.D. research during his years at Cornell University from 1941 to 1946. He used isotopic labeling techniques to study the mechanisms (how the atoms or molecules actually react) of the redox reactions of oxychlorine species and related molecules in aqueous solutions. This work brought him the American Chemical Society (ACS) Award for Nuclear Applications in Chemistry in 1955.

It was only as an assistant professor at the University of Chicago, when he taught a course in coordination chemistry, that he began to work in this field. Although much was known about the composition, structure, and reactivity of inorganic coordination compounds (complexes) by 1950, little was known about the mechanisms involved.

Taube explained reactivity as a unified concept based on the configuration of the electrons of the central metal ion and on the influence of the ligands (groups bonded around the central ion) of the coordination compound. He originated the valuable concept of inner (inert) and outer (labile) spheres to correlate the rates of ligand substitution reactions of complexes.

One of the leading pioneers in modern inorganic chemistry, Taube established the basis for various conceptual advances and investigated many aspects of chemical reactivity using new techniques. His research on electron transfer in metal complexes not only forms the basis for modern inorganic chemistry but also has led to a fuller understanding of the biochemical reactions that maintain life.

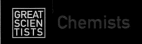

The Mechanism of an Electron Transfer Reaction

Taube's study of one electron transfer reaction exemplifies his new way of looking at such processes.

In the reaction between the inert pentaam-minechlorocobalt(III) ion and the labile hexa-aquachromium(II) ion the products are the penta-aquachlorochromium(III) ion and the penta-ammineaquacobalt(II) ion. The electron transfer is thus connected with a chloride ion transfer from cobalt to chromium. Before Taube's work, however, no knowledge existed of how the reaction takes place.

According to Taube, the chloride ligand in the inert cobalt(III) reactant neither could have left the cobalt coordination sphere before electron transfer nor could have entered the coordination sphere of the inert chromium(III) product after electron transfer.

Taube proved experimentally with a radioactively labeled chloride ion that the chloride ion was part of both the cobalt and the chromium coordination spheres at the moment of electron transfer. He found that, in forming, the chromium(III) product picks up almost no radioactivity, demonstrating that the transfer is direct; the chloride ion bridges the two metal centers before the chromium(II) reactant is oxidized.

Thus, Taube demonstrated that formation of ligand bridges between two interacting complexes is one of the fundamental mechanisms of electron transfer in such complexes.

Bibliography

Gray, Harry B. and James P. Coliman. "The 1983 Nobel Prize in Chemistry." *Science* 222 (1983).
Milgrom, Lionel and Ian Anderson. "Understanding the Electron." *New Scientist* 100 (October, 1983).

Later Work

Taube's 380 articles include work on mixed valence ions in a series of iron, ruthenium, and osmium complexes; intramolecular electron transfer between metal ions applied to biological systems; molecular nitrogen complexes; and transition metal organometallic compounds. Despite his retirement in 1986, he continued to be active in research until 2001.

Taube had many hobbies including gardening and listening to 78 rpm vocal records. He died in his home on the Stanford campus in 2005.

Bibliography

By Taube

"The Exchange of Water Between Aqueous Chromic Ion and Solvent," *Journal of Chemical Physics,* 1950 (with John P. Hunt).
"Rates and Mechanisms of Substitution in Inorganic Complexes in Solution," *Chemical Reviews,* 1952.
"Observations on the Mechanism of Electron Transfer in Solution," *Journal of the American Chemical Society,* 1953 (with Howard Myers and Ronald L. Rich).
Electron Transfer Reactions of Complex Ions in Solution, 1970.
"Electron Transfer Between Metal Complexes: Retrospective," *Science,* 1984.

About Taube

Walsh, Jerry. "Henry Taube." In *Nobel Laureates in Chemistry, 1901-1992,* edited by Laylin K. James. Washington, D.C.: American Chemical Society, 1993.
"Henry Taube" Stanford Report, October 3, 2001, http://news.stanford.edu/news/2001/october3/taube-103.html
Hargittai, István. "Interview: Henry Taube." *The Chemical Intelligencer* 3 (1997).

(George B. Kauffman)

Moddie Daniel Taylor

Discipline: Chemistry

Contribution: During World War II, Taylor worked on the Manhattan Project, the U.S. program to build an atomic bomb.

Mar. 3, 1912	Born in Nymph, Alabama
1935	Graduates from Lincoln University as valedictorian
1935-1939	Works as an instructor at Lincoln
1939-1941	Promoted to full professor at Lincoln
1939	Earns a master's degree from the University of Chicago
1943	Awarded a Ph.D. in chemistry from the University of Chicago
1943-1945	Serves as an associate chemist on the Manhattan Project
1948	Hired as an associate professor at Howard University in Washington, D.C.
1959	Promoted to full professor at Howard
1960	Publishes *First Principles of Chemistry*, a college-level chemistry textbook
1965	Appointed by President Lyndon B. Johnson to serve on the Assay Commission
1969-1976	Serves as head of the chemistry department at Howard University
Sept. 15, 1976	Dies in Washington, D.C.

Early Life

Moddie Daniel Taylor was born on March 3, 1912, to an African American family in Nymph, Alabama, and grew up in St. Louis, where his father worked as a postal clerk. After his graduation from Charles H. Sumner High School in 1931, Taylor attended Lincoln University in Jefferson City, Missouri.

That same year, Taylor began teaching at Lincoln University, first as an instructor and then, from 1939 to 1941, as a full professor. Meanwhile, he had enrolled in the University of Chicago's graduate chemistry program. He received his master's degree in 1939 and a Ph.D. in 1943.

The Manhattan Project

From 1943 until 1945, Taylor worked as an associate chemist on the Manhattan Project, the U.S. government's program to build an atomic bomb. At the University of Chicago, he joined a team that helped to develop the process of separating plutonium from uranium 238.

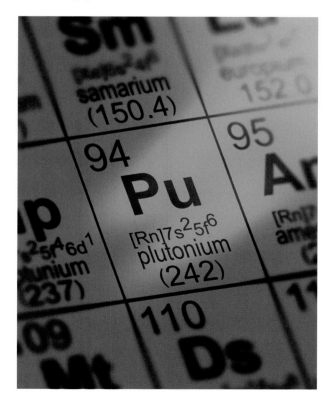

Taylor was involved in the production of plutonium for the Manhattan Project. Plutonium is needed as fuel for an atomic bomb.

Separating Plutonium from Uranium

While working for the Manhattan Project, Taylor was part of a team that developed a chemical method for separating plutonium from irradiated uranium 238.

Uranium naturally occurs in two isotopes. Uranium 235 is fissionable, which means that the nucleus will split when hit by neutrons. Uranium 238, which is 140 times more common, will absorb neutrons but will not split. When uranium 238 absorbs neutrons, however, it eventually becomes plutonium, which is fissionable—and therefore good atomic bomb fuel.

It was discovered that plutonium could be produced inside atomic "piles" within nuclear reactors. When a chain reaction began, uranium 238 within the pile absorbed neutrons produced by the fission process and eventually turned into plutonium. After several days, a considerable amount of plutonium could be produced.

Scientists had to cope with the problem of how to separate the plutonium from the uranium, which is highly toxic. It was eventually found that bismuth phosphate could serve as a carrier— a catalytic agent used to transfer one element to another—for plutonium.

A plutonium separation plant was set up in Hanford, Washington, that used techniques developed by the University of Chicago research team that included Taylor. Uranium from the reactor containing plutonium was immersed in water, which absorbed the toxic radiation, and was dragged through canals to the plant. There, the plutonium was separated from the uranium using the bismuth phosphate process.

Bibliography

Little, Monroe Jr. "Forgotten Pioneers of the Atomic Age." *The Indianapolis Star*, February 26, 1996, p. AO 5.

Groueff, Stephane. *The Manhattan Project*. New York: Bantam Books, 1967.

Fermi, Laura. *The Story of Atomic Energy*. New York: Random House, 1962.

The process was perfected, and plutonium was used in the first atomic explosive device tested at Jornada del Muerto, New Mexico, as well as in the bomb that was dropped on Nagasaki, Japan. For his work on the Manhattan Project, Taylor was awarded a Certificate of Merit from Secretary of War Henry Stimson.

Return to Teaching

After the war, Taylor returned to Lincoln University. In 1948, he was hired as an associate professor of chemistry at Howard University in Washington, D.C. He became a full professor in 1959 and headed the chemistry department from 1969 until 1976.

In 1960, he published *First Principles of Chemistry*, a college-level chemistry textbook. That same year, he received the Manufacturing Chemists Association award as one of six outstanding college chemistry teachers in the United States.

Taylor served on a number of boards and commissions. He served on the examinations committee for the college board's chemistry achievement test during the 1960s. In 1965, President Lyndon B. Johnson appointed him to serve on the Assay Commission. Taylor retired in 1976. On September 15 of that year, he died in Washington, D.C.

Bibliography

By Taylor
First Principles of Chemistry, 1960

About Taylor
Overton, Vivian Sommers. *Blacks in Science and Medicine*. New York: Hemisphere, 1990.

Washington Greene, Henry. *Holders of Doctorates Among American Negroes*. Newton, Mass.: Crofton, 1974.

(Lawrence K. Orr)

Harold Clayton Urey

Disciplines: Astronomy, biology, chemistry, and physics

Contribution: Urey was awarded the 1934 Nobel Prize in Chemistry for his work that led to the discovery of deuterium (heavy hydrogen).

Apr. 29, 1893	Born in Walkerton, Indiana
1911-1914	Teaches in rural schools in Indiana and Montana
1914-1917	Studies at Montana State University
1923	Earns a Ph.D. from the University of California, Berkeley
1924	Works with Niels Bohr in Copenhagen, Denmark
1925-1929	Works as associate in chemistry at The Johns Hopkins University
1930	Serves as associate professor of chemistry at Columbia University
1932	Discovers deuterium
1934	Wins the Nobel Prize in Chemistry
1940	Becomes a member of the Manhattan Project
1945-1958	Conducts nuclear studies at the University of Chicago
1951	The Urey-Miller experiment produces amino acids
1952	Named Martin A. Ryerson Distinguished Service Professor
1971	Receives the Kepler Medal from the American Association for the Advancement of Science
1973	Receives the Priestley Medal from the American Chemical Society
Jan. 5, 1981	Dies in La Jolla, California

Early Life

Harold Clayton Urey was born in the small rural community of Walkerton, Indiana, on April 29, 1893. Perhaps his future interest in teaching and science came from his father, Samuel Clayton Urey, who was a schoolteacher and lay minister in the Church of the Brethren. Unfortunately, his father died when Harold was only six years old. His mother, Cora Reinoehl Urey, later remarried. Harold had a sister, Martha, and a brother, Clarence. Two half sisters, Florence and Ina, were from his mother's second marriage. His stepfather was also a Brethren minister, and Harold grew up with a sincere respect for learning and education.

Urey was fortunate to be able to complete high school, and he looked forward to attending college. Most people at that time did not have the opportunity to further their education much beyond elementary school. Times were hard, and they had to either work on the farm or in the city.

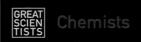

The Discovery of Deuterium and Its Implications

Deuterium (heavy hydrogen) is a relatively rare isotope; there are 5,000 atoms of ordinary hydrogen for every one of deuterium.

Frederick Soddy first discovered isotopes of various elements in 1913. Finding isotopes of heavier elements was difficult enough, but isolating an isotope of a light element such as hydrogen was thought to be nearly impossible. Urey developed an experiment that would produce the desired result if heavy hydrogen actually existed.

The technique developed by Urey to identify heavy hydrogen required the vaporization of liquid hydrogen. His hypothesis suggested that the lighter form of hydrogen would evaporate first, leaving behind the heavier isotope.

In Urey's experiment, he began with 4 liters (1 gallon) of liquid hydrogen that were allowed to evaporate very slowly. In the end, only 1 milliliter (0.03 oz) of liquid hydrogen was left. When he examined the product with a spectroscope, he found the exact predicted absorption lines for heavy hydrogen. The result was the discovery of deuterium.

Following the discovery of deuterium came the identification of several other isotopes, among them oxygen, nitrogen, carbon, and sulfur. It is the combination of deuterium and heavy oxygen that produces so-called heavy water, which was critical to the manufacture of the atomic bomb. Its principal use is to slow down the reaction rate in a nuclear fission reaction.

An additional discovery to result from Urey's work was the fact that isotopes tend to differ chemically from each other, if only in small ways. It was the belief that since the isotopes of a given element have a similar electronic configuration, they should have identical chemical properties.

Urey found a small difference in the reaction rates of isotopes because they have a characteristic difference in mass.

Urey's experience with isotopes became extremely important during World War II. Two German scientists, Otto Hahn and Fritz Strassman, discovered the principle of nuclear fission in 1939. Once this was known, the potential for creating a bomb became obvious. In 1940, Urey was invited to join the Uranium Committee for the Manhattan Project, the U.S. program to build an atomic bomb. His role was to separate uranium 235 from its heavier form, uranium 238. His success led to the development of the atomic bomb. After the war, Urey continued his work and extracted another isotope of hydrogen, called tritium, which was used to develop the hydrogen bomb.

Although Urey's discoveries concerning the isotopes of hydrogen led to weapons of mass destruction, they had other uses as well. After World War II he turned his attention to the relationship of oxygen isotopes to past climates.

Urey noted that in warmer climatic periods, organisms consume more of the lighter oxygen isotope and less of the heavier form. During cooler periods, the difference between the two isotopes is much less. From this fact, Urey was able to develop an "oxygen thermometer" based on oxygen isotope ratios found in the shells of sea creatures. This process is widely used today for the prediction of climatic changes, both past and present.

Bibliography

Calvin, Melvin. *Chemical Evolution*. New York: Oxford University Press, 1969.

Goldsmith, Donald and Tobias Owen. *The Search for Life in the Universe*. Menlo Park, Calif.: Benjamin/ Cummings, 1980.

Urey did not have the money to go directly to college, so he took a job teaching in country schools from 1911 to 1914 in order to pay for his education.

Beginning an Academic Life

At the age of twenty-one, Urey was able to enroll at Montana State University. At this early stage of his life, he chose biology as his course of study. His first original research work dealt with microorganisms found in the Missoula River. After three years of study, he was awarded a bachelor of science degree in zoology in 1917.

That year, the United States entered World War I. Because of his religious beliefs, Urey did not serve in the military. He did his part for the war effort by working in a chemical plant that developed high explosives, putting his scientific training to good use.

When World War I ended, Urey returned to Montana State University and taught chemistry there until 1921. His desire for additional knowledge took him to the University of California, Berkeley, where he enrolled into a doctorate program in physical chemistry. He received his degree in 1923. His research dealt with the calculations of heat capacities and entropies of various gases through the use of a spectroscope.

After receiving his doctorate, Urey traveled to Copenhagen, Denmark, to work and study with the famous physicist Niels Bohr. Bohr was working on the basic structure of the atom, and this research greatly excited Urey. It was this experience that developed Urey's interest in several atoms and their related isotopes.

A Promising Career

In 1925 Urey accepted an important position within the chemistry department at The Johns Hopkins University in Baltimore, Maryland. This would be the beginning of an exceptional career. It was also during this time that he married Frieda Daum, who was also a scientist. They were married on June 12, 1926, in Lawrence, Kansas, and had four children: Gertrude Elizabeth, Frieda Rebecca, Mary Alice, and John Clayton.

The turning point in Urey's professional life came in 1929 when he left Johns Hopkins to become an associate professor of chemistry at Columbia University in New York City. One year later, Urey and a colleague, Arthur E. Ruark, wrote a book entitled *Atoms, Molecules, and Quanta*, which was hailed as the first comprehensive English-language textbook on atomic structure. It was also significant in linking the new field of quantum physics to chemistry.

International Acclaim

The highpoint in Urey's career came in 1932, with the discovery of the isotope deuterium. Along with his coworkers Ferdinand Brick-wedde and George M. Murphy, they were able to separate the deuterium isotope from the more common form of hydrogen. This discovery opened the door for a better understanding of isotopes in general and led to the discovery of many more for other elements.

For his work in the discovery of deuterium, Urey was awarded the 1934 Nobel Prize in Chemistry. Columbia University also recognized his accomplishment by appointing him Ernest Kempler Adams Fellow and later promoting him to professor of chemistry. In addition to these honors, Urey became the first editor of the prestigious publication *Journal of Chemical Physics*.

All these accomplishments were more than most scientists achieve in a lifetime, but there was much more in the future for Urey. The coming of World War II would place him at the center of the development of the atomic bomb. His research would be critical to the separation of the two isotopes of uranium that was required.

After the war, Urey's research interests varied. He would seek answers for the origin of the solar system and of life itself. Urey died in 1981.

Bibliography

By Urey

Atoms, Molecules, and Quanta, 1930 (with Arthur E. Ruark).

"On the Relative Abundances of Isotopes," *Physical Review,* 1931 (with C. A. Bradley, Jr.).

"A Hypothesis Regarding the Origin of the Movement of the Earth's Crust," *Science,* 1949.

The Planets: Their Origins and Development, 1952.

"The Origin of the Earth" in Nuclear Geology: *A Symposium on Nuclear Phenomena in the Earth Sciences,* 1954.

About Urey

Brickwedde, Ferdinand G. "Harold Urey and the Discovery of Deuterium." *Physics Today* (September, 1982).

Silverstein, Alvin and Virginia. *Harold Urey: The Man Who Explored from Earth to Moon.* New York: J. Day, 1970.

Brush, Stephen G. "Nickel for Your Thoughts: Urey and the Origin of the Moon." *Science* 217 (1982).

Sagan, Carl. "Obituary: Harold Clayton Urey, 1893-1981." *Icarus* 48 (1981).

(Paul P. Sipiera)

Jacobus Henricus van't Hoff

Disciplines: Chemistry and physics

Contribution: An early worker in the field of theoretical chemistry, van't Hoff won the Nobel Prize in Chemistry for his work on chemical dynamics and osmotic pressure in solutions.

Aug. 30, 1852	Born in Rotterdam, the Netherlands
1871	Receives a degree in engineering from the University of Delft
1874	Receives a doctorate from the University of Utrecht
1875	Teaches at the Royal Veterinary School in Utrecht
1877	Appointed to the faculty of the University of Amsterdam
1887	Founds and edits, with Wilhelm Ostwald, the journal *Zeitschrift für physikalische Chemie*
1893	Wins the Davy Medal of the Royal Society of London
1894	Appointed Chevalier of the Legion of Honor
1896	Named a professor of experimental physics at the University of Berlin
1901	Elected president of the German Chemical Society
1901	Awarded the first Nobel Prize in Chemistry
1908	Directs his work toward the study of enzymes
Mar. 1, 1911	Dies in Steglitz (now Berlin), Germany

Early Life

Jacobus Henricus van't Hoff (pronounced "vahnt hawf"), following the usual Dutch education through the secondary level, entered the Polytechnic School at Delft at his parents' urging. Although he had already demonstrated an interest in pure science, his father believed that better career opportunities existed in the field of technology. Van't Hoff earned a technology diploma in 1871 with the highest score on the final examination.

A Career Is Chosen

A short stint working as a technologist in a sugar factory convinced van't Hoff that such a life would be dreary and unchallenging. Thus, his own decision to follow a career in pure science was made. He studied mathematics for a year at Leyden and then went to Bonn, where he studied chemistry with Friedrich August Kekule von Stradonitz.

From there, van't Hoff moved to Paris to broaden his chemical studies with Charles Adolphe Wurtz

and returned to the Netherlands to receive a doctorate, summa cum laude, under Ernst Mulder at the University of Utrecht in 1874. From that point, he continued with an academic career.

A Reputation Is Established

Van't Hoff stayed in Utrecht for three years and, in 1877, received an appointment as lecturer (later professor) at the University of Amsterdam, where he remained for eighteen years. He completed his career at the University of Berlin, continuing there as a research professor until his death.

Van't Hoff's doctoral dissertation was judged to be routine and uninspired; it was most likely offered as the safest course to the degree because he was already at work on a much more important and controversial work. His publication of a pamphlet concerning the three-dimensional nature of molecules had the scientific community in a buzz. This pamphlet was expanded into his first publication, *La Chimie dans l'espace* (1875; *Chemistry in Space*, 1891).

It was on the strength of the gradual acceptance of this stereochemical work that van't Hoff received his appointment at Amsterdam. While holding this position, he did most of his groundbreaking research on chemical dynamics and equilibrium. This work and van't Hoff's writings at the time form one of the pillars supporting the new field of physical chemistry.

The Mature Scientist

His shift to the University of Berlin in 1896 signaled a change in van't Hoff's work. He spent much time traveling, lecturing, and enjoying the fame that he had earned.

In 1901, he was awarded the first Nobel Prize in Chemistry. In his research, he dropped theoretical work and instead developed a systematic, methodical approach applying chemistry to geological problems, resulting in the publication of more than fifty papers.

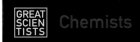

The Structure and Movement of Molecules

Many of the outwardly measurable chemical and physical properties of a substance can be explained by considering the structure and movement of the molecules of which the substance is made.

Prior to van't Hoff's work, molecules were thought of as static, two-dimensional objects. Van't Hoff pursued their three-dimensional character and their dynamics, which provided explanations in several areas of chemistry.

His findings ushered in the field of stereochemistry, the study of spatial relationships of atoms within molecules. Differing stereochemical arrangements of atoms accounted for the variety of properties found for molecules all having the same chemical formula. In particular, this concept explained the property of optical isomerism, in which molecules with identical formulas exhibit different responses to polarized light. These isomers differ from one another as do right and left hands.

Van't Hoff used his mathematical insight to describe the motion of molecules and their collisions with one another in order to lay the foundation for the branch of chemistry called kinetics. Further theorizing led him to the explanation of chemical equilibrium, the point at which no net change in the concentrations of chemicals in a reacting system occurs. He showed that this occurrence could be explained by both forward and reverse reactions taking place at equal rates. His idea of molecules in motion also provided an explanation of osmotic pressure. Osmotic pressure arises when solutions of differing concentrations are separated by a semipermeable membrane, an effect that is very important in understanding biological cell function.

Bibliography

Pauling, Linus and Roger Hayward. *The Architecture of Molecules*. San Francisco: W. H. Freeman, 1964.

Bard, Allen J. *Chemical Equilibrium*. New York: Harper & Row, 1966.

Connors, Kenneth A. *Chemical Kinetics: The Study of Reaction Rates in Solution*. New York: VCH, 1990.

Tinoco, Ignacio Jr., Kenneth Sauer, and James C. Wang. *Physical Chemistry: Principles and Applications in Biological Sciences*. Englewood Cliffs, N.J.: Prentice Hall, 1995.

Eliel, Ernest L. *Stereochemistry of Carbon Compounds*. New York: McGraw-Hill, 1962.

In 1908, a revitalized van't Hoff returned to theoretical chemistry and directed his efforts at understanding the action of enzymes as biological catalysts. Although few publications resulted from this work, those that exist show important insights.

Van't Hoff died in 1911.

Bibliography

By van't Hoff

Ansichten über die organische Chemie, 1878-1881.

Études de dynamique chimique, 1884.

Vorlesungen über theoretische und physikalische Chemie, 1898-1900 (3 vols.; *Lectures on Theoretical and Physical Chemistry*, 1899-1900, 3 vols.).

Zur Bildung der ozeanischen Salzablagerungen, 1905-1909 (2 vols.).

About van't Hoff

Hudson, Claude S. "The Basic Work of Fischer and van't Hoff in Carbohydrate Chemistry." *The Journal of Chemical Education* 30 (1953).

Harrow, Benjamin. "The Meeting of Ostwald, Arrhenius, and van't Hoff." *The Journal of Chemical Education* 7 (1930).

(Kenneth H. Brown)

Sir Geoffrey Wilkinson

Discipline: Chemistry

Contribution: Wilkinson was a pioneer in analyzing the chemistry of organometallic "sandwich" compounds.

July 14, 1921	Born in Springside, Yorkshire, England
1941	Earns a B.S. from Imperial College, London University
1943-1946	Serves as a junior scientific officer in the Atomic Energy Project in Canada
1946	Earns a Ph.D. from Imperial College
1946-1950	Works at the Lawrence Radiation Laboratory
1950-1951	Research associate at the Massachusetts Institute of Technology (MIT)
1951-1955	Assistant professor at Harvard University
1955-1978	Chair of inorganic chemistry, Imperial College
1965	Elected a Fellow of the Royal Society of London
1973	Wins the Nobel Prize in Chemistry
1978-1988	Appointed Sir Edward Frankland Professor of Inorganic Chemistry, Imperial College
1983-1996	Founds and edits the journal *Polyhedron*
1996	Wins the Davy Medal of the Royal Society of London
Sept. 26, 1996	Dies in London, England

Early Life

Geoffrey Wilkinson, the oldest of three children, was born in Springside. His father and paternal grandfather were house painters, and his mother worked in the local cotton mill. Wilkinson was introduced to chemistry by his uncle, who owned a small chemical factory and who allowed Geoff (as he preferred to be called by students and colleagues) to play in the laboratory and accompany him on visits to chemical companies.

Through a Royal Scholarship, Wilkinson attended the Imperial College of Science and Technology in London from 1939 to 1941. After graduating, he continued to conduct research there under H. V. A. Briscoe before joining a number of chemists developing nuclear energy in Canada from 1943 to 1946.

For the next four years, he worked with Glenn T. Seaborg at the University of California, Berkeley, using a cyclotron to study radioisotopes of the lanthanides (the so-called rare Earth elements).

Sandwich Compounds

An unusually stable organic iron complex called ferrocene led to the recognition of a hitherto unknown type of chemical bonding and to the discovery of countless completely new organometallic compounds.

In 1951, a new and unusually stable complex between one iron atom and two cyclopentadienide anions was reported by T. J. Kealy and P. L. Pauson. They assigned to the complex the structure of a central iron atom with a single σ bond on either side attached to one of the five carbon atoms of the flat, planar cyclopentadienide ring.

Wilkinson immediately recognized that this structure could not account for the compound's stability. He proposed that all five carbon atoms of each ring contribute equally to the π-bonding to the iron atom, resulting in a "sandwich" in which the iron atom is centered between two "slices" of cyclopentadienide "bread."

Robert B. Woodward had the same idea, and Wilkinson collaborated with him to prove the correctness of this structure through measurements of the compound's infrared and ultraviolet spectra, magnetic susceptibility, and dipole moment. Ernst Otto Fischer and W. Pfab independently confirmed the structure by X-ray diffraction.

Woodward found that the aromatic character of the cyclopentadienide rings was similar enough to that of benzene to permit the compound, subsequently named "ferrocene" in analogy with benzene, to undergo classical electrophilic ("electron-loving") aromatic substitution reactions. Wilkinson prepared ruthenium and cobalt analogues.

The entire class of transition metal and cyclopentadienyl compounds, termed "metallocenes," became known as sandwich compounds.

Bibliography

Miller, S. A., J. A. Tebboth, and J. F. Tremaine. "Dicyclopentadienyliron." *Journal of the Chemical Society* (1952).

Kauffman, George B. "The Discovery of Ferrocene, the First Sandwich Compound." *Journal of Chemical Education* 60 (March, 1983).

Kealy, T. J. and P. L. Pauson. "A New Type of Organo-Iron Compound." *Nature* 168 (1951).

According to Seaborg, who presented him with the American Chemical Society's Centennial Foreign Fellowship in 1976, Wilkinson "has made more isotopes of the chemical elements than any other human being." He even accomplished the ancient alchemists' dream of transmuting another element into gold.

Organometallic Chemistry

Because Briscoe advised Wilkinson that he was unlikely to find an academic position in nuclear chemistry in England, in 1950 Wilkinson became a research associate at the Massachusetts Institute of Technology (MIT), where he returned to his first interest as a student—transition metal complexes such as carbonyls (carbon monoxide compounds). In 1951, Wilkinson became an assistant professor at Harvard University, largely because of his background in nuclear research. Although he carried out some nuclear chemistry there, since he had already begun work on olefin complexes at MIT, he was extremely interested in T. J. Kealy and P. L. Pauson's discovery of an iron and cyclopentadienyl complex in 1951. Together with future Nobel chemistry laureate Robert B. Woodward, he recognized this complex's remarkable molecular structure as a "sandwich compound," work that led to his own Nobel Prize in Chemistry in 1973.

In 1955, Wilkinson succeeded Briscoe in the chair of inorganic chemistry at Imperial College, the only such established chair in the United Kingdom. There, he spent the remaining four decades of his life, working with a relatively small number of students and postdoctoral fellows, almost entirely on the transition metal organometallic complexes.

Wilkinson prepared hundreds of new complexes of ruthenium, rhodium, rhenium, and olefins. His discovery of the so-called Wilkinson's catalyst led to methods for the synthesis of pharmaceuticals. His rhodium catalysts for the industrial hydroformylation of olefins to produce fuels ("syngas") and the resulting patents enabled him to support his research group after his retirement in 1988.

Wilkinson was elected to the Royal Society of London in 1965 and was knighted in 1976. He died suddenly of cardiac arrest in his London home in 1996 at the age of seventy-five.

Bibliography

By Wilkinson

"The Structure of Iron *bis*-Cyclopentadienyl," *Journal of the American Chemical Society*, 1952 (with M. Rosenblum et al).

Advanced Inorganic Chemistry: A Comprehensive Text, 1962 (with Cotton).

"The Iron Sandwich: A Recollection of the First Four Months," *Journal of Organometallic Chemistry*, 1975.

Basic Inorganic Chemistry, 1976 (with Cotton).

About Wilkinson

Thomas, John Meurig and Edward Abel. "Geoffrey Wilkinson (1921-96)." *Nature* 384 (November 21, 1996).

Green, Malcolm and William P. Griffith. "Prof. Sir Geoffrey Wilkinson." *The Independent* (October 1, 1996).

Griffith, W. P. "Sir Geoffrey Wilkinson 1921-96." *Chemistry in Britain* 33 (January, 1997).

(George B. Kauffman)

Georg Wittig

Discipline: Chemistry

Contribution: Wittig developed a broad and versatile method for joining carbon units. The Wittig reaction has provided a means of introducing double bonds in specific locations and is used in the synthesis of pharmaceuticals and other complex molecules.

June 16, 1897	Born in Berlin, Germany
1923	Earns a Ph.D. in chemistry from Marburg University
1926	Appointed to the faculty at Marburg as a lecturer
1932-1937	Acts as director of the Technische Hochschule in Braunschweig
1937-1944	Serves as a Special Professor at the University of Freiburg
1944	Accepts an offer to become institute director at the University of Tübingen
1953	Receives the Adolf von Baeyer Medal from the Society of German Chemists
1956-1967	Teaches chemistry at Heidelberg University
1973	Wins the Roger Adams Award of the American Chemical Society
1979	Awarded the Nobel Prize in Chemistry jointly with Herbert C. Brown
1980	Accepts the German Ordens Grosses Verdienstkreuz Award
Aug. 26, 1987	Dies in Heidelberg, West Germany

Early Life

Georg Wittig (pronounced "VIH-tihk") was born in Berlin on June 16, 1897. He attended school at the Wilhelms Gymnasium in Kassel. In 1916, he began studies at the University of Tübingen, but his undergraduate work was interrupted by service in the military during World War I. For part of this period, he was a prisoner of war in Great Britain.

In 1923, Wittig received his Ph.D. from Marburg University, where he studied chemistry under Karl von Auwers. For the next several years, he taught and conducted research at Marburg, Braunschweig, and Freiburg universities. In his early career, he focused on questions of mechanism and theory rather than on synthesis. He studied diradicale, carbanions, bonding, and molecular structure.

Seminal Discoveries

Wittig became institute director at Tübingen in 1944. It was there that his pioneering work on the preparation of alkenes, carbon compounds with double bonds, was performed using phosphorus ylides.

Wittig did not set out to discover a useful synthetic method. He was doing research on the nature of pentavalent group V compounds when an unexpected product formed. Wittig named this unstable nitrogen compound an ylide. He proceeded to repeat the reaction with the element under nitrogen in the periodic chart, phosphorus. The phosphorous ylide was much more stable than the nitrogen one and opened the door to the development of the Wittig reaction.

Practical Applications

In 1956, Wittig moved to Heidelberg University, where he continued to extend the utility of the Wittig reaction. He reacted ylides with numerous carbonyl compounds and demonstrated the wide scope of his method. By the early 1960s, more than a hundred papers on the applications of the Wittig reaction had appeared.

The chemical company BASF engaged Wittig as a consultant for an industrial-scale preparation of vitamin A using an ylide intermediate. Wittig also developed a boron compound that was sold commercially for the determination of sodium ions.

An accomplished pianist, Wittig's continued interest in music was reflected in the name of the article that he wrote on phosphorous chemistry in 1964: "Variations on the Theme by Staudinger." Hermann Staudinger, a German chemist, had done early work on phosphorous ylides.

Retirement: Idyllic Times

Wittig became professor emeritus at Heidelberg in 1967 and produced fifty papers in the decade after his retirement. He received the Nobel Prize in Chemistry in 1979, sharing the honor with Herbert C. Brown. The following year, the German government awarded Wittig the Ordens Grosses Verdienstkreuz its award of highest service. Wittig died on August 26, 1987, in Heidelberg.

The Wittig Reaction

Organic chemicals are characterized by linked chains of carbon atoms. The Wittig reaction provides a means of adding carbon atoms together to produce carbons joined by double bonds.

In the Wittig reaction, a carbon doubly bonded to an oxygen (an aldehyde or ketone) reacts with a phosphorus ylide to give an olefin or alkene.

Vitamin A acetate can be prepared by reactions shown in the accompanying figure.

Initially, a phosphine (1) reacts with an alkyl halide (2) to form a phosphonium salt (3). This salt is then treated with a strong base to remove a molecule of hydrogen halide and generate the phosphorus ylide (4). Phosphorous ylides are rather stable. The ylide adds to the carbonyl group (5) to give intermediates that eliminate phosphine oxide and generate the new carbon-carbon bonds, as shown in vitamin A acetate (6).

The Wittig reaction is very general and widely applied. A great variety of aldehydes and ketones can be used. The reaction has proven useful in the synthesis of natural compounds such as vitamins A and D and the steroid precursor squalene. Beta carotene, the orange-colored component of carrots, has also been prepared by a Wittig reaction.

Bibliography

Smith, Michael B. *Organic Synthesis*. New York: McGraw-Hill, 1994.

Johnson, William A. *Ylid Chemistry*. New York: Academic Press, 1966. (adapted from Wittig's "From Diyls to Ylides to My Idyll," *Science*, 1980).

The Formation of Vitamin A Acetate by a Wittig Reaction

Bibliography

By Wittig

Stereochemie, 1930.

"Variations on a Theme by Staudinger," *Pure and Applied Chemistry*, 1964.

"From Diyls to Ylides to My Idyll," *Science*, 1980.

About Wittig

Shaw, Robert. "George Wittig: Virtuoso of Chemical Synthesis." *Nature* 282 (1979).

McMurray, Emily J., ed. *Notable Twentieth-Century Scientists*. New York: Gale Research, 1995.

(Helen M. Burke)

Friedrich Wöhler

Disciplines: Chemistry and medicine

Contribution: Wöhler synthesized urea from ammonium cyanate, thus advancing knowledge of isomerism and striking a blow against the theory of vitalism.

July 31, 1800	Born in Escherheim, near Frankfurt am Main, Germany
1823	Earns an M.D. at the University of Heidelberg
1823-1824	Studies chemical analysis with Jöns Jakob Berzelius in Sweden
1825-1831	Teaches in Berlin
1828	Publishes a description of the synthesis of urea
1831-1836	Teaches in Kassel
1832	With Justus von Liebig, prepares a series of benzoyl derivatives
1836-1882	Serves as a professor of chemistry and pharmacy at the University of Göttingen
1838-1845	Translates Berzelius' textbooks into German
1845	Publishes a method for preparing aluminum
1854	Elected a foreign member of the Royal Society of London
1857	Discovers the first silicon hydrides
1862	Prepares acetylene from calcium carbide
1864	Elected a foreign associate of the Institut de France
1872	Awarded the Copley Medal of the Royal Society of London
Sept. 23, 1882	Dies in Göttingen, Germany

Early Life

Blessed with lively scientific curiosity and supportive parents, Friedrich Wöhler (pronounced "VOY-luhr") received an excellent education in public school and at the Gymnasium and took additional instruction in music and languages.

After a year at Marburg University, Wöhler transferred to the University of Heidelberg, where he was awarded a doctorate in medicine in 1823. With the recommendation of his chemistry professor, Leopold Gmelin, Wöhler spent a year in Stockholm studying with Jöns Jakob Berzelius, a master of analytical chemistry.

Wöhler married his cousin Franziska in 1828 and they had two children before she died in 1832. In 1834, Wöhler married Julie Pfeiffer, with whom he had four daughters.

Berlin and Kassel

Extending his work on cyanates, Wöhler achieved the synthesis of urea (a component of urine) from

The Synthesis of Urea

The synthesis of urea (an organic compound) from ammonium cyanate (an inorganic compound) contradicts the theory of vitalism.

The reaction of silver cyanate and ammonium chloride produces a precipitate of silver chloride that can be filtered out, leaving a water solution of ammonium cyanate (a).

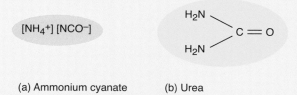

[NH$_4^+$] [NCO$^-$]

(a) Ammonium cyanate   (b) Urea

N is nitrogen, H is hydrogen, C is carbon, and O is oxygen.

From the water solution of (a), Wöhler obtained crystals that he recognized as urea (b) by certain of its reactions, which were also exhibited by a sample of urea obtained from urine. Ammonium cyanate rapidly forms urea when heated in water solution. Wöhler made only a slight reference to the theoretical significance of the synthesis in his publication on the subject, but he was more effusive in a letter that he wrote to his friend Jöns Jakob Berzelius.

The theory of vitalism, which had existed under a variety of names since at least the time of Aristotle, held that living organisms possessed a "life force" that operated outside the realm of ordinary laboratory experiments. Thus, it was believed that no product of natural origin could ever be prepared in the laboratory.

The theory of vitalism was often contradicted, and it faded in importance over time. History has tended to give Wöhler the credit for ending vitalism and founding modern organic chemistry. Hardly a chemistry text exists that does not refer to Wöhler's achievement in 1828 on the opening page of the organic chemistry chapter.

Bibliography

Philosophy of Nature. Moritz Schlick. Translated by Amethe Von Zeppelin. New York: Greenwood Press, 1949.

"Woehler's Urea and Its Vital Force?—A Verdict from the Chemists." John H. Brook. *Ambix* 15 (1968).

"Wöhler's Preparation of Urea and the Fate of Vitalism." Timothy O. Lipman. *Journal of Chemical Education* 41, no 8 (1964).

ammonium cyanate, gaining considerable fame for this blow against the theory of vitalism.

Wöhler befriended Justus von Liebig, a professor at the University of Giessen, who was working on compounds called fulminates. Fulminates and cyanates turned out to provide one of the first examples of the phenomenon of isomerism: compounds with the same elemental composition but different properties.

Research

In further collaboration with Liebig, Wöhler established the existence of a "benzoyl radical," a group of atoms that remained constant in a series of compounds derived from bitter almond oil.

A substance in almonds called amygdalin yields glucose, hydrogen cyanide, and benzal-dehyde when acted on by an enzyme called emulsin, also present in almonds.

Wöhler clarified most of the chemistry of amygdalin, the first example of a common type of natural product called glycosides, and showed that emulsin could be inactivated by boiling.

In his other research, Wöhler prepared aluminum from aluminum chloride and potassium, and he also prepared beryllium.

He worked out a method for extracting nickel from ore deposits near Kassel, and a refinery was built there. He suggested the use of nickel in coinage. In 1831, the first edition of his textbook *Grundriss der unorganischen Chemie* (fundamentals of inorganic chemistry) was published. It would run through fifteen editions.

Göttingen

A professorship at the University of Göttingen in 1836 brought Wöhler impressive teaching and administrative duties, and it also made him responsible for inspecting apothecary shops in the province of Hannover. He produced the books *Grundriss der organischen Chemie* (1840; *Wöhler's Outlines of Organic Chemistry*, 1873) and *Practische Übungen in der Chemischen Analyse* (1853; practical exercises in analytical chemistry), as well as a translation of a chemistry textbook by Berzelius. Wöhler's research achievements included syntheses of phosphorus, acetylene, and the first silicon hydrides.

Colleagues

Students flocked to Göttingen from many countries, including the United States. Among those who heard Wöhler's lectures was Ira Remsen, a U.S. chemist who later became president of The Johns Hopkins University and founded the first graduate program in chemistry in the United States.

Loved and respected by students and colleagues and honored by scientific societies in Germany, France, and England, Wöhler maintained an active interest in chemical research until his death in Göttingen in 1882.

Bibliography

By Wöhler

Grundriss der unorganischen Chemie, 1831.

Grundriss der organischen Chemie, 1840 (*Wöhler's Outlines of Organic Chemistry*, 1873).

Beispiele zur Übung in der analytischen Chemie, 1849 (examples for practice in analytical chemistry).

Practische Übungen in der Chemischen Analyse, 1853 (practical exercises in chemical analysis).

Wallach, O., ed. *Aus Justus Liebigs und Friedrich Wöhlers Briefwechsel 1829-1873*, 1888 (from Justus Liebig's and Friedrich Wöhler's correspondence, 1829-1873).

About Wöhler

Hofmann, A. W. Hofmann. "Friedrich Wöhler." in *Great Chemists*, edited by Eduard Farber. New York: Interscience, 1961.

Keen, Robin. "Friedrich Wöhler." in *Dictionary of Scientific Biography*, edited by Charles Coulston Gillispie. Vol. 14. New York: Charles Scribner's Sons, 1980.

Richet, G. "An Unrecognized Renal Physiologist: Friedrich Wöhler." *American Journal of Nephrology* 15, no. 6 (1995).

(*John R. Phillips*)

Glossary

Acetyl: A grouping of atoms, usually designated by the formula CH_3CO, which remains stable through a variety of chemical reactions.

Adiabatic: Occurring without the gain or loss of heat.

Alpha particle: A product of radioactive decay, identical to a helium atom that has lost two electrons.

Amino acid: Any organic molecule containing both at least one amine and one carboxyl (COOH) group.

Atom: The smallest unit of an element.

Atomic number: The number of protons in the atomic nucleus of a given element, which determines that element's location in the periodic table.

Base: A chemical that gains a positively charged hydrogen ion in a reaction. *Compare* **Acid**.

Bond: Any of several forces by which atoms or ions are held together.

Cloud chamber: An apparatus for detecting the path of particles through the trail of drops of liquid formed on ions produced by passing charged particles through a supersaturated vapor.

Decay: The disintegration of a subatomic particle into a combination of new particles.

Dipole: A pair of equal but opposite electrical charges or magnetic poles.

Electron: A stable elementary particle with a negative charge that orbits the atomic nucleus. *Compare* **Neutron**, **Proton**.

Element: A substance composed of atoms which all have the same number of protons in their nuclei.

Enzyme: A protein catalyst for a chemical reaction.

Equilibrium: The state of a reaction in which the forward and reverse reactions occur at equal rates so that there is no change in the concentrations of reactants.

Fission: The breaking apart of large atoms into smaller fragments, with the creation of energy. *Compare* **Fusion**.

Fusion: The joining of two light nuclei to form a larger one, with the release of great amounts of energy. *Compare* **Fission**.

Half-life: The time needed for half of some initial number of identical radioactive particles to decay.

Handedness: A property in which forms can be classified as right-handed or left-handed. These forms differ from the mirror image of the object but not from the rotated object.

Infrared light: Electromagnetic radiation with a wavelength just longer than the visible spectrum.

Inorganic: Compounds not containing carbon. *Compare* **Organic**.

Ion: An atom or molecule that has attained a net electrical charge by gaining or losing electrons.

Isotope: A variant of an element that has the same number of protons but a different number of neutrons.

Light elements: Elements with an atomic number less than 50. They have a low binding energy and may undergo fusion if sufficient excitation energy is provided.

Molecule: A stable group of atoms held together by chemical forces and entering into characteristic chemical reactions.

Neutron: An uncharged particle in all atomic nuclei except those of hydrogen. *Compare* **Electron**, **Proton**.

Nucleus: The dense central portion of an atom containing protons and neutrons.

Organic: Pertaining to any aspect of living matter; any chemical compound containing carbon. *Compare* **Inorganic**.

Particle: Any very small piece of matter, such as a molecule or atom.

Periodic table: A table of the elements of increasing atomic number organized into horizontal rows (periods) and vertical columns (groups) that illustrates the similarities in chemical properties of members of each group.

Phlogiston: A hypothetical substance thought to combine with metallic ores to form metals, presumed to have negative mass.

Photon: A massless particle that carries electromagnetic force.

Polymer: A long chain of identical chemical units that are linked to form a single large molecule.

Positron: An elementary particle identical to an electron except for its positive charge, the antiparticle of the electron. *Compare* **Electron**.

Potential energy: The capacity of a body to do work as a result of its position relative to other bodies. *Compare* **Kinetic energy**.

Proton: A positively charged particle in the atomic nucleus. *Compare* **Electron**, **Neutron**.

Quanta (*sing.* **quantum):** Units of any physical quantity whose values are restricted to multiples of a basic unit.

Quantum mechanics: The modern theory of matter and electromagnetic radiation in which many characteristics are quantized.

Radiation: The process of emitting energy in any form.

Radical: An atom or stable group of atoms with at least one unpaired electron, which makes the group chemically reactive.

Radioactivity: The emission of subatomic particles from unstable nuclei.

Reagent: One of the substances involved in a chemical reaction.

Relativity: The theory that recognizes the universality of the speed of light and the dependence of measurements of space, time, and mechanical properties on the motion of the observer relative to the motion of the object being observed.

Scattering: The change of direction of a particle produced by a collision with another particle or system of particles.

Spectroscopy: The branch of physics concerned with electromagnetic spectra.

Spectrum (*pl.* **spectra):** A plot of the intensity of radiation as a function of a given quantity, usually wavelength or frequency.

Stereochemistry: The scientific study of the spatial arrangement of atoms in molecules.

Subatomic: Pertaining to something smaller than the atom.

Superconductor: Any material that loses its electrical resistance at low temperatures.

Thermodynamics: The branch of physics that studies the change of energy from one form to another, especially the transformations between heat and work.

Valence: A number that indicates the bonds that atoms of an element form with other atoms.